second life®
the official guide

By Michael Rymaszewski, Wagner James Au,
Mark Wallace, Catherine Winters, Cory Ondrejka,
Benjamin Batstone-Cunningham, and Second Life
residents from around the world

Foreword by Philip Rosedale, Linden Lab Founder and CEO

BICENTENNIAL
1807
WILEY
2007
BICENTENNIAL

ISBN-10: 0-470-09608-X
ISBN-13: 978-0-470-09608-6

This book is printed on acid-free paper.

Library of Congress Cataloging-in-Publication Data is available from the publisher.

Printed in the United States of America.

10   9   8   7   6   5   4   3

CONTENTS

INTRO
CHAPTER 1
CHAPTER 2
CHAPTER 3
CHAPTER 4
CHAPTER 5
CHAPTER 6
CHAPTER 7
CHAPTER 8
CHAPTER 9
CHAPTER 10
CHAPTER 11
CHAPTER 12
CHAPTER 13
APPENDICES

iii

FOREWORD

When *Second Life* launched in 2003, running on just 16 servers with barely 1,000 dedicated users, it was the culmination of a kind of dream for me. One of the things I'd always been interested in, ever since I was a young boy, was how we manipulate the world around us. The world had so much *stuff* in it; there was always something I wanted to change, something I wanted to add, something I wanted to build out of the things I saw around me. That, to me, was magical: seeing the world change shape in response to the ideas in my head. One of the things I wanted to do when we started developing *Second Life* almost a decade ago was to give anyone a chance to work that same magic.

Fast-forward three years and that's exactly what we have. *Second Life* now runs on more than 3,000 servers and has close to a million registered users, but the fundamental idea of the world hasn't changed: it's a place where you can turn the pictures in your head into a kind of pixelated reality. It's a venue for self-expression that's among the richest and most satisfying out there. In *Second Life*, if you see something you want to build or change, the ability to do so is at your fingertips. The world is a place you experience, but more importantly, it's a place you create.

And those million users—you—have created quite a world. You add millions of objects to *Second Life*—in the form of cars, clothes, castles, and every other kind of thing you can imagine—every day. You spend close to $5 million there every month; and that's money you spend not on the things Linden Lab creates, but on the things that other users have created and added to the world. To me, that's the beauty of *Second Life*: all we've created is a platform, an almost empty world; where we got lucky is in the fact that you came along and breathed life into it. If *Second Life* is a world at all, it's because you've created it.

When Wiley approached us about this book, it seemed like a great opportunity to let even more people be involved in that process of creation. Like *Second Life* itself, the book developed as a collaboration. Michael Rymaszewski and the other authors have been helped by any number of residents who've contributed their thoughts and experiences throughout the text. Here you'll find information, tips, stories, profiles, and even some secrets that should make a great offline resource for everyone, but especially for new residents. If you're looking for a way to get on your feet quickly in *Second Life*, this book is a great choice.

For those brand-new to virtual worlds, you need not fear. *Second Life*'s geography, society, culture, and technology are all laid out here in easy-to-understand terms. There's a wealth of information and practical advice about creating and customizing your avatar, building objects, earning money, becoming part of a community, and more. Those who want to peek under the hood will be especially interested by Chapter 8, which was cowritten by Ben Batstone-Cunningham (a programmer at Linden Lab) and Cory Ondrejka (chief technology officer at Linden Lab and the man responsible for the "physics" that underpin the world). In other chapters, profiles of *Second Life* residents give a look at how various people have found their place in the world, be it socially, through business ventures, as game developers, or simply as visitors to the fascinating society that's emerging as a result of their efforts.

The main purpose of this book is to allow you to more easily become part of that society yourself. *Second Life* is growing every day; all it takes to get in on the action is a computer, an Internet connection, and an open mind. There's a lot of stuff in *Second Life*, but there's always room for more. I look forward to seeing what you add to the world you find there.

—Philip Rosedale
CEO and Founder, Linden Lab

INTRO
CHAPTER 1
CHAPTER 2
CHAPTER 3
CHAPTER 4
CHAPTER 5
CHAPTER 6
CHAPTER 7
CHAPTER 8
CHAPTER 9
CHAPTER 10
CHAPTER 11
CHAPTER 12
CHAPTER 13
APPENDICES

DEDICATION

To Olga, who inspired me to get a second life

—Michael Rymaszewski

ACKNOWLEDGMENTS

It's not easy to write a guide to a virtual world, a place that exists in cyberspace. There were voices raised that said it's just impossible—and without many extra voices, that might have well been true. Just like *Second Life*, this book has been created thanks to many people contributing to its content.

So, a very big thank-you to Cory Ondrejka, Catherine Winters, Wagner James Au, Ben Batstone-Cunningham, and Mark Wallace, who authored selected chapters. Willem Knibbe at Wiley was the person who actually conceived this book and made sure it became reality. Candace English edited it so that it reads as well as it does, and Patrick Cunningham made it look as good as it does. At Linden Lab, Catherine Smith exhibited a saint-like patience in dealing with numerous requests for help and extra information. Jonhenry Righter contributed greatly to the book's look, John "Pathfinder Linden" Lester provided an excellent appendix for educators, and Torley Linden, Jeff Luan, Jeska Dzwigalski, Kara Jordan, Tom Verre, Eric Call, James Cook, Beth Goza, Michael Blum, Kelly Washington, Richard Nelson, Daniel Smith, Joe Miller, Daniel Huebner, and many other Linden Lab employees reviewed the text and contributed valuable input.

Last but not least, many *SL* residents contributed quotes on selected topics—little pearls of wisdom that will improve the quality of your virtual life.

Thank you, guys. You're the kind of people one hopes to meet when starting another life.

—Michael Rymaszewski

ABOUT THE AUTHORS

Michael Rymaszewski is a veteran writer who has authored more than 20 strategy guides. His *Age of Empires III: Sybex Official Strategies and Secrets* was named a Best Computer & Internet Book of 2005 by Amazon.com. Michael's other published work includes reviews, strategy articles, short fiction, coffee table books, and video/TV movie scripts. He is also a video game writer and designer for City Interactive. Michael authored Chapters 1, 2, 4, 5, 6, 9, and 10.

Wagner James Au writes New World Notes (`http://nwn.blogs.com`) and covers the culture and business of high technology and gaming for GigaOM.com, Kotaku.com, Salon.com, and Wired. He's also written for the *Los Angeles Times*, *Lingua Franca*, *Smart Business*, and *Game Developer*, among other publications and websites, primarily on game culture and the game industry, along with politics, film, and pop culture. He's also a screenwriter (his script *Future Tense* was optioned by Canal Plus in 2001), and as a game developer, wrote for Electronics Arts' groundbreaking conspiracy thriller *Majestic*, and was a designer on *America's Army: Soldiers*. His work as the embedded journalist for *Second Life* has been featured in the BBC, the *Washington Post*, NPR's *All Things Considered*, CNN International, MSNBC, *Wired* magazine, News.com, *New Scientist*, *Popular Science*, and the *San Jose Mercury News*, among many other publications. He's also a consultant for businesses and nonprofits developing a presence in *Second Life* and is a part-time coordinator/promoter for Creative Commons' efforts in *Second Life*. He's developing his work in *Second Life* into an upcoming book of his own. You can contact him at `wjamesau@well.com`. James wrote Chapters 11 and 12.

Mark Wallace is the editor of 3pointD.com, a widely read blog covering virtual worlds and other 3D online technologies. His writing on virtual worlds, video games, and other topics has appeared in *The New York Times*, *Financial Times*, *Wired*, *GQ*, and many other publications. He has written regularly on online games for *The Escapist* (`www.escapistmagazine.com`), and since January 2005 has run the *Second Life Herald* (`www.secondlifeherald.com`), a popular online newspaper covering virtual worlds. With *Herald*

INTRO
CHAPTER 1
CHAPTER 2
CHAPTER 3
CHAPTER 4
CHAPTER 5
CHAPTER 6
CHAPTER 7
CHAPTER 8
CHAPTER 9
CHAPTER 10
CHAPTER 11
CHAPTER 12
CHAPTER 13
APPENDICES

founder Peter Ludlow, he is coauthor of the forthcoming *Only a Game: A Cyberspace Murder on the Bleeding Edge between Real and Online Worlds*. He played his first video game, the text-based game *Adventure*, in 1978 on aPDP-11. He lives in Brooklyn. Mark wrote Chapters 3 and 13.

Catherine Winters is one of the longest-tenured residents still active within the *Second Life* community. In 2003, she cofounded the LSL Wiki, the collaborative *Second Life* programming site that has grown to become the definitive reference manual for LSL scripting. A prolific scripter and content creator within *Second Life*, Catherine is one of the few *SL* residents to have made *Second Life* her primary source of real-world income. In her first life, Catherine lives in Vancouver, British Columbia. She enjoys cycling and downhill skiing, as well as curling up with a good book. Her personal web log can be found at `www.CatherineOmega.com`. Catherine authored Chapter 7.

Cory Ondrejka: Cory Ondrejka is chief technical officer at Linden Lab. He leads the *Second Life* development team in creating and leveraging such technologies as distributed physical simulation, 3D streaming, and real-time, in-world editors. He also spearheaded the decision to allow users to retain IP rights to their creations, helped craft Linden's virtual real-estate policy, and created the Linden Scripting Language. Cory coauthored Chapter 8.

Ben Batstone-Cunningham is a Linden Lab programmer and scripting expert. On a brisk morning in February 2002, while cutting a Quantum Physics class, Ben read in the paper about a virtual world where anything was possible. He signed up for the alpha test of what was then called *LindenWorld* and quickly became addicted. Several months later, having become proficient with the tools, he was invited to work for Linden Lab in creating the freshly renamed *Second Life*. Several years later, he is still happily addicted, and still creating scripts for Linden Lab—including example content for residents to learn from. Ben coauthored Chapter 8.

INTRODUCTION

When you visit a new place—city, country, continent—a good guide comes in really handy. You need a guide that will go beyond advice on which sights are worth seeing and where to stay; a guide that will tell you about the people who inhabit your new destination, the local laws, best places to pick up bargains, and whether it's OK to drink the tap water.

Second Life is a virtual world. A whole world, virtual or not, definitely merits a guide. But how can one give advice and provide guidance about a world that's changing constantly, and much faster than what we call the real world? It's difficult enough when dealing with a land that consists of solid soil and rock; how does one handle a land made out of bytes, a place that consists of pixels on your monitor? In *Second Life*, changes that would take millenia of groaning and straining in the real world can be completed within a few hours. If real life is all about evolution, *Second Life* is evolution squared. How do you write a guide to a place like that?

Well, to begin with, you focus on things that are there to stay. *Second Life* is and always will be a representation of the world as we know it. It has been conceived by and is being created by humans, and people tend to do things in a certain way. It doesn't matter whether the world they're in is virtual or "real." Real is what exists in the mind. We may live in an enlightened age, but emotions and fantasies rule just like they always did (if you disagree, watch the evening news). And while we may be vastly different from each other on the outside, inside we're all the same: blood, guts, and plenty of dreams. Even the dreams are the same: everyone wants love, success, happiness. The people who don't are either dead or ready to die.

All these banal truths become even more true in *Second Life*. It lets you concentrate single-mindedly on the pursuit of your own, private happiness. You don't need to deal with all the mundane stuff that eats up a lot of time on planet Earth, and you're free to do what you want. The few restrictions that do apply in *SL* are nonintrusive, and simply represent common sense applied to a social situation. In fact, the only thing that may obstruct you in your virtual pursuit of real happiness is real life. Well, what do you expect? It's not easy to live two lives in the same timeframe.

We hope this guide will make it easier. Here's what you'll find inside:

Chapter 1 introduces *Second Life*: what it is about, how it came into being, and how it has evolved since its beginning. It discusses basic *SL* concepts and rules, including types of *SL* memberships and their benefits.

INTRO
CHAPTER 1
CHAPTER 2
CHAPTER 3
CHAPTER 4
CHAPTER 5
CHAPTER 6
CHAPTER 7
CHAPTER 8
CHAPTER 9
CHAPTER 10
CHAPTER 11
CHAPTER 12
CHAPTER 13
APPENDICES

Chapter 2 guides you through the process of getting acquainted with *Second Life*. It discusses the *SL* interface, views, and movement within the virtual world, as well as virtual land ownership. It also covers *SL* resident groups and communities.

Chapter 3 takes you on a tour of the virtual world, just as if you were touring a location in the real world. It lists a number of must-sees for the *SL* tourist; places that represent what might be called the culture of *Second Life*.

Chapter 4 deals with a pretty delicate subject: your appearance in *Second Life*. It discusses the myriad considerations involved in choosing a good *SL* name for yourself, and the complex task of making your *SL* avatar look the way you want it to look.

Chapter 5 reviews the hundreds of gifts you receive when you enter the virtual world for the first time. These are contained in a special folder called the Library, and they are often overlooked by new *SL* residents.

Chapter 6 advises you on how to manage and tame the *SL* monster known as the Inventory. Your avatar's Inventory is where you keep all your belongings in *Second Life*, including readymade houses, spaceships, and hundreds of cool things to wear. The number of your Inventory items reaches four figures even before you arrive on the *SL* mainland, and getting a good grip on your Inventory is very important—otherwise, you're likely to spend many hours of online time just looking for stuff.

Chapter 7 expertly guides you through the process of creating new objects in the virtual world. It reveals the intricacies of the mysterious prim, explains the *SL* building and object-editing tools, and lets you gain an understanding of the almost-infinite possibilities for creating new stuff in *Second Life*.

Chapter 8 focuses on LSL (the Linden Scripting Language), which is used to write scripts that animate objects in *Second Life*. It explains how LSL works, and what you should know to make it work for you. Together with Chapter 7, it provides all the basic info you need to join in one of the most rewarding activities in *Second Life*: creating new content.

Chapter 9 discusses *SL* persona, career, and lifestyle choices with the aid of concrete examples. It features many contributions by longtime *SL* residents, in which they reveal who they are and how they spend their time in the virtual world. Chapter 9 was co-authored by *SL* residents Angel Fluffy, Baccara Rhodes, Cheri Horton, Desmond Shang, Forseti Svarog, Francis Chung, Iris Ophelia, Tao Takashi, and Taras Balderdash.

Chapter 10 talks about making money in *Second Life*. Yes, it's possible to make real money in a virtual setting, and this chapter tells you what's involved. It reviews *SL*'s most popular paying jobs, discussing the required skills and comparing earning potential, and it alerts you to the considerations involved in running a virtual business.

Chapter 11 features portraits of interesting *SL* people—residents whose presence in the virtual world has had a lasting impact of one kind or another.

Chapter 12 describes noteworthy events in *SL* history, such as the famous prim tax revolt.

Finally, **Chapter 13** examines the real-life lessons and real-world value of *Second Life*'s virtual world. Yes, there's real life in cyberspace, and this concluding chapter talks about the implications.

Four appendices round out this guide. Appendix A, by John "Pathfinder Linden" Lester, is addressed to real-world educators interested in taking advantage of a virtual environment. Appendix B contains a glossary of special terms and slang, and Appendix C directs you to sites that contain valuable *SL* info. Appendix D explains *SL*'s pull-down menu functions.

In addition, this guide is accompanied by a CD that includes special animations, character templates, and textures created by Linden Lab exclusively for this book, as well as the best of *SL*-resident-created *machinima*, or computer-generated movies. The disc also guides new users through the installation process and includes a code that grants a special object the first time you enter the metaverse.

We hope you'll find this book as enjoyable as it is useful. See you in *Second Life*.

CREDITS

Acquisitions Editor: Willem Knibbe

Developmental Editor: Candace English

Technical Editor: Mark Wallace

Production Editors: Patrick Cunningham, Sarah Groff-Palermo

Production Manager: Tim Tate

Vice President and Executive Group Publisher: Richard Swadley

Vice President and Executive Publisher: Joseph B. Wikert

Vice President and Publisher: Dan Brodnitz

Book Designer & Compositor: Patrick Cunningham

Proofreader: Asha Johnson

Cover Designer: Ryan Sneed

Cover Image: Jonhenry Righter

INTRO

CHAPTER 1
CHAPTER 2
CHAPTER 3
CHAPTER 4
CHAPTER 5
CHAPTER 6
CHAPTER 7
CHAPTER 8
CHAPTER 9
CHAPTER 10
CHAPTER 11
CHAPTER 12
CHAPTER 13
APPENDICES

PART I
GETTING A SECOND LIFE

CHAPTER 1

WHAT IS SECOND LIFE?

Second Life is a virtual world. No, *Second Life* is a 3D online digital world imagined, created, and owned by its residents. But hang on, there's more: critical authorities have defined *Second Life* as a *metaverse*—dig that? Everyone on the same page? All the statements above are true. *Second Life* is basically anything you want it to be. It's your virtual life, after all, and what you do with it is up to you.

Second Life is a virtual environment in which almost all of the content is created by users—people like you. You are the one who determines what *Second Life* means to you. Do you enjoy meeting people online, talking to them and doing things together in real time? Welcome to *Second Life*. Do you enjoy creating stuff and making it come alive? Welcome to *Second Life*. Do you enjoy running a business and making money—real money? Welcome to *Second Life*. The list of possible *Second Life* activities is as long as you can imagine.

This chapter discusses basic *Second Life* concepts, rules, and activities. Some of these—for example, benefits linked to given type of *SL* memberships—are subject to frequent changes. However, certain basic principles remain constant and are covered here.

CONTENTS

A BRIEF HISTORY OF SECOND LIFE

Second Life was conceived by Philip Rosedale. Like all artists, he'd always wanted to create a masterpiece that represents the world in a microcosm. Instead of paint, words, marble, or clay, he used bytes. Philip Rosedale started working on the concept that would become *Second Life* (initially, it was called *Linden World*) in 1991. Beta testing began in November 2002, and it was opened to the public just six months later. The beta version included a teleporting fee, as well as a tax on prims (short for "primitives") on top of land-maintenance costs; fees were charged for rezzing and maintaining all resident-created objects in the virtual world. On the surface, this step seemed very sensible, as every extra prim places a tiny extra burden on the hardware that runs *Second Life*'s virtual world. However, taxing residents' creations wasn't a wise move in a political sense, and it led to big consequences down the line.

On June 23rd, 2003, *Second Life* went live. In October of that year, a major update introduced a host of new features: improved search functions and world map, new land-management options, a new copyright/permission system for resident creations, and many groundbreaking graphic improvements. However, the update also included tools to minimize tax evasion. It sought to counterbalance this by introducing a new stipend called *dwell*, which essentially rewarded people for socializing. Creative *SL* residents were appalled that thoughtless socialites were being rewarded, while creators of new *SL* content were still penalized through prim tax.

The crackdown on prim-tax evaders brought drama and dissent; some *SL* resident groups fell apart, and themed communities were hit particularly hard: making an area reflect a certain theme requires plenty of new prims. The stage was set for a very real-life development; a grass-roots social movement began to form in the virtual world. Within a few weeks, a revolution was underway. In December 2003, the revolutionaries won: an entirely new tax system based on land ownership *sans* the prim tax was introduced in a subsequent update. That update also introduced the concept of SL time (same as Pacific Standard Time) and a number of new scripting and interface features.

More updates and improvements followed, and landmark updates introduced custom animations and gestures (June 2004), the LindeX currency exchange (October 2005), and an end to stipends for Basic membership plans (May 2006).

NOTE

ADDITIONAL INFO:
MORE SL HISTORY

If you're interested in SL *history, refer to Chapter 11 and visit the Second Life Historical Museum. You'll find the museum's landmark in the* SL Guidebook *that you can obtain on Help Island; if for some reasons you didn't, use the* SL Search *function. The museum exhibits are updated as* Second Life *evolves and include many resident creations as well as illustrated presentations of memorable events in* SL *history. You'll also find extra info in* Second Life's *History Wiki at* `http://history.secondserver.net/index.php/Main_Page`. *Like the museum exhibits, the History Wiki is updated constantly with fresh entries and articles as* Second Life *continues to grow and evolve.*

CHAPTER 1

HOW DOES IT WORK?

From your point of view, *SL* works as if you were a god in real life. Not an almighty god, perhaps—more like one of those mythological minor gods, who tended to specialize in certain areas, get drunk, have sex, fight, and (most important) cast spells left, right, and center. Regardless of who you are in *Second Life*, you're able to "cast spells" too (Figure 1.1). And just like a mythological god, you're able to fly, and teleport wherever you like in an instant.

Figure 1.1: Abracadabra, one, two, three—pow!

INTRO
CHAPTER 1
CHAPTER 2
CHAPTER 3
CHAPTER 4
CHAPTER 5
CHAPTER 6
CHAPTER 7
CHAPTER 8
CHAPTER 9
CHAPTER 10
CHAPTER 11
CHAPTER 12
CHAPTER 13
APPENDICES

CHAPTER 1

INTRO

PART I

PART II

PART III

APPENDICES

HOW DOES IT WORK?

You can also change your appearance whenever you want to, and to whatever you like. In case you've ever dreamed of pulling a Zeus number and wooing someone as a swan, *Second Life* offers you the opportunity.

The *SL* virtual world imitates the real world that you know, and hopefully like. It consists of interlinked regions that contain land, water, *and* sky (*SL* lets you build castles in the sky). Each region has an area of 65,536 *Second Life* square meters.

NOTE

ADDITIONAL INFO:
REGIONS AS SIMS

SL residents often refer to regions as sims—short for simulators. This is because originally, one server or simulator held one entire region. Now there are two regions per server, but the old name has stuck.

SL regions are both geographical and administrative units: they are governed by rules and regulations that may change from region to region. The entire *Second Life* world is divided into areas that can include any number of regions governed by a given set of rules. For example, a separate area called Teen grid is reserved for *SL* members between the ages of 13 and 17. Members in that age group are not allowed into the main adult area, and vice versa. You'll find more info on *SL* mores, customs, and social etiquette later in this chapter, and in Chapter 2.

Second Life is populated by avatars: virtual representations of *SL* members. The *SL* world also contains a great variety of objects. Ranging from palaces to pebbles, almost all the objects in *Second Life* have been created by *SL* citizens. Creating new objects—clothes, guns, spaceships—is one of the most popular *SL* activities, and the driving force behind *SL* commerce. *Second Life* keeps track of everything that's happening in its virtual world by assigning unique identifiers not only to in-world objects and avatars, but also to anything that has significance (see the "How *Second Life* Keeps Track of Things" sidebar).

SIDEBAR

FROM LINDEN LAB:
HOW SECOND LIFE KEEPS TRACK OF THINGS

A UUID (Universally Unique Identifier) is a 16-byte string that looks like this: 987fc1b0-bd3b-47fb-8506-2b1ffbec8984—it's 8 characters, 4 characters, 4 characters, 4 characters, 12 characters, all separated with hyphens.

Across the Second Life *platform*, we use *UUIDs* in a variety of places where we want to represent a complex bundle of data with a smaller, simpler reference—a *UUID* is only *16* bytes long. Some of the data that have a *UUID* "name" include the following:

- *Avatar agents.*

- *Land parcels. As you create, subdivide, merge, or otherwise modify parcels, they get a new UUID every time.*

- *Groups. Every group that is made gets a UUID.*

- *Regions. They not only have a unique name, but they also have unique UUIDs.*

- *Simulator states, which are snapshots of a region. These are periodically saved and given a UUID.*

- *Money transactions and inventory transactions.*

- *Your login sessions.*

- *Folders in your inventory.*

- *Any snapshot you take.*

- *Every event or classified ad you create.*

- *Assets, which are sharable resources including textures, objects, landmarks, clothing, and almost anything that goes in your inventory.*

What does this mean? Well, any of the data above is guaranteed to be unique across space and time—that is to say, if you have a texture and you know its UUID, you can be confident that no other texture had, has, or will have the same UUID.

Many LSL functions take a UUID and operate on the texture/sound/ inventory item with that UUID. For example, you must give llSetTexture() the UUID of the texture you want to set your object to.

—Jeff Luan, Linden Lab

INTRO
CHAPTER 1
CHAPTER 2
CHAPTER 3
CHAPTER 4
CHAPTER 5
CHAPTER 6
CHAPTER 7
CHAPTER 8
CHAPTER 9
CHAPTER 10
CHAPTER 11
CHAPTER 12
CHAPTER 13
APPENDICES

1

INTRO

PART I

PART II

PART III

APPENDICES

HOW DOES IT WORK?

THE MAGIC PRIM

Almost all the objects you see in *Second Life* are created or built from solids (3D geometric shapes) called prims. Each region can support 15,000 prims (plus a reserve of around 10 percent to let it handle moving objects).

Prims can assume any shape you want, and they come in a variety of shapes to make transformations easier. And you can make prims look any way you want by applying selected textures to their surfaces (Figure 1.2). They can be given certain qualities and features (such as transparency or the ability to flex/bend with the wind), they can be linked together, and they can be made to *do* things by a script written in LSL—*Second Life*'s

Figure 1.2: Your ability to create and manipulate prims is probably the most godlike feature of Second Life.

scripting language. For example, in *Second Life* a dog that moves and barks is an animated object made of linked prims, scripted to move in a certain way and play custom sound effects. You'll find a detailed discussion of prim- and scripting-related issues in Chapters 7 and 8.

You don't have to be a building and scripting guru to acquire and enjoy all the objects you'd like to have in *Second Life*. Like in real life, you can buy them, using real-world money or Linden dollars. But unlike in real life, you can also count on being given tons of cool freebies the moment your avatar enters the *SL* world. The Library folder in your avatar's Inventory is packed with stuff—follow the advice in Chapter 5 of this guide, and check it out. Many new *SL* citizens don't, and some of them subsequently spend a lot of Linden dollars to buy items they already have in their Libraries from a smiling con man (or con woman). Yes, those exist in *Second Life*, too.

FROM LINDEN LAB:
LINDEN PLANTS

Linden plants from the Library are special objects with unique properties. Although they appear to be much more complex than prims, each plant counts as a single prim—something to keep in mind when you become a proud landowner and want to do some landscaping.

SL MONEY

As you know by now, *Second Life* has its own currency: the Linden dollar. Linden dollars are exchangeable for real-life dollars. The exchange rate fluctuates; predictably, it's determined by money supply (which is influenced by ongoing tweaks to *SL* stipends and bonuses, as well as the ratio between new Premium and Basic accounts started by fresh *SL* residents—the differences between these two account types are discussed in the section at the end of this chapter).

At the time of writing, US$1 is worth nearly 275 Linden dollars. Historical highs had the exchange rate hovering in the low two hundreds, while a relatively recent low saw an exchange rate of well over L$300 to US$1. Inside *Second Life*, a Linden dollar has much more purchasing power than real-life money, of course.

You can obtain Linden dollars in a variety of ways (which are described in Chapter 10). Very roughly, *SL* income sources correspond to the income sources in real life. You may opt to take a virtual job—the *SL* Classifieds always feature many job ads—or you may want to try turning a profit by running your own business. If you're lucky and skilful, you can make money gambling; if you're talented, you can design and create saleable items; if you're none of the above, you can sit in a "camping chair" and make something like L$3 every 15 minutes. L$3 is roughly worth one US cent, but it can buy you a lot of nice items in *Second Life!* You can also buy Linden dollars at a number of third-party currency exchanges, paying in US dollars or euros. This is often the wisest course, letting you spend your *SL* time on activities other than making money.

Depending on the membership plan you choose, you may also receive Linden dollars when you begin your *SL* membership. This is discussed in more detail later in this chapter.

INTRO
CHAPTER 1
CHAPTER 2
CHAPTER 3
CHAPTER 4
CHAPTER 5
CHAPTER 6
CHAPTER 7
CHAPTER 8
CHAPTER 9
CHAPTER 10
CHAPTER 11
CHAPTER 12
CHAPTER 13
APPENDICES

NOTE

ADDITIONAL INFO:
THE BEST THINGS IN SECOND LIFE ARE FREE

Just like in real life, you don't have to have money to enjoy the best Second Life *has to offer. Making new friends is free of charge, and so is having a fun time doing something you like with people you like. Yes, owning a few things that bring private joy is nice, but you'll find out that in* Second Life *you can get lots of very nice stuff for free. Check the* SL *Classifieds for offers by* SL *merchants, and do not forget to visit* SL *Boutique at* `http://www.slboutique.com`. *Its catalog always features plenty of special offers that let you get great stuff for free, or for the symbolic price of L$1. And as explained in Chapter 10, in* SL *you can make a bunch of Linden dollars by sitting in a chair for 15 minutes.*

YOU AND YOUR AVATAR

In *Second Life*'s virtual world, your avatar represents you. You can change your avatar's appearance as often as you like. *SL* tools include a powerful avatar-appearance editor, and on top of that every avatar comes with a Library full of goodies, including a number of complete alternate avatars. Very broadly, an avatar consists of shape (the body) and outfit (what's worn on the body, plus any body attachments). You'll find a discussion of avatar-appearance editing options in Chapter 4, and more details about the Library in Chapter 5.

The vast majority of *SL* citizens opt to stay human in *Second Life*. But some choose avatars based on fictional characters from real-life movies, comic strips, or books. There are more vampires in *Second Life* than in all of Transylvania (they are very friendly vampires, for the most part). The Furries—*SL* people who choose to be represented by furry animal avatars—are another large group. Interestingly, some groups have grown so big and have become so highly organized that they're referred to as *micronations*.

Your avatar choices say a lot about who you are; to the people you encounter in the *SL* world, your avatar *is* who you are. It's true, too—your avatar choices reflect your personality and mentality. It's good to keep that in mind (Figure 1.3).

Avatar choices do not affect your access to *Second Life* options and privileges *except* when they breach community standards. So you may want to think twice before you attach a striking appendage to your avatar prior to a stroll through the streets of *Second Life*. Of course, you are free to be just about as radical as you want on land that you own, or on any privately or group-owned land whose owners allow anything and everything. This and other aspects of land ownership are discussed in Chapter 2.

Figure 1.3: I wonder if that's really me...

WHAT TO DO WITH YOUR NEW LIFE

As you know by now, *Second Life* gives you the freedom to pursue your dreams and interests. For some residents, this means having as much virtual sex as possible; for others, it means shooting at other people, possibly while piloting a spaceship. You'll find examples of various *SL* lifestyles in Chapters 9 and 11.

Virtual hedonism is fun, but do not let it blind you to other possible *SL* activities. For many residents, *Second Life* primarily represents a great opportunity to develop their talents as creators and artists. In addition to building and scripting, *Second Life* lets you take photographs and make movies. If you feel talented in one of these areas, you could gain more than just applause: the top prize at a *Second Life* movie festival may be as high as L$100,000 (roughly US$400). Chapter 3 discusses these activities in more detail.

For a lot of *SL* citizens, the virtual world is simply a great place to meet other people (Figure 1.4). It is also a great place to play with others: as explained earlier, *Second Life* allows all kinds of virtual social interaction. Whatever takes place in *Second Life* takes place by mutual consent: anyone who does not like what's going on can leave the world with a single mouse click.

INTRO

CHAPTER 1

CHAPTER 2

CHAPTER 3

CHAPTER 4

CHAPTER 5

CHAPTER 6

CHAPTER 7

CHAPTER 8

CHAPTER 9

CHAPTER 10

CHAPTER 11

CHAPTER 12

CHAPTER 13

APPENDICES

However, a general principle applies to all activities: no matter what they are, there is a place for them somewhere in *Second Life*. If you're exceptionally hard to satisfy, then you'll want to acquire private land and set your own rules. Many *SL* residents form groups to purchase land and set their own rules to pursue shared interests. However, land ownership is permitted only with Premium *SL* membership; see the relevant section further on in this chapter for more details.

ADDITIONAL INFO:
ROLE PLAYING

Role playing is very popular among SL residents, and areas are specially themed to enhance the role-playing experience. If you've always dreamed of living in the Victorian era or in the Wild West, you can—see Chapters 2 and 3 for more info. Interestingly, one of the most popular forms of individual role play in Second Life *is real-life males appearing as virtual females—in one online poll, 18.6% of male members confessed to living their second life as the opposite sex.*

SL RULES AND ETIQUETTE

Second Life's community standards are listed on a notecard in your Library (Notecards folder). There are six cardinal sins (called "the Big Six"):

- **Intolerance.** Just like in real life, being derogatory or demeaning with regard to another person's race, ethnicity, gender, religion, or sexual orientation is a big no-no.

- **Harassment.** Harassment can take very many forms in a virtual world, but the forms have a common denominator: someone gets upset. If you see your actions or words are upsetting someone, stop.

- **Assault.** This includes pushing, shooting, and shoving another *SL* resident in an area marked as Safe (Safe status is displayed as an icon on the top info bar). Making fellow residents miserable by targeting them with scripted objects is forbidden, too.

- **Disclosure.** Information about another resident can be freely shared only if it is displayed in the resident's profile, or if you have the affected resident's consent

INTRO
CHAPTER 1
CHAPTER 2
CHAPTER 3
CHAPTER 4
CHAPTER 5
CHAPTER 6
CHAPTER 7
CHAPTER 8
CHAPTER 9
CHAPTER 10
CHAPTER 11
CHAPTER 12
CHAPTER 13
APPENDICES

CHAPTER 1

INTRO

PART I

PART II

PART III

APPENDICES

HOW DOES IT WORK?

to share extra information. This includes residents' real life data as well as their conversations—posting or otherwise sharing conversation logs requires prior consent of the people affected.

- **Indecency.** It's simple: if what you want to do can be offensive to other people, do it on private land in Mature areas.

- **Disturbing the peace.** Briefly, don't be a pest. Every resident is entitled to an enjoyable, peaceful second life.

As you can see, *SL* community standards are pretty reasonable and straightforward, and they amount to this: don't interfere with other people's enjoyment of their virtual experience. If what you want to do constitutes a threat to other people's enjoyment, do it at home—that means on land owned by yourself or by a group of *SL* citizens who share your special interests. Otherwise, just employ the same common sense you use in real life to decide what

Figure 1.5: You may find a new friend among the dragons, vampires, and gangstas of **Second Life.**

sort of behavior is acceptable. This will leave you with a comfortable safety margin— *Second Life* is a more relaxed social environment than the real world, and the people inhabiting its world are markedly friendlier than you're used to in real life (Figure 1.5). It's interesting to note *Second Life* is particularly appreciated by women; see the "Being a Woman in *Second Life*" sidebar.

"SL is a world where women have equality to a much greater extent than in RL. The primary advantage men have over women in RL, which influences many things, is physical strength. Here I am just as strong as any man. I don't need him to move or lift something. I can truly do anything men can do. So I have an equal opportunity to do anything I want to try.

"Also, the good-old-boy networks do not exist. Men aren't given advantages just because they are men.

"I don't have to split my time between a man, children, and doing what I want to do. I don't have to feel guilty if I chose work over children. If a woman wants to devote full time to making money, she can easily do so and not feel guilty.

"The second advantage is harder to explain. It has to do with a sense of security. Here, I can get all the attention and positive affirmation without the downside. I don't have to worry about unwanted attention. I do not have to fear the male's greater physical strength

"The last thing that comes to mind is that the little girl inside can be a beautiful as she likes. All the wishes 'if only I...' can come true. We can be as glamorous, sexy, trampish, or whatever as we wish. We are not judged by men on looks we can't do anything about."

—Jennifer McLuhan

"Personally, I enjoy SL for a lot of reasons... this world has opportunities for everybody; where you go and how well you do is based on your imagination and your talent, not your connections or your gender or any other thing that influences RL opportunities.

"I enjoy it because I love being able to do so many things that aren't possible in the real world... and because I love having the tools to turn anything from my imagination into reality. I love being able to meet so many people who I'd never have a chance to meet in RL.

"And yes, I enjoy SL because I love being able to look as good as I want, being able to change my look in an instant, being able to look completely different from my RL self.

"And I totally understand the security thing... it's great to have control here, to not have to worry about my personal safety. That's equally true for anyone here, male or female, but it's particularly significant for women, I think."

—*Ilianexsi Sojourner*

"I wanted to see what it would be like to play a male, so here's how it went:

"Went shopping. Limited choices! Men have limited choices in Second Life and real life. I guess it would be difficult making male lingerie or something sexy for men. The clothes were as pricey as female, but there wasn't much to buy. No wonder why there are so many female avatars.

"Went to a few clubs and found that men get catty like women, especially over other women. A guy wanted to kick my ass just for talking to his virtual girlfriend.

"I told people that I am a scripter and no questions were asked, but when I was a female avatar questions were asked, including 'Are you a male in RL?'

"I thought it would be easier to be a male, but not really. Women have more choices of clothing, hair, shoes, etc."

—*Damien Ferris*

NOTE

ADDITIONAL INFO:
COMMUNITY RULES

Make sure you read the Community Standards notecard! Taking out an SL membership means you automatically agree to respect SL rules. Penalties include suspension and banishment from Second Life.

MEMBERSHIP TYPES

As *Second Life* marches on, it evolves. Accordingly, membership plans can and do change. However, it's a safe bet that future variations will include the two membership types that are available at the time of writing. These are Basic membership and Premium membership, and both let you have lots of fun (see the "Membership Type Choices" sidebar).

RESIDENTS SPEAK:
MEMBERSHIP TYPE CHOICES

"Well, I am a free [Basic] member and can honestly say I'm having a ball here. Sure, if you want to own land you have to pay for a Premium account, but if your goal is simply to meet people and have fun at events you can easily do that for free. If you want extra L$ to buy clothes or whatever, you could use the camping chairs or dance pads. You can also attend games like trivia contests and bingo and maybe win some L$. I won L$100 last night at an '80s trivia event.

"There are so many cool things to see at SL that I never get bored just looking around. If you want a home you can always rent land and get a free house at a yard sale (I'm doing this right now).

Have fun, because that is the best part of SL!"

—Hedgie Till

"I have been playing (minus an absence last fall/winter) for a year and a half. Up until last month still wore freebie jeans. I have a Premium account and spent very few L$, yet I still manage to have fun and create and feel that I am getting all of the game.

"It all depends on your perception of 'all of the game.' Do you want to spend money on all sorts of gadgets, or do you want to create, explore, and try all sorts of different things?

"I don't see why a free account member cannot have the same

CHAPTER 1

INTRO

PART I

PART II

PART III

APPENDICES

← experience that a Premium account member does, aside from owning land. Do you really need a house? Are you actually going to sleep in SL?

"Get out, explore the world, experiment with building and scripting; most of all, enjoy yourself!!! Welcome to Second Life."

—Artemis Cain

NOTE

ADDITIONAL INFO:
A DUAL-ACCOUNT LIFE

For current information about Second Life membership plans, visit http://secondlife.com/whatis/plans.php. Consider establishing a free Basic membership right away to get a taste of what Second Life is like, and subsequently open a second, Premium account that lets you own land. It is always worth your while to have two Second Life accounts, as it lets you easily back up your Inventory.

BASIC MEMBERSHIP

A Basic membership plan entitles you to enter *Second Life* completely free of charge. It lets you enjoy all of *Second Life*'s activities and privileges except for one: you cannot own land in the *SL* world. (The consequences of this are explained later in this chapter.)

You may open additional Basic membership accounts; at the time of writing, each extra Basic account costs US$9.95. In spite of the cost, this might be a wise step if you have many Inventory items that you'd hate to lose. Creating a second account lets you create an alternate avatar, and having an alternate avatar lets you back up your Inventory. This might not sound like a big deal if you've just started out as an *SL* resident. But after you've spent some time in *Second Life*, your Inventory is likely to contain many thousands of items, and at least a few one-off specimens that cannot be copied. The process of backing up your Inventory is described in Chapter 6.

PREMIUM MEMBERSHIP

Premium membership lets you own land. It can be argued that this feature has less and less significance as *SL* develops—renting space is increasingly popular among residents. The advantages and disadvantages of land ownership are discussed in Chapters 2 and 10; however, be aware that having space of your own in *Second Life* is important. It lets you store items outside an avatar's Inventory (see Chapter 6 for details).

Premium membership costs vary depending on how you choose to pay. At the time of writing, the base rate of $9.95 per month shrinks to $6 when paid in an annual lump sum. Regardless of payment plan, you receive the coveted land-ownership rights plus a L$1,000 signup bonus and a weekly stipend of L$400. Note that all the quoted numbers are subject to change; please visit `http://secondlife.com/whatis/plans.php` for updated info.

There is no limit on how much land you can own in *Second Life*. However, the cost of owning land increases with the size of your real-estate holdings. This and other practical issues are discussed in the next chapter.

CHAPTER 2

GETTING STARTED

Living a life means making choices, and you'll be making plenty from the moment you log onto *Second Life* for the first time.

There is a third-person view and a first-person view. There are pull-down menus at the top of the screen and a button menu at the bottom. Should you stay on Help Island for a while, or dive into the action on the mainland right away? And once you've arrived on the mainland, what should you do next?

This chapter will help you sort out those and other issues that appear the moment you begin your virtual existence. It is intended mainly for new *SL* denizens, but it can also be very helpful to anyone who has been impatient and dived headfirst into *Second Life*. If you've ever wished you could return to Help Island, if only to grab some of the new freebies that have become available there, this chapter's for you, too.

CONTENTS

TAKING CONTROL OF YOUR SECOND LIFE

Being familiar with the *Second Life* interface enriches your virtual experience: almost every button, menu, and options panel is a doorway to new possibilities. The sections that follow synthesize all the interface info for your convenience. You'll find some extra information in the guides, and how-to instructions in the *Second Life* Knowledge Base (http://secondlife.com/knowledgebase).

ADDITIONAL INFO:
KEYBOARD SHORTCUTS

To obtain a list of **SL** *keyboard shortcuts, visit* http://secondlife. com/knowledgebase/article.php?id=075. *It's a good idea to print the list and keep it handy until you've memorized the shortcuts you use. The camera-control shortcuts are particularly helpful.*

FIRST STEPS

If you intend to become a new *SL* resident, begin by checking whether your system allows you to have a second life. At the time of writing, the system requirements are as follows. (Please note that this book is written with the assumption that you're using a PC as the portal to your second life. If you're using a Mac, please refer to http:// secondlife.com/corporate/sysreqs.php.)

- High-speed Internet connection
- **Operating system:** Windows XP (Service Pack 2) **or** Windows 2000 (Service Pack 4)
- **Computer Processor:** 800MHz Pentium III or better
- **Memory:** 256MB or better
- **Video/graphics card:** NVIDIA GeForce 2, GeForce 4mx, or better *or* ATI Radeon 8500, 9250, or better

To view the latest system requirements, please visit http://secondlife.com/corporate/sysreqs.php. If you're running a firewall, note that *Second Life* needs to connect to ports 443/TCP, 12035/UDP, 12036/UDP, and 13000-13050/UDP. You should configure your firewall to allow outbound traffic on those ports, and related inbound traffic.

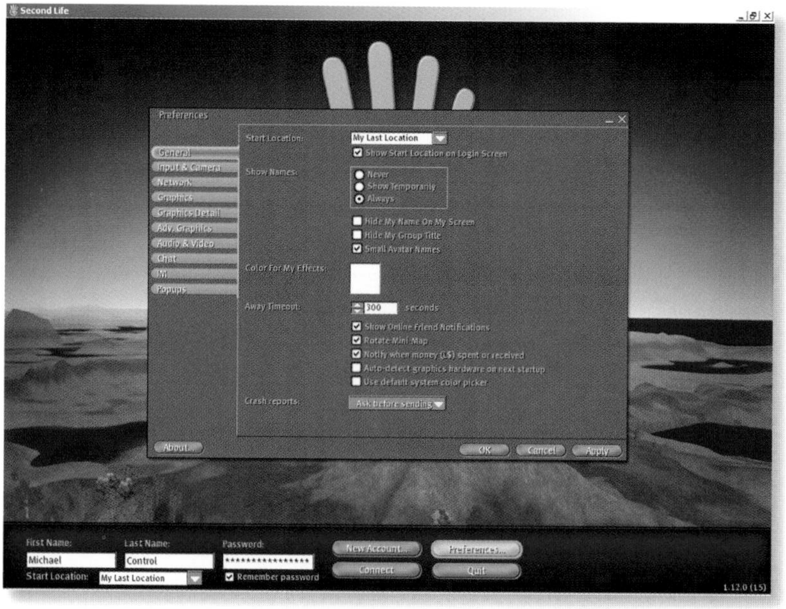

Upon logging into *Second Life*, you're presented with a login screen that contains

Figure 2.1: Adjusting the settings on the Preferences panel can optimize SL performance on your computer.

an important button: Preferences (Figure 2.1). Many new *SL* citizens are so eager to enter the virtual world that they never check it out. If you've been one of them, click it the next time you log in. It opens the Preferences panel, which contains 10 tabs:

- **General.** This tab offers basic *SL* options such as avatar name and title display, notifications of friends online and of money spent or received, etc.

- **Input and Camera.** This lets you adjust mouse sensitivity in mouselook (first-person view) and a quality called camera springiness. If you're after precision, use the sliders to reduce mouse sensitivity and camera springiness to 0.

- **Network.** You need to configure settings here if you're logging onto *Second Life* from inside a LAN. You can also lower maximum bandwidth if you have a slow connection (the default of 500 kbps is comfortably in excess of actual available bandwidth).

- **Graphics.** This tab presents basic graphic settings such as screen resolution and draw distance. Draw distance determines how far you can see in the virtual world. Lowering draw distance and screen resolution can improve performance if you have a relatively slow system or an old video card.

INTRO
CHAPTER 1
CHAPTER 2
CHAPTER 3
CHAPTER 4
CHAPTER 5
CHAPTER 6
CHAPTER 7
CHAPTER 8
CHAPTER 9
CHAPTER 10
CHAPTER 11
CHAPTER 12
CHAPTER 13
APPENDICES

INTRO

PART I

PART II

PART III

APPENDICES

TAKING CONTROL OF
YOUR SECOND LIFE

Graphics Detail. This lets you adjust the amount of detail visible in the virtual world. Lower settings improve performance on slow systems/old video cards. Note that some options, such as Enable Ripple Water, may be disabled if your system or video card is not up to par.

Adv. Graphics. More graphic-detail choices await here; their effects are explained in the submenu. Generally, lowering the displayed default values improves performance.

Audio and Video. You'll definitely want to review the default choices on this submenu. They include audio muting, playing streaming music and videos, SFX volume, etc.

Chat. This lets you switch chat bubbles on and off, change the color and size of displayed text, and adjust miscellaneous chat settings.

IM. This tab opens a small submenu with instant-messaging options.

Popups. Here you can choose which messages you want to see displayed in the world.

Take the time to review the default settings in the Preferences panel, and adjust them as appropriate for your system and Internet connection. If you'd like more info on what individual options can do for you, visit `http://secondlife.com/knowledgebase/article.php?id=087` to read more about them.

> **NOTE**
> **ADDITIONAL INFO:**
> **THE STATISTIC BAR**
>
> *To get detailed info on how well* Second Life *is running on your computer, activate the Statistic Bar by pressing CTRL + Shift + 1. Visit* `http://secondlife.com/knowledgebase/article.php?id=091` *to find out more.*

WHAT'S ON THE MENU

Second Life's main screen features a top bar and a bottom bar. Both are packed fairly tightly with features. Many of these, though not all, are discussed in the *SL*

Knowledge Base at http://secondlife.com/knowledgebase/category.php?id=19. The following sections review what is what.

The top bar includes a set of Windows-style pull-down menus (Figure 2.2). Some of the commands available through the pull-down menus are *not* accessible through any other menu or shortcut. You'll find a full list of pull-down menu commands and an explanation of what each command means in Appendix D.

Figure 2.2: The pull-down menus contain commands and helpful shortcuts, such as the one to the LSL scripting guide.

To the right of the pull-down menus, you'll see icons showing whether any activities are disallowed in your avatar's present location. If you are unsure what an icon means, hover your mouse cursor over it to bring up a tooltip. Your avatar's location—name of region, map coordinates, area rating, etc. —is shown right next to the icons.

Moving farther right, you'll see a clock displaying Pacific Standard Time. Residents call it "SL time." Money comes next: the little round Linden-dollar icon lets you buy *SL* currency through the LindeX (Basic members should note this requires credit card info). Your current L$ balance is next: it's updated instantly following every financial transaction. Finally, at the extreme left of the top bar, you'll see packet-loss and bandwidth indicators. Pay attention to these; high packet loss and low bandwidth may mean it's wise to cancel that planned visit to a busy nightclub.

THE BOTTOM LINE

The bottom bar features a row of buttons. From left to right, here's what is what:

INTRO

CHAPTER 1

CHAPTER 2

CHAPTER 3

CHAPTER 4

CHAPTER 5

CHAPTER 6

CHAPTER 7

CHAPTER 8

CHAPTER 9

CHAPTER 10

CHAPTER 11

CHAPTER 12

CHAPTER 13

APPENDICES

IM opens the Instant Message panel. If you have unread IMs from other *SL* residents, you'll see their names on tabs along the bottom of the panel. Click on a tab to read the IM from the named resident.

Chat opens the Chat box for typing text, but pressing the Enter key is much simpler and has the same effect.

Friends opens a panel listing all the *SL* people who've agreed to be your friend and tells you which are currently online. It acts as a small administrative center for common *SL* actions such as sending IMs, offering teleports to your current location, etc.

Fly toggles the Fly mode and is quite useful despite the convenient keyboard shortcuts (Page Up/Page Down is the default). Clicking it to stop flying will let you watch an entertaining animation as your avatar descends for a semihard landing (depending on how high you've been soaring around).

Snapshot opens the Snapshot Preview panel for taking snaps of the virtual world. Set all the options, such as snapshot size, resolution, image quality, etc. here.

Build opens the Build panel, and it's active only if the land you're on allows building (a sandbox area, your own land).

Mini-Map opens a mini-map in the upper-right corner of the screen. It can be useful when trying to find your way somewhere, or in busy, crowded areas such as commercial malls and entertainment complexes.

Map is, hands down, the most powerful button of them all. It opens a resizeable, rescaleable map of the *SL* world that's much more than a map. It includes Search functions and is also an interface for instant travel: double-clicking on any spot teleports your avatar to that location. In the virtual world, activities such as walking or driving a vehicle are entertainment choices, not necessities. Now you know why most of the roads and streets in *Second Life* are empty.

Inventory opens the Inventory panel (CTRL + I is the shortcut).

Note that the button menu may be inaccessible if you've set your Windows taskbar to stay on top of other application windows; in that case, right-click the Windows taskbar and select Properties to make the necessary changes.

ADDITIONAL INFO:
THE PIE MENU

Right-clicking on almost anything in the virtual world brings up a pie menu. The menu's options are context-sensitive and depend on the properties of what you clicked on. To find out more about SL pie menus, visit `http://secondlife.com/knowledgebase/article.php?id=133.`

VIEWS AND MOVEMENT

The standard *SL* view is the "follow" mode, with the camera behind and slightly above your avatar. However, some people find the mouselook or first-person view to be far more convenient when moving around. If walking down a street and keeping to the pavement proves a comically difficult exercise using the standard view, switch to mouselook. Mouselook is also great for flying: you'll fly in the direction indicated by your mouse cursor. Thus, you can turn, ascend, and descend by moving your mouse—it feels as if you were flying a plane.

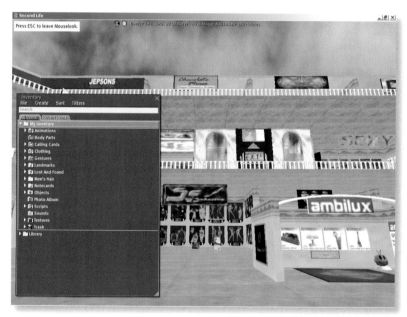

Figure 2.3: Use keyboard shortcuts for menu functions in mouselook.

You cannot access the onscreen menus in mouselook, which is quite a drawback. However, you can still use shortcut keys to execute commands: for example, open your Inventory by pressing CTRL + I (Figure 2.3). Keeping the ALT key depressed lets you move the mouse cursor without changing the view; once the cursor is over a panel, you can let go of the key and proceed to do what you wanted to do (for

INTRO
CHAPTER 1
CHAPTER 2
CHAPTER 3
CHAPTER 4
CHAPTER 5
CHAPTER 6
CHAPTER 7
CHAPTER 8
CHAPTER 9
CHAPTER 10
CHAPTER 11
CHAPTER 12
CHAPTER 13
APPENDICES

example, rearrange Inventory items). The ALT key also lets you move the camera around and zoom in and out while in the standard "follow" view.

NOTE

ADDITIONAL INFO:
FLIGHT PACKS

The SL marketplace features all types of aircraft as well as many models of "flight packs." These can be very sophisticated and very affordable—see the "Flying High in Second Life" sidebar for a few examples of aircraft for sale. Chapter 3 discusses Abbott's Aerodrome, a popular place to purchase aircraft.

SIDEBAR

ADDITIONAL INFO:
FLYING HIGH IN SECOND LIFE

DefCon 1 Aerospace Vehicles (free demo flights)

Sponsored by Marlin Engineering. Some of the best flying vehicles in Second Life, smooth and responsive flight model...sleek stylish looks, low prim for low lag. Nice features and reasonable price, one- and two-person fighters L$500, five-person shuttle L$600.

Intelligent flight assist / jetpack @ Aodhan's Forge

It's no ordinary jetpack. The Scarab was designed with your convenience in mind. Making a flight pack go fast is easy, but what really matters is making a flight pack do what you want it to do...automatically. The Scarab almost completely takes away the fumbling with typed commands while giving you the flight assist you need, when you need it. Details at SL.AodhansForge.com.

DreamTech Aeronautics

Specializing in airships of various kinds, historic, futuristic, and fantastic. Visit us for a test flight today!

Zeppelins, airships, flying ships, aircraft, blimps, sailboats, sailing, yachts, teleporters, teleportation system.

← CRYSTALTECH *Vehicles*

Home of the unbeaten most realistic vehicle models in SL!

Vehicles store. Get spaceships, choppers/helicopters, and jetfighters. All featuring physical smooth flight.

As mentioned earlier, "ordinary" movement—walking, flying, driving a vehicle, or taking the streetcar—is a source of entertainment and an opportunity to socialize; it's not a necessity. The introduction of instant teleporting, free of charge, any time and anywhere, has made all other modes of movement unnecessary except when inside small, confined spaces. But a drive in a virtual car, a stroll around a shopping mall, or a visit to a nightclub can be entertaining. Walking and flying are definitely the preferred movement modes when you're sightseeing. The *SL* world contains more interesting places to visit than most tourist hotspots in the real world; you'll find more details in Chapter 3.

NOTE

ADDITIONAL INFO:
SETTING LANDMARKS

Set landmarks on the SL map to move quickly between your favorite places, or to arrive in specific spots, such as a venue for an event you want to attend. Visit http://secondlife.com/knowledgebase/category. php?id=22 *for detailed info on navigation and movement in Second Life.*

CHAPTER 2

LEARNING ABOUT SECOND LIFE

Second Life offers you almost as many choices as real life does. Visit the *Second Life* Knowledge Base right at the start of your new existence, if only to review all the topics covered—it will help you get an idea of what's possible. The Knowledge Base is updated constantly as new features become available, so it's a good idea to revisit it on a regular basis. The guides and how-to articles featured there are a great way to find out more about how things work in the virtual world. The Knowledge Base is complemented by the *Second Life* Wiki. These two sources contain invaluable

INTRO
CHAPTER 1
CHAPTER 2
CHAPTER 3
CHAPTER 4
CHAPTER 5
CHAPTER 6
CHAPTER 7
CHAPTER 8
CHAPTER 9
CHAPTER 10
CHAPTER 11
CHAPTER 12
CHAPTER 13
APPENDICES

information, regardless of whether your interest is in running a virtual business, making movies, or socializing and role playing.

> **ADDITIONAL INFO:**
> ## SEARCHING THE KNOWLEDGE BASE
>
> *Puzzled about something? Enter the appropriate keyword into the SL Knowledge Base search box. Chances are you'll find a whole series of articles, guides, and tutorials related to your chosen subject.*

If you need a little personal guidance, acquire a mentor. Mentors are volunteers who are longtime *SL* residents. Most often, they specialize in a particular skill or knowledge area—for example, creating new virtual objects with prims. You'll encounter some mentors on Help Island. And if you don't come across a mentor in the arrival area on the *SL* mainland, use the search function: enter "mentor" and pick the All tab on the Search panel. You can refine your search further to find a mentor who is knowledgeable about a topic you're interested in.

ORIENTATION ISLAND AND HELP ISLAND

Your virtual existence begins on Orientation Island. The short tutorial offered there will teach you a few basics, but not more than that. Your next stop will be Help Island (Figure 2.4), and this is where you should stay awhile. In addition to snapping up the freebies from the Freebie Shop, you should definitely visit the tutorials and demo areas. If you don't understand something clearly, ask the mentors on duty in the Help Island arrival area.

> **ADDITIONAL INFO:**
> ## RETURNING TO YOUR ROOTS
>
> *Your avatar cannot return to Orientation or Help Island once it has arrived on the mainland, but you can. You can start a new basic account at no charge and revisit the two islands. Creating a second or alternate avatar is a wise step, since it lets you back up your Inventory (see Chapter 6).*

Make sure you collect and keep all the notecards from Help Island; you'll be seeing and experiencing too many new things to remember everything. In particular, the Explorer Guidebook (which tells you where to go on the mainland if you want to repeat Orientation Island tutorials) and Real Life Education Places notecards are worth keeping when you're doing your first big Inventory cleanup prior to departing for the mainland.

Figure 2.4: Make sure you explore all of Help Island.

Once you've arrived on the mainland, use the Search function to find out where you can learn more about various aspects of *Second Life*. Choices range from attending classes and courses at one of the many schools and universities to learning how to be a good servant to an *SL* master. The classes and courses available aren't limited to *Second Life* subjects; you may pick up valuable real-life skills!

MAINLAND CHOICES

Once you're on the mainland, your priorities are shaped by the kind of virtual life you want to live. But regardless of your interests, you'll make two choices early on: whether to have a place of your own in the virtual world, and whether to remain a lone wolf or become part of a specific community.

FORMING AND JOINING GROUPS

Any two *SL* residents, regardless of membership plan type, can form a group (right-click on your avatar and choose Groups from the pie menu). The resident who

INTRO
CHAPTER 1
CHAPTER 2
CHAPTER 3
CHAPTER 4
CHAPTER 5
CHAPTER 6
CHAPTER 7
CHAPTER 8
CHAPTER 9
CHAPTER 10
CHAPTER 11
CHAPTER 12
CHAPTER 13
APPENDICES

CHAPTER 2

INTRO

PART I

PART II

PART III

APPENDICES

LEARNING ABOUT SECOND LIFE

initiated this process becomes the group's founder and enjoys special privileges. It is interesting to note that group rules in general have evolved from a democratic, open model toward a more authoritarian one with *SL* updates. It seems that the young age of virtual society made formally organized communities too immature for democracy, resulting in the breakup of many ambitious enterprises. At the time of writing, group rules are slightly reminiscent of a monarchy, with the founder designating successors to carry on the work: you'll find details at `http://secondlife.com/app/help/new/groups.php`. The new authoritarian group structure promises to be helpful to the long-term survival of many organized *SL* communities.

Organized communities greatly enrich the virtual world (Figure 2.5). There are no restrictions on community size or the degree of their organizational development, and some even resemble micronations. However, many communities—and estate owners—have goals other than expansion (see the "Groups and Communities" sidebar). If you look around, you're sure to find many groups whose goals or activities appeal to you. You

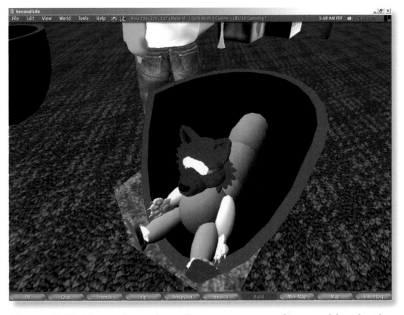

Figure 2.5: There is a place for everyone and everything in the virtual world.

can belong to as many as 25 different groups, including those that you started yourself.

SIDEBAR

ADDITIONAL INFO:
GROUPS AND COMMUNITIES

"The Neualtenburg Projekt is a private land cooperative formed in 2004 now occupying one entire simulator or "sim" of 64 virtual acres in Second Life acquired directly from Linden Lab in May 2005. It attempts to

simulate the look and feel of a functioning Bavarian city with residential, commercial and public spaces. The cooperative has a democratic republican government with three branches and a constitution. The simulated city is open to the public, but participation in the government requires the acquisition of virtual land in the city. Acquisition of land constitutes agreement to abide by various specific standards of building and activity in the city.

Title to the entire sim is actually "owned" (licensed from Linden Lab) by an avatar as "Estate Owner." This status allows the treasurer to deed land to ownership groups and to reclaim land from those groups. For its convenience, Neualtenburg has chosen to appoint the "alt" of its treasurer to accept title to the land as estate owner on behalf of the municipality.

In return for a one-time payment, resident's ownership groups receive grant deeds to particular parcels, allowing them rights to use specific parcels of virtual land as long as they conform to the city's land use regulations and payment of monthly land use fees in the nature of property tax. Residents' rights may be terminated and their virtual property reclaimed by the city for breach of the various covenants and agreements. Residents in good standing may sell their virtual land rights to third parties approved by the city."

—from "The Neualtenburg Projekt Summary" by Frank Lardner

Earlier today I have formed the Second Life chapter of the Socialist Party. In doing this, I hope to provide an alternative way for individuals to commune, interact, and produce. I also hope to utilize Party membership to launch some in-world political activism. Our goal isn't to overthrow the free market of Second Life or anything like that, as most people seem to enjoy virtual capitalism, we just want there to be options. If anybody is interested in helping out with SPSL, then instant message Lenin Camus.

Also, for members in need, I'm offering some free rent homes."

—Lenin Camus

"Caledon is a small, windswept forested country at a temperate latitude. Wild creatures, country estate life, sights and sounds that were common well over 100 years ago are the hallmark of the land.

Technology is approximately that of the 19th century, though some astonishing breakthroughs have provided for incredible wonders. Ground vehicles, airships, and even a device known as a Telehub are made possible through the power of exotic material properties and the wonders of steam technology. (The Steampunk community has a strong presence in Caledon, including The Manor, headquarters of the Steampunks group.)

The government is an expansionist monarchy, supported by a strong aristocracy (i.e., residents). Caledon offers the opportunity for residents to take their turn at "Stewardship," a post which can involve answering questions, restarting sims, banning obvious griefers, etc."

—from SL *History Wiki: The Independent State of Caledon*

COMMUNITY LAND

A group is an association of two or more residents sharing common aims and/or interests. However, groups may and frequently do own land that is purchased from Linden Lab by the estate owner, or donated by individual group members.

NOTE
ADDITIONAL INFO:
THE BENEFITS OF COMMUNITY LAND

The land-ownership structure in SL rewards residents who form organized communities: member land-tier donations to group estates receive a 10% bonus. Thus, donating 512 square meters of tier results in the group being able to hold 563 square meters.

Land ownership in *Second Life* does not require a Premium membership plan when the land in question is purchased from an estate owner. The intricacies involved are explained in detail in the *Second Life* Knowledge Base: just keep in mind that becoming an estate owner—purchasing land from Linden Lab—does require Premium membership and can carry significant extra costs.

OWNING VIRTUAL LAND

Owning land in *Second Life* carries land-use costs. Your Premium membership includes land-use costs for up to 512 square meters of real estate. If you want to own more, the costs increase. Table 2.1 displays land area/associated land-use costs at the time of writing.

Table 2.1: Land-Use Costs

ADDITIONAL LAND (OVER 512 SQ METERS)	MAXIMUM AREA (IN SQUARE METERS)	MONTHLY LAND-USE FEE
1/128 Region	512 sq. meters	US$5
1/64 Region	1,024 sq. meters	US$8
1/32 Region	2,048 sq. meters	US$15
1/16 Region	4,096 sq. meters	US$25
1/8 Region	8,192 sq. meters	US$40
1/4 Region	16,384 sq. meters	US$75
1/2 Region	32,768 sq. meters	US$125
Entire Region	65,536 sq. meters	US$195

Land Use Fees are always charged monthly and are determined by peak land ownership within the period for which they apply. If you're a real-estate speculator beginning and ending the month with 512 square meters but hitting a peak 10,000 square meters midway through the month, you'll pay Land Use Fees for 1/4 Region (US$75). Note that donating land to a group does not absolve you of carrying its Land Use Fees. However, a Basic membership plan holder who buys land from an estate owner does not have to pay land-upkeep fees *unless* this is specified in the land covenant. However, owners of land in organized communities often make periodical payments such as land "taxes" that defray Land Use Fees to the estate owner or administrator.

If you look at the table data carefully, you should notice a pattern: the more land you own, the less it costs per square meter. This is unlikely to change even if the fees do. This can have important implications on trading for profit in the land market. Chapter 10 discusses more ways to make money in *Second Life*.

INTRO
CHAPTER 1
CHAPTER 2
CHAPTER 3
CHAPTER 4
CHAPTER 5
CHAPTER 6
CHAPTER 7
CHAPTER 8
CHAPTER 9
CHAPTER 10
CHAPTER 11
CHAPTER 12
CHAPTER 13
APPENDICES

ADDITIONAL INFO:
REAL-ESTATE RICHES

At the time of writing, the richest SL resident is Anshe Chung—a real-estate tycoon whose virtual holdings, as reported by the real-world magazine Business Week, are rumored to be worth around a quarter million real-life US dollars.

There is no limit on your virtual land holdings. If you like, you can order and purchase your very own made-to-order island from Linden Lab. *Second Life* islands cannot be smaller than a single region (65,536 square meters). At the time of writing, the two island sizes on offer are one and four regions. Note that regardless of the island's starting size, extra land in the form of additional island may be added to the island at a later date, if there is room around the island on the map.

Owning a little personal empire is not cheap. At the time of writing, island-setup fees are US$1,250 for a one-region island and $5,000 for the four-region model. In addition, island owners pay standard Land Use Fees. Visit `http://secondlife.com/community/land-islands.php` for up-to-date island-ownership info, and `http://secondlife.com/whatis/landpricing.php` to check on current Land Use Fees.

Figure 2.6: You rule your land through the About Land panel.

Before you commit to joining any groups or buying real estate, it's wise to get an idea of the lay of the land and have a comprehensive picture of what goes on where. Accordingly, the next chapter takes you on a tour of the *SL* mainland.

ADDITIONAL INFO:
THE ABOUT LAND PANEL

Right-click on land you own and select About Land to open a panel with many land-management options (Figure 2.6). These include restricting access, issuing permission to run scripts, playing music, banning specific residents, etc. Note that when you buy land from an estate owner, land-management options may be modified in accordance with the land covenant.

CHAPTER 3

THE GRAND TOUR

A hundred years ago, young men of position were sent on a "grand tour" of Europe to round out their cultural education. A hundred years from now, young men and women may make a similar tour of virtual worlds. Now's your chance to get a head start. If you visit all the spots in this chapter, you'll not only have a good grounding in *Second Life*'s cultural history, but you'll also get a look at a few of the most robust communities on the grid, and you'll have peeked at a few places most people won't know about. The only question is, what are you going to do with your education?

CONTENTS

WHERE TO BEGIN?

Spend enough time with Philip Rosedale, founder and CEO of Linden Lab, and you'll eventually hear him talk about "the event horizon of content creation." There was a time, Philip wistfully recalls, when a body could take in all the new content that was added to the *Second Life* grid every day—every house, every car, every new dress or hairdo that the residents had created. But that point was passed more than a year ago, according to Rosedale. These days, you're lucky to be able to visit a fraction of what's added to the virtual world every 24 hours.

How do you figure out what's worth seeing then? One way is to check out what other people are checking out. *Second Life*'s "search" interface includes a list of the most popular places on the grid. These are the places that have climbed to the top of the list over many months; it features old standbys with good staying power, but the latest hot nightclub might not have made it onto the list yet. You can also look on the Picks tab of other residents' profiles, where people list their favorite places in the world. To get to them, just click the Teleport button or Show on Map to see where you're going. Each location in this chapter is indicated by the name of a region followed by three numbers: the X, Y, and Z coordinates within the region (indicating east-west location, north-south location, and height, respectively). Taken together, these coordinates describe any location on the grid.

Of course, the best way to figure out the latest trends is just to keep your eyes open and your ear to the ground. But trends come and go—perhaps surprisingly, *Second Life* features a great deal of content that's stuck around longer than most people expected it would. Builds like Eddie Escher's Seacliff towers have been around for two years or more. Other establishments have been around even longer.

Choosing the ones that are both stable additions and must-see spots isn't easy. There's no doubt that the list below is biased toward a few of the places I find most interesting on the grid. However, it also includes places I rarely visit but that stick out as institutions in *Second Life* (The Edge nightclub, for instance). I've tried to include oldies but goodies, a few of the spots that have drawn the most attention from a wider audience (the Svarga "living sim," for instance), and a few lesser-known but still-important hangouts that might not make it onto everyone's list.

CHAPTER 3

INTRO

PART I

PART II

PART III

APPENDICES

WHERE TO BEGIN?

DESTINATIONS FOR NEWCOMERS

Many *Second Life* locations are designed expressly for those new to the world. From Linden-run welcome areas and sandboxes to resident-run nightclubs and outreach organizations, there's always a helping hand available to those who've just set foot in this strange new world.

AHERN WELCOME AREA—AHERN (12, 12, 40)

The intersection of the Ahern, Bonifacio, Dore, and Morris sims marks the main welcome area at which new residents enter *Second Life*. Pick up freebies, practice building, or get pointers on the latest must-see sites. *SL* veterans often hang out here, lending a helping hand to those just learning how to find their way. Drop in if you have a question, or if you feel like being of service; just remember: no shooting or selling allowed.

NEW CITIZENS PLAZA—KUULA (54, 175, 29)

New to *Second Life* and unsure where to begin? Lots of great information can be had at New Citizens Plaza, an open resource for newbies that's stocked with plenty of free stuff, pointers to interesting places and more free stuff, guides to getting around, and helpful staffers willing to lend a hand. The most heartening thing about the place? It's run entirely by residents, so you can be sure you're getting the inside scoop.

THE SHELTER—ISABEL (44, 244, 79)

The Shelter is one of the rare *SL* social spaces that's both welcoming to new residents and completely free of sexual content. Travis Lambert describes his newbie-friendly nightclub as more of a rec center than a disco. The Shelter bills itself as "the friendliest spot in SL," and its staff takes pains to help out newbies, showering them with free gifts and showing them the ropes. Dance parties feature pop tunes from the 1980s and '90s, and free game shows, lotteries, and contests help give new residents a financial leg up. If dancing's not your bag, hang by the pool on the patio out back. For Lambert, it's important that the Shelter feel as comfortable as a living

INTRO
PART I
PART II
PART III
APPENDICES
DESTINATIONS FOR NEWCOMERS
44

room. "I think it's turned into a place people feel good about and consider their first home when they come to *SL*," he says.

THE SANDBOXES

The sandboxes provide a place for *SL*'s landless residents to get their build on, though you can often find accomplished builders stretching out in them as well. Public sandboxes have all builds wiped every 12 hours, so be sure to save a copy. Private sandboxes vary. Both are great places to get building tips and meet new friends—and occasionally to feel the push of a griefer's gun. Here's a list of public sandboxes, ordered from busiest to loneliest:

Sandbox Island (Figures 3.1 and 3.2)

Goguen Sandbox

Cordova Sandbox

Newcomb Sandbox

Morris Sandbox

Figure 3.1: Sandbox Island at the height of newbie building...

Figure 3.2. ...and right after a wipe

YADNI'S JUNKYARD—LEDA (210, 28, 54)

The blue-skinned YadNi Monde is one of *Second Life*'s most accomplished builders. An imposing presence in person, YadNi maintains one of the best resources for newbies at his junkyard in the Leda sim, where any number of textures, clothing, vehicles, toys, and other objects are available at bargain-basement prices of L$1 for a box full of junk. But it's useful junk, to be sure. The junkyard is an invaluable stop, and a good place to revisit for new additions.

IVORY TOWER LIBRARY OF PRIMITIVES—NATOMA (210, 164, 27)

A self-guided, self-paced, comprehensive building tutorial, the Ivory Tower has launched any number of successful *Second Life* building careers. Even 30 minutes spent here will prove valuable if you plan on doing any building at all. The explanations are clear and concise, and sample objects are provided to illustrate the concepts being taught.

STUFF TO SEE

Second Life has no shortage of locations that are interesting in and of themselves. Many of the places listed in the Stuff to See category also have activities associated with them—like shopping in the anime sim of Nakama—but these are also simply some of the most striking areas of the virtual world.

ARMORD COMPLEX—MIRAMARE (192, 38, 33)

One of the oldest neighborhoods in *SL*, the skyscraping towers of the ARMORD complex in Miramare (Figure 3.3) feature jetpacks, sci-fi mech-bot armor suits, *Tron*-style lightcycles, and the FURMORD line of furry mech helmets—all for sale at reasonable *SL* prices. Check out the observation deck at the space needle (a reproduction of the Seattle tower), the explorers' maps, and the science experiments—including a working toaster!

INTRO
CHAPTER 1
CHAPTER 2
CHAPTER 3
CHAPTER 4
CHAPTER 5
CHAPTER 6
CHAPTER 7
CHAPTER 8
CHAPTER 9
CHAPTER 10
CHAPTER 11
CHAPTER 12
CHAPTER 13
APPENDICES

CHAPTER 3

INTRO

PART I

PART II

PART III

APPENDICES

STUFF TO SEE

Figure 3.3: The towers of ARMORD

Figure 3.4: The virtual ecosystem at work

SVARGA (7, 123, 22)

SL resident Laukosargas Svarog spent a year creating Svarga (Figure 3.4), a functioning ecosystem in which the sun and the wind, the birds and the bees are all crucial to the continued growth of the plants and animals. Drop in to feed the birds and watch the grass grow.

RAMBLER COUNTY, TEXAS—GLUPHISIA (240, 62, 93)

Check out Nash Rambler's detailed re-creation of a rural Texas town, complete with general store, water tower, church, farm, and rutting deer. Catch Nash at home to enjoy his southern hospitality.

SCI-FI GEEKS MUSEUM AND THEATER—INDIGO (74, 212, 22)

Take the helm of a Klingon Bird of Prey or the USS *Defiant* from *Star Trek* at the Sci-Fi Geeks Museum. Both ships feature intricately re-created interiors (best navigated in mouselook). The museum also sports a functioning holodeck and a theater that shows a rotation of sci-fi-movie trailers. If you're lucky, you may even meet your Lieutenant Uhura here, so wear your dress uniform (Figure 3.5).

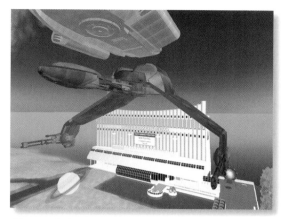

Figure 3.5: Prepare to be boarded.

Figure 3.6: Spaceport Alpha

INTERNATIONAL SPACEFLIGHT MUSEUM—SPACEPORT ALPHA (47, 77, 24)

Impressive scale models of rockets from throughout the history of space flight adorn this outdoor museum (Figure 3.6), which also includes a clockwork solar-system model; an amphitheater where lectures and music events take place; and a gift shop featuring art, apparel, and working Archer rockets, complete with smoke and fire trail. Look out for passersby before you light one off.

ANIME PARADISE—NAKAMA (128, 127, 21)

For fans of the Japanese cartoon style known as anime, Nakama is the place to be. Four *ku*, or neighborhoods, are devoted to anime styles from seedy to cute to slice-of-life to stories set in feudal-era Japan. Although there's a slight shortage of the art itself, there's no lack of outfits and other accessories that can make your second life more colorfully Japanese-style.

BLACKLIBRARY—HYPERBOREA (92, 58, 23)

Wandering Yaffle's extensive collection of game-related writing draws a vibrant, intellectual crowd to his _blacklibrary, named for the http://alwaysblack.com site

INTRO
CHAPTER 1
CHAPTER 2
CHAPTER 3
CHAPTER 4
CHAPTER 5
CHAPTER 6
CHAPTER 7
CHAPTER 8
CHAPTER 9
CHAPTER 10
CHAPTER 11
CHAPTER 12
CHAPTER 13
APPENDICES

INTRO

PART I

PART II

PART III

APPENDICES

STUFF TO SEE

it links to. Visit the art gallery or just hang out in the _blackbored, the underground bar named for the site's discussion forums.

THE PORT (251, 79, 26)

Billed as "an arena and an archive for projects that create new links between first and *Second Life*," the Port presents a vast, futuristic facade crisscrossed with network links and data representations in the style of William Gibson's *Neuromancer* (in which "cyberspace" was coined). A challenging place to make sense of, the Port will at least spark your thinking as to how your online life relates to your offline one.

THE FUTURE (133, 211, 65)

An entire sim packed with unique visions of—what else?—the future; from architecture to landscapes to art, The Future is an ever-changing wonderland of futuristic builds, vehicles, and hangouts, and one of the most visually delightful places in *SL*.

SEACLIFF (168, 200, 24)

Filled with the stunning structures of Eddie Escher, Fallingwater Cellardoor, and Reitsuki Kojima, Seacliff boasts some of the most satisfyingly fanciful architecture in *Second Life*. A lovely place for a virtual picnic.

SIDEBAR

RESIDENTS SPEAK:
SEASIDE VILLAGE BY THE FOREST OF KAHRUVEL

"One of my absolute favorite places in Second Life *is the Seaside Village (Figure 3.7) near the Forest of Kahruvel—Cowell (152, 79, 26). It's peaceful and charming and convenient to the forest, which is in and of itself a fantastic place for exploring, games of hide-and-go-seek, picnics, or pretty much any outdoor activity you can think of. The village, though, is my favorite because it looks and, more importantly, it feels like a real place I know and haven't been to for a very long*

> *time. It makes me nostalgic for sitting on a patio drinking wine and eating olives and cheese with friends I also haven't seen for a very long time."*
>
> —Chance Takashi

Figure 3.7: The Seaside Village: you might as well be in Greece.

NOVA ALBION "CITY" SIMS

SL architect Lordfly Digeridoo has been a resident of a place called Nova Albion since January 2004. Consisting of the four "city" sims of Grignano, Miramare, Sistiana, and Barcola (where twice as many objects can be built as elsewhere), Nova Albion was designed with a pre-arranged layout of roads, sidewalks, and trolleys before residents were allowed to move in. "The idea was to get a city feel going," says Digeridoo. "Dozens moved in, toyed with the city idea, then left. Now there's only a handful of residents there, but they've collectively kept the theme going informally, as well as coming up with distinct neighborhoods: Miramare is best known for shiny, techno-future builds; Grignano is known for brick-and-mortar brownstones and artistic havens." Barcola and Sistiana are the slums, often being graced with factories, warehouses, and the like.

Barcola

Grignano

Miramare

Sistiana

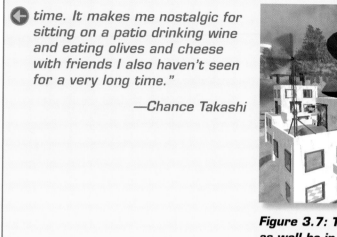

INTRO
CHAPTER 1
CHAPTER 2
CHAPTER 3
CHAPTER 4
CHAPTER 5
CHAPTER 6
CHAPTER 7
CHAPTER 8
CHAPTER 9
CHAPTER 10
CHAPTER 11
CHAPTER 12
CHAPTER 13
APPENDICES

CHAPTER 3

INTRO

PART I

PART II

PART III

APPENDICES

Figure 3.8: Hobo village or welcome area?   **Figure 3.9: Churning out absurdity**

HOBO VILLAGE—CALLETA (151, 201, 31)

Masquerading as a broken-down trainyard, this impressively detailed build (Figure 3.8) is really a Linden-run area with information for new residents, and a real hobo village complete with cardboard boxes and outdoor bathtub for "homeless" *SL* residents.

SOMETHING AWFUL—BAKU (128, 128, 33)

Known in *Second Life* as the W-Hats, this community of refugees from the forums at http://www.somethingawful.com specializes in creating the most outrageously offensive builds in *SL*—though also some of the most impressive. Their home in the Baku sim (Figure 3.9) is a constantly shifting melange of polluted factories, natural disasters, lovingly re-created assassination scenes, and some of the murkiest irony anywhere on the Internet.

OIL RIG—ANWR (105, 170, 40)

With almost everything on the grid built by residents, the few Linden constructions are worth noting on any grand tour. One of the most impressive is the oil rig in the ANWR sim (Figure 3.10) along the corridor that connects the mainland with the northern continent. Besides being highly detailed, the oil rig has also been the site of informal chats between residents and *SL* head honcho Philip Linden. Be sure to explore the interior, and find out just where all those prims come from in the first place.

Figure 3.10: The heart of prim production on the grid

Figure 3.11: Magellan Linden's wrecked exploration craft

MAGELLAN LINDEN CRASH SITE—COLUMBIA (170, 110, 29)

A crashed airship still lies at the site (Figure 3.11), where the explorer Magellan Linden "discovered" *SL*'s northern continent. Little has been heard from Magellan since he stumbled on the remains of a strange moth-worshipping civilization that briefly provided the fictional excuse for *SL*'s northward expansion.

MOTH TEMPLE—IRIS (202, 138, 30)

Among the ruins left by the moth-worshippers is this grand temple to an unknown moth god (Figure 3.12). It's well worth a midnight visit, and it's said that the moth god still visits on occasion, though the apparition has never been documented. The nearby roller coaster at Phantom Island—Istar (90, 204, 21)—is worth a spin as well.

Figure 3.12: Though the moth gods are gone, their temple still stands.

INTRO
CHAPTER 1
CHAPTER 2
CHAPTER 3
CHAPTER 4
CHAPTER 5
CHAPTER 6
CHAPTER 7
CHAPTER 8
CHAPTER 9
CHAPTER 10
CHAPTER 11
CHAPTER 12
CHAPTER 13
APPENDICES

STUFF TO DO

From shootouts to NASCAR heats, full-sail regattas or free-love grottos, *Second Life* provides no shortage of things to do and places to explore for those who like to lead an active virtual existence.

JESSIE COMBAT SIM (127, 128, 40)

The Jessie sim (Figure 3.13) is one of the few places in *SL* where an avatar can take damage and even "die" (i.e., be teleported to one's home location). Come heavily armed, and prepare for an exchange of fire.

Figure 3.13: The dangerous environs of Jessie

SILVER MOTORSPORTS COMPLEX—SILVER ISLAND (131, 121, 22)

Race stock cars, funny cars, and more at Gremlin Glitterbuck's motorsport complex, the first place in *SL* where you could make left turns all day. Customize your ride and get in on the competitive action at the twice-weekly races too.

SIDEBAR

FROM LINDEN LAB:
TOP PLACES TO BE SEEN IN RED PRIM SHOES

🟦 *Sailing the high seas on a Flying Tako sailboat at Starboards Yacht Club—in my SF Designs loafers (Hollywood, 96, 149, 25)*

◀ 🧊 *Diving deep to explore the beautiful underwater caves, gardens, and fish at Cave Rua—in Jumpda Shark's free scuba flippers (Rua, 167, 44, 7)*

🧊 *Dancing and groovin' to the live music of Cylindrian Rutabaga at the Blarney Stone Irish Pub—in Silfie Minogue Cascade Stilettos (Dublin, 81, 81, 25)*

🧊 *Making people guess what I'm building out of tortured prims during a Prim Challenge edugame at Teazer University—in Shiny Things Sleek Boots (Beyond the Prim, 106, 253, 241)*

🧊 *Fishin' on the dock of the bay and hopin' for a big fish at Neo-Realms Fishing Camp—in Boing Fromage Ankle Wrap Flats (Hearts Enchanted, 203, 192, 24)*

—Red Linden

NEO-REALMS FISHING CAMP—HEARTS ENCHANTED (203, 192, 24)

When Sweegy Manilow created the Neo-Realms fishing camp (Figure 3.14), he had no idea it would become one of *SL*'s most popular sporting destinations. Residents flock from all over the grid to cast in fishing tournaments, practice their catch-and-release technique, test new rods, or just socialize with the anglers who are almost always in attendance. Join up in-world and check standings at `http://fish.neorealms.com/`.

Figure 3.14: See what you can hook at Neo-Realms.

CHAPTER 3

INTRO

PART I

PART II

PART III

APPENDICES

STUFF TO DO

HOLLYWOOD SPORTS AND ENTERTAINMENT COMPLEX— HOLLYWOOD (141, 53, 25)

Featuring a yachting harbor, a nine-hole golf course, and a virtual Grauman's Chinese Theater and Hollywood Bowl, the Hollywood sim has enough to entertain a visitor for hours. Both sailing and golf take *SL*'s embedded wind data into account, making for a surprisingly realistic sporting experience. Just don't forget to tip the caddies.

XTASIA—SRI SYADASTI (88, 161, 30)

Located near the Xcite "private parts" emporium at Eventide (126, 130, 26), the Xtasia "isle of temptation" provides *SL* residents with a place to try out their new purchases in privacy—or in public, if that's how you roll. The Club Med of cybersex, its "lush gardens" are clothing-optional and come with a warning that all who enter must be at least 18 years old.

STARLIGHT ROOM—STARLIGHT ISLE (149, 209, 37)

The most heavily visited spot in all of *Second Life* in mid 2006, the Starlight Room and High Rollers Casino features not only 1940s-styled gambling tables, but camping chairs where avatars desperate for funds can earn pennies for doing nothing but sitting around. It's also not a bad place to gamble, and it's definitely worth a visit if only to drink in the weird absentee culture of camping chairs.

FAIRCHANG ISLAND (178, 173, 38)

Go sailing, explore underwater tunnels, visit a coral garden, and take part in other aquatic diversions on Garth and Pituca FairChang's water sim. Head next door to the peaceful FairChang Resort to explore waterfront living possibilities.

SAILING THE SOUTHEAST SEAS

"My favorite place is the best area for sailing in SL. It's the island archipelago on the north side of the southeastern continent. The Lindens did a wonderful job creating an interesting and natural-looking landscape here, with a lot of protected water and a couple protected islands. I usually start sailing from Sanchon sim, then head through Jinsil, Haengbok, Joseon, Toedamgol, Cheongdam, Sandeulbaram, Banpo, and Jilseo. Both the casual sailors and serious yacht-racers frequent this region. There are also occasional pirate battles."

—Pixeleen Mistral

COMMUNITIES

One of the strengths of *Second Life* is what it makes possible in terms of community-building. All over the grid, groups of like-minded people have come together to make "real" their fantasies of what life could or should be. While some communities are less formal, with only simple rules of etiquette to keep the peace, others, like the Gorean sims, work on a social structure so complex that they have their own libraries and classes in proper behavior. Whether you're interested in joining one or simply in seeing the kinds of minisocieties that are emerging in these unique corners of cyberspace, a number of *SL* communities are well worth checking out.

INDEPENDENT STATE OF CALEDON (190, 190, 23)

Not many fictional cultures can support seven sims' worth of peacefully coexisting avatars, but in *Second Life* the Independent State of Caledon has found a stable foundation in "steampunk," a kind of mechanical version of science fiction set among Victorian surroundings. The steampunk sims feature all manner of fantastic clanking and puffing contraptions—as well as occasionally anachronistic speech patterns. If you're into the steampunk aesthetic or just curious to see how the legacies of Jules Verne, H.G. Wells, Mervyn Peake, and K.W. Jeter have evolved, don a hoop skirt and drop in.

INTRO
CHAPTER 1
CHAPTER 2
CHAPTER 3
CHAPTER 4
CHAPTER 5
CHAPTER 6
CHAPTER 7
CHAPTER 8
CHAPTER 9
CHAPTER 10
CHAPTER 11
CHAPTER 12
CHAPTER 13
APPENDICES

LUSKWOOD—LUSK (195, 112, 52)

Despite what you may have heard, not all the furries of *Second Life* are in it for the mature content. To pick up a starter furry avatar and meet the like-minded or just curious, head to the leafy enclave of Luskwood, heart of the mainland furry community.

LUXOR PYRAMID—FURNATION PRIME (129, 185, 34)

For a more adult version of furry fandom, look to the FurNation sims (Figure 3.15), starting at the Luxor Pyramid in FurNation Prime, where anything goes. If you're feeling adventurous, dive into the Ark nearby.

Figure 3.15: The furry paradise of Luxor Pyramid

GOREAN SIMS—PORT COS (11, 118, 27)

Fans of John (Lange) Norman's sci-fi novels, in which women are sexual chattel, have re-created the regimented milieu of the planet Gor in impressive detail. If you're not interested in being "collared," you can tour the Gorean sims as an observer, starting in Port Cos. Don't forget to read the elaborate bylaws and city laws, and check into the Scribary for more information. Despite its adult content, the Gorean sims are among the most richly realized communities in *Second Life*.

SIDEBAR

FROM LINDEN LAB:
COOL THINGS IN TEEN SECOND LIFE

🔹 **The Meiji Monster.** *A gigantic, Asian-styled serpent beautifully textured in orange-and-white koi scales, created by master prim*

crafter Kurenai Meiji, rises from the depths and threaten visitors to the nearby info hub. A sign warns, "Don't Feed the Meiji Monster—Por Favor, No Alimente Los Meiji Monstruos."

Behemoth. *The region named after the Teen Grid's first resident has been maintained as a full 16 acres of lush woodlands with three giant cedar trees. Lover of nature Malarthi Behemoth threatens to take a chunk out of any developer, Linden or otherwise, who threatens this pristine natural environment.*

Global Kids Islands. *Global Kids is an 18-year-old, NYC-based educational program that realized Teen Second Life was an ideal environment for translating their global youth-development programs online—whether through engaging residents in interactive world issues like global inequality or the genocide in Darfur, or using the environment as a platform for their after-school youth leaders to create socially conscious games, animated movies (machinima), or social actions.*

Crystal Garden. *Sumptuous event space and everything you need for birthdays, weddings, or sweet-16 parties, from dresses to cakes. From the chapel (complete with staging rooms) to the banquet hall, it's a slice of real life in Second Life.*

The Inverse Skate Park. *Huge skate park equipped with music running 24/7 and complete with skate shop, goths, furries, and goth furries often seen grinding the rails and loitering in one of the grid's most interactive environments.*

—Blue Linden

INTRO
CHAPTER 1
CHAPTER 2
CHAPTER 3
CHAPTER 4
CHAPTER 5
CHAPTER 6
CHAPTER 7
CHAPTER 8
CHAPTER 9
CHAPTER 10
CHAPTER 11
CHAPTER 12
CHAPTER 13
APPENDICES

BETTER WORLD ISLAND (149, 147, 25)

Devoted to helping create a better world, Better World Island, sponsored in part by Omidyar.net, the socially responsible investing group of eBay founder Pierre Omidyar (a major investor in Linden Lab), contains consciousness-raising exhibits on life in a refugee camp in Darfur, Somalia, and the plight of Iraqi schoolchildren, as well as the Serendipity Retreat Center and a center for performing arts. Drop in and see how you can make a difference.

INTRO

PART I

PART II

PART III

APPENDICES

COMMUNITIES

A GALAXY FAR, FAR AWAY—DANTOOINE (128, 128, 41)

If *Star Wars* is your thing, visit the Dantooine sim. Named for a planet that housed a rebel base in the original *Star Wars* movie, Dantooine is home to a thriving community of *Star Wars* role-players, including Sith, Jedi, clones, and various other kinds of spacefarers and bounty hunters. Visit the Jedi Temple to pay your respects.

NEXUS PRIME, CYBERPUNK CITY OF THE FUTURE— GIBSON (186, 236, 106)

The vaguely dystopian city of Nexus Prime towers above the Gibson and Bonifacio sims. An elaborate role-playing experiment in cyberpunk living, Nexus Prime offers the full range of products and services found in any other *SL* community—plus a colorful historical narrative, cyberpunk slums, and an underground sewer you may find yourself trapped in if you're not careful.

ELVEN SIMS

The elves provide a rare peaceful refuge from the riotous clang of the wider world. With their flowing robes, the rich colors of their surroundings, and the pointed ears that are their hallmarks, the elves have established lands that provide an unmistakable role-playing opportunity, or just a nice diversion from the virtual rat race:

Elf Haven

Elf Harbour

ElvenGlen

ElvenMoor

ElvenMyst

ElvenVale

Figure 3.16: Life in the virtual suburbs

Figure 3.17: Get your Doodle pad at Patch Lamington's Doodle House.

"ZONED" SIMS

While Linden Lab lets residents build what they please, they also provide a few sims zoned as suburban enclaves, including Boardman (Figure 3.16), Blumfield, and Brown. They're worth a visit to see how the company's vision of a welcoming environment contrasts with what residents actually build. Just as in the real world, the suburbs can be a bit soulless, but creative residents have managed to add their own touches here and there to liven things up. Don't miss Patch Lamington's Doodle House (Figure 3.17): teleport there from Blumfield.

Boardman (128, 128, 22)

Blumfield (142, 74, 26)

Brown (130, 128, 22)

NIGHTSPOTS AND ENTERTAINMENT

With a population of residents from all over the real world, many of *Second Life*'s nightspots stay open round the clock. Although a number of clubs come and go like the alts some residents don to check out the seamier side of the nightlife behind a screen of anonymity, some have become better established over the years. Whether it's dancing and music, cybersex, vampires, or just good conversation, there's something for everyone.

CHAPTER 3

INTRO

PART I

PART II

PART III

APPENDICES

NIGHTSPOTS AND ENTERTAINMENT

FROM LINDEN LAB:

THE CREEPIEST PLACES IN SL

- **Sanctum Sanctorum (225, 126, 62).** *A beautiful combination of classic architecture and eerie landscaping make this island a must-visit. There is plenty to do, with a shopping area and nightclub. But when the sun sets and you find yourself alone, this can be quite a creepy place.*

- **Crimson Falls Insane Asylum—Crimson Falls (149, 129, 20).** *The entire region has a weathered, abandoned feel that gives it an eerie air, but the insane asylum perched atop the hill puts this town over the top. It's evident from the stained textures inside of the condemned building that bad things happened here. You can almost smell the metallic stink of unwashed lunatics.*

- **Spook House Amusement Ride—Noyo (77, 154, 33).** *A classic-style amusement ride is a perfect way to get started on the creepy side of SL. Brilliantly condensed into a few meters of space, this is horror concentrate!*

- **Taco (128, 128, 10).** *Nothing is more unsettling than Taco. Everything seems cheerful and happy on the surface. But beneath the expertly crafted builds and textures, there has to lurk some sort of hidden creepy force of doom or despair.*

- **Transylvania (177, 90, 30).** *Living up to its namesake, Transylvania is a vampire hotspot. Graffiti of the resident bloodsuckers' names covers a wall in front of one of the island's many gothic horror-inspired buildings. Boasting a cemetery, castle, museum, mall, and other builds, this location is 16 square acres of creepy.*

—Bub Linden

VAMPIRE EMPIRE—TRANSYLVANIA (177, 90, 30)

The Vampire Empire nightclub is at the heart of a sprawling two-sim goth entertainment complex filled with all things pale-skinned and bloody. Pentagrams decorate stone courtyards near fanged avatars dancing to the latest death metal.

Beyond a swimming pool filled with blood stands a vampire cathedral that plays host to elaborate goth weddings, an intricately imagined castle, and a small Gothique Mall in case you left your eyeliner at home. Head to the Sweet Oblivion lounge for a drink and steer clear of the bodies impaled on spikes in the garden out back.

THE EDGE—EDGE (126, 126, 101)

One of the most popular nightclubs in *SL*, The Edge features dancing and DJs at all hours of the day or night, as well as prizes and various kinds of "best avatar" contests—your punk-rock duds, your swimsuit, or just that sexy body shape you've been keeping in your inventory could win you hundreds of Linden dollars. Though its crowds aren't exactly a cross-section of *SL*, The Edge can be a good place to meet residents who are out for a good time—whatever that might mean to them or you.

SUTHERLAND DAM CLUB—SUTHERLAND (199, 8, 24)

Prokofy Neva's "discussion club" occupies the inner structure of the imposing Sutherland dam, an enormous Linden-built structure that keeps the virtual waters low in the Sutherland sim. Drop by Friday evenings for some vital debate with one of *Second Life*'s most outspoken residents in one of the coolest interiors in all the virtual land.

FROM LINDEN LAB:
GAMING IN SECOND LIFE

You've probably heard of Tringo, the game created by Kermitt Quirk that went on to become a Game Boy game. Here are my favorite Second Life *games:*

- *Dark Life—Navora (59, 46, 23). Multiplayer fantasy RPG created by Mark Busch, Crash Prefect, and Pirate Cotton.*

- *Castle Wars—Montmartre (61, 197, 151). Multiplayer destruction by RacerX Gullwing.*

> ⬅ 📦 ***Patterns—Pi (103, 59, 24).*** *Two-person board game from Lasivian Leandros and Racer Plisskin.*
>
> 📦 ***The Pot Healer Adventure—Numbakulla (214, 17, 22).*** *Mystery game made by Moopf Murray.*
>
> —Ivy Linden

PLAYERS SHACK—SEMANG (185, 160, 26)

No Playboy mansion, the Players Shack—home to Marilyn Murphy, publisher of *Players*, *SL*'s original girlie mag—features a regular coterie of scantily clad female avatars (Figure 3.18). Pick up the latest issue for pictorials, interviews, and more.

Figure 3.18: A rare glimpse inside the Players Shack

SIDEBAR

RESIDENTS SPEAK:
THE ELBOW ROOM—MARE (104, 44, 57)

"In a time of big splashy corporate events spanning multiple sims with elaborate builds and strategic publicity, the Elbow Room has never sat on more than 512 square meters of land. [That] is the smallest parcel size in Second Life and is commonly considered too small of a plot to 'live on.' But using the minimal prims allotted to [that parcel size], proprietor Elex Dusk has managed to maximize his small space to host dancing, social events, games, and some of the best parties in Second Life. The Elbow Room has been around for more than two years, and regulars will tell you that the consistency and quality of the events keeps them coming back."

—Johnny Ming

STUFF TO BUY

There's no more-popular activity in *Second Life* than shopping, which could easily fill a whole chapter itself. Here's a highly selective list including a few old favorites and a few places you may never have heard of. Just don't spend all your Linden dollars in one place.

TABLEAU BOARDWALK—TABLEAU (244, 183, 24)

Founded by a group of émigrés from *The Sims Online*, the shops at the boardwalk in the Tableau sim feature inexpensive hipster fashions by designers Nylon Pinkney and Toast Bard, classy shoes and handbags by Ingrid Ingersoll, and that rarest of *Second Life* fashion commodities, tasteful men's clothing, by Barnesworth Anubis.

NYTE'N'DAY—COUTURE ISLE (7, 128, 49)

Nyte Caligari and Elikapeka Tiramisu's spacious Nyte'N'Day shops on Couture Isle are refreshing in their simplicity: visit The Salon for hair, The Boutique for clothing and shoes, and The Body Shop for skins. Plus wings, bling, and more.

REZOLUTION SUPERSTORE—LINDA (19, 245, 21)

A towering Ikea of the mind, the REZOLUTION Superstore features a huge range of textures, gadgets, structures, furniture, and outfits in four distinct styles. Color-coded and laid out in a skyscraper complete with showrooms, chances are REZOLUTION has whatever you need to furnish your second life in style. Mix and match for best results.

ABBOTT'S AERODROME—ABBOTTS (116, 170, 64)

In operation since February 2004, Abbott's is *SL*'s oldest and best-known airfield, featuring aircraft and more from revered vehicle-maker Cubey Terra and friends. Jet

CHAPTER 3

INTRO

PART I

PART II

PART III

APPENDICES

planes, gliders, helicopters, dirigibles, jetpacks, parachutes, test flights, experimental craft, and more. If it flies, chances are you can get it at Abbott's.

MIDNIGHT CITY (114, 141, 26)

It's always midnight in Midnight City. One of *Second Life*'s oldest continuously operating shopping malls, Midnight City features high-profile designers like Torrid and Mistress Midnight, Launa Fauna, Barnesworth Anubis, proprietor Aimee Weber, and prefab architect Lordfly Digeridoo. In addition to the clothes, accessories, and architecture, Midnight City features a social scene all its own.

SIDEBAR

ADDITIONAL INFO:
SHOP 'TIL YOU DROP

If you did nothing but shop in Second Life, *you'd still never run out of new places to see and new things to drop your hard-earned L$ on. In the interest of keeping you busy a while longer, here are some additional places to check out once you've bought out the stock at the other shops discussed in this chapter:*

- ***Carduccis* Guns & Weapons—Yongchon (219, 113, 30).** *Just what it sounds like, including quick-draw scripts, shields, and other gadgets of war. A must-stop before a visit to Jessie.*

- **The Darkness—Purden (141, 108, 129).** *A vast emporium of goth paraphernalia, featuring everything from fangs to wings, pale white skins, bondage equipment, leather outfits, and more.*

- **Panache Island Home Store—Panache (126, 127, 38).** *Popular hair and skins from designers Zyrra and HoseQueen Maclean.*

- **Lukas Designs—Jin Ho (128, 120, 69).** *It's the rare shop that sells good hair, skins, clothing, and accessories specifically designed for men.*

- **PixelDolls—Chartreuse (215, 94, 23).** *Fashion designer Nephilaine Protagonist rocketed to fame with her PixelDolls*

line and is now the subject of a documentary film thanks to her business.

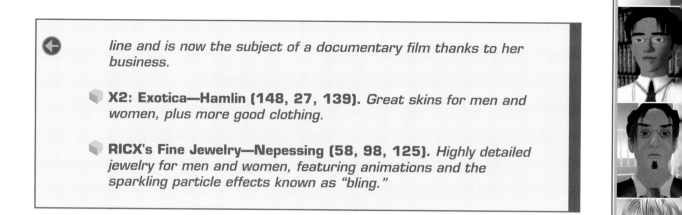

- ● **X2: Exotica—Hamlin (148, 27, 139).** *Great skins for men and women, plus more good clothing.*

- ● **RICX's Fine Jewelry—Nepessing (58, 98, 125).** *Highly detailed jewelry for men and women, featuring animations and the sparkling particle effects known as "bling."*

DOMINUS MOTOR COMPANY—CHARTREUSE (68, 26, 30)

Francis Chung is probably *Second Life*'s most accomplished vehicle builder. Drive off with one of her Dominus Shadows here.

CHAPTER 3

PLACES TO LIVE

Basic account holders may not own land, but that doesn't mean they can't have a place to call their own. Many residents set up shop as landlords, renting space to those who don't care to buy their own real estate. This section discusses some of the more-colorful places to take out a week-to-week lease.

SLEEZYWOOD TRAILER PARK—SLEEZYWOOD (113, 185, 22)

Down on your luck? Need a place to park your Airstream for a month or two? For just L$225 a week, you can get a small plot of land at the SLeezyWood Trailer Park (Figure 3.19). Set out your lawn chair, grab a beer, and make like virtual white trash—at least until the sheriff shows up with your eviction notice.

INTRO
CHAPTER 1
CHAPTER 2
CHAPTER 3
CHAPTER 4
CHAPTER 5
CHAPTER 6
CHAPTER 7
CHAPTER 8
CHAPTER 9
CHAPTER 10
CHAPTER 11
CHAPTER 12
CHAPTER 13
APPENDICES

CHAPTER 3

INTRO

PART I

PART II

PART III

APPENDICES

PLACES TO LIVE

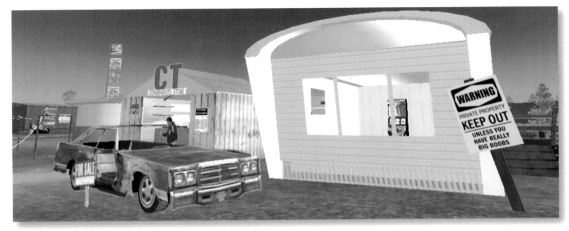

Figure 3.19: Life with the virtual white trash

DREAMLAND (128, 128, 22)

Land baron Anshe Chung maintains her own minicontinent consisting of several dozen sims off the northwest coast of Linden Lab's own northern land mass. Large enough to feature zoned regions for Japanese speakers, gay and lesbian communities, commercial ventures, and a variety of landscapes, Dreamland is the paragon of user-created commerce and worth a visit either to see how deep Anshe's impact has been or to find a dream home of your own.

SOUTHERN CALIFORNIA SIMS

To see how the upper crust lives, visit the three Southern California sims:

Beverly Hills

Venice Beach

Los Angeles

It's more like a re-creation of the world of *Grand Theft Auto: San Andreas* than of the real world. The shopping is geared toward wedding dresses and formalwear, the houses are built on McMansion scale, and downtown is deserted at night. And in case LA isn't rich enough for you, there's even an incongruous replica of Dubai's mega-expensive Burj Al Arab hotel to tour.

THE PROFESSIONALS

Not surprisingly, there's a lot in *Second Life* that just isn't easily classified. This section covers the companies that have sprung up lately, as well as some of their projects and an odd corner of the grid that may be worth checking out to satisfy your curiosity about what the real geeks are up to in *SL*.

RESIDENTS SPEAK:
THE PI DEVELOPER'S SIM—PI (128, 131, 76)

"One of my favorite places in Second Life is the island of Pi. Pi is a sim inhabited by talented software and content developers. It was created to provide these developers with an affordable place that has plenty of room to build and is not bogged down by lag nor constantly running out of prims. Why does that make it one of my favorite places? Because it is always changing and there is always a new project going on. It also means most all of it is very clever and smartly done. As a developer myself, I find there are always other developers willing to lend a hand, give a demonstration, and even some give you some free stuff if you are nice enough."

—Jeremy Flagstaff

THE INFINITE MIND (209, 76, 46)

The first national radio show to go virtual, *The Infinite Mind* does a regular broadcast from within *Second Life*. *The Infinite Mind* sim features the show's broadcast studio, the offices of virtual-world services company Infinite Visions Media, a museum, a lecture hall, and more.

ALOFT HOTEL—ALOFT ISLAND (68, 70, 27)

In one of the most interesting real-world projects in *Second Life*, Starwood Hotels has prototyped its new Aloft hotel line on an island in *SL* and chronicled the development

CHAPTER 3

INTRO

PART I

PART II

PART III

APPENDICES

THE PROFESSIONALS

of the project on a blog at http://www.virtualaloft.com/. Stroll around the grounds and let Starwood know if the new low-frills luxury package is the way to go. Would you rent a room in this virtual world?

NEW GLOBE THEATRE—MILLIONS OF US (128, 127, 23)

Produced by virtual-world services company Millions of Us (run by ex–Linden Lab employee Reuben Steiger), this scale model of the new Globe Theatre designed by the architectural firm of Sir Norman Foster has hosted plays, performances, and speeches.

ADIDAS (104, 183, 55)

Branding agency Rivers Run Red—located at Avalon (193, 158, 39)—brought Adidas to *Second Life*, complete with the bounce-happy Adidas a3 Microrides available in-world.

PNC PARK—BASEBALL (196, 117, 26)

This re-creation of a real-life baseball stadium by the Electric Sheep Company—whose offices you can visit at The Infinite Mind (49, 207, 601)—has been used to host simulcasts of Major League Baseball's Home Run Derby and other events.

PART II

LIVING A SECOND LIFE

CHAPTER 4

CHANGING YOUR APPEARANCE

As you know from Chapter 1, *Second Life* offers you the opportunity to be reborn in many ways. This is especially true of your avatar's appearance. You can change your avatar's appearance as often as you like, and you can be as crazy as you like. You can enter the world as a fire-breathing dragon, turn into a vampire halfway through your online session, and eventually log out as a middle-aged, bald, beer-bellied male construction worker with a long, furry tail.

The importance of avatar appearance becomes obvious the moment you enter *Second Life*: the arrival lot on Orientation Island is often packed with freshly born avatars whose appearance is being edited by their owners. Every resident begins *Second Life* as an attractive young male or female in jeans and T-shirt, and almost every resident immediately begins working to make their avatar their own. This chapter discusses this process, explains the options available, and offers practical hints and notes. All this advice is only advice: feel free to choose your own path through *Second Life*. But whatever you do, remember that your presence in the virtual world is defined by your appearance.

CONTENTS

FIRST CHOICES

Your first big "avatar appearance" choice is made even before you enter *Second Life*. You make it when you choose your *SL* name (Figure 4.1). Your avatar's name is displayed for all to see, and it always has a major impact on how others perceive you. A seven-foot-tall hunk called Daisy Pony is definitely perceived differently than a seven-foot-tall hunk called Rocky Balboa! As this demonstrates, avatar appearance is a sum of many parts. Generally speaking, these are as follows:

- **Avatar name.** Your avatar's name is very important: you get to choose it only once (it cannot be changed). Choose a name that fits your image, and make sure you can live with it for a long, long time. It's not easy, especially for first-time users, who choose a name with very little advance knowledge of what avatars can look like. A safe way out is to pick a name you'd be comfortable with in real life—however, at the same time you want an avatar name that's attractive and memorable.

- **Avatar shape.** This goes beyond silhouette: basically, avatar shape includes all body parts and body features (body thickness, height, shape of head, eyes, nose, etc.).

- **Avatar skin.** Avatar skin is what you see covering avatar shape in the absence of any clothing. Its appearance may be changed with *SL* tools. However, to get realistic-looking human skin, you'll have to acquire a custom skin. Skins which are created using an external application such as Adobe Photoshop, then imported/uploaded into *Second Life* at a nominal fee. Luckily, you don't have to make one to own one; there are lots of very sharp custom skins for sale, and you can also get a good freebie skin if you look around.

- **Avatar hair and eyes.** Avatar hair and eyes constitute a separate category because although they're body features, they can also be worn as attachments (prim hair, eyes worn as attachments that cover the default eyes). You'll find more hair and eye details later in this chapter.

- **Avatar attachments.** This, predictably, includes clothes and any other objects that can be attached to an avatar's shape (a hat, a gun, hair).

- **Avatar animations.** Each avatar comes with a set of animations that grow with almost every *SL* update. However, longtime *SL* citizens view the standard

animations with disdain. You can buy custom animations that will make your avatar move with extra grace. Creating custom animations involves using an external application (many *SL* citizens use Poser) and writing an override script in LSL (*Second Life*'s scripting language) so that custom animations are played instead of the defaults. You can acquire freebie animations too if you look around. As you might have guessed, if you're interested in virtual sex, custom animations (and attachments too) are a must.

CHOOSING YOUR NAME

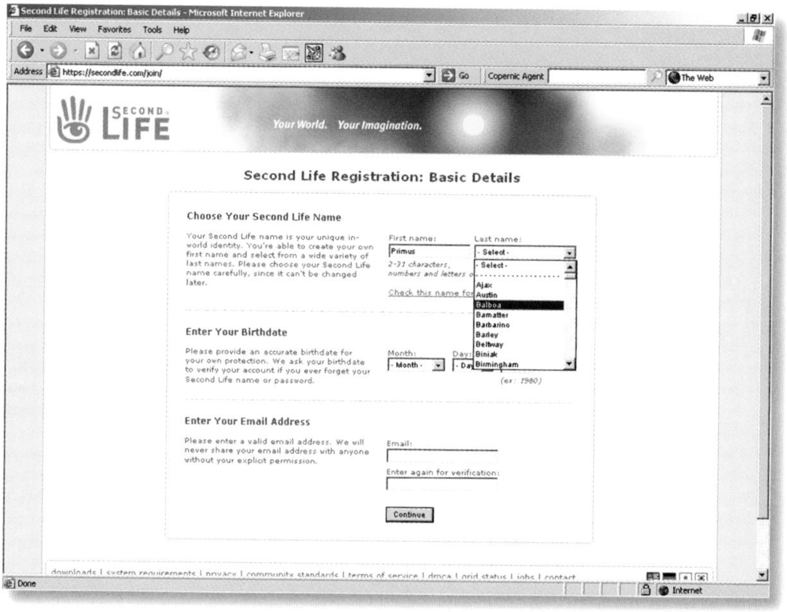

At the time of writing, the options here aren't unlimited—you have to choose a last name from those available at the time. However, the list (which changes periodically) always features plenty of choices, and of course you can give yourself any first name you like—as long as someone else isn't already using the same first-name/last-name combination. If you encounter this problem, a small tweak can put things right: popular solutions include changing the

Figure 4.1: Your avatar is officially born the moment you give it a name.

spelling of the first name to get a unique combination—for example, "Oskar Peterson" instead of "Oscar Peterson." Other widely used solutions are to make the first letter of your first name lowercase, (as in "sandy" instead of "Sandy") or to add a letter (for example, your middle initial: "John A. Smith" becomes "JohnA Smith").

Remember that the name you've chosen won't appear in isolation; it will be viewed in combination with your avatar. Therefore, you should consider how it will fit the appearance of the avatar(s) you intend to use in *Second Life*. Are you going to switch between sexes? If so, you might want to consider an "unisex" name: for

INTRO

CHAPTER 1

CHAPTER 2

CHAPTER 3

CHAPTER 4

CHAPTER 5

CHAPTER 6

CHAPTER 7

CHAPTER 8

CHAPTER 9

CHAPTER 10

CHAPTER 11

CHAPTER 12

CHAPTER 13

APPENDICES

CHAPTER 4

INTRO

PART I

PART II

PART III

APPENDICES

FIRST CHOICES

example, Sandy Sprocket or RobertA Hansen. Is your avatar's appearance going to be outrageous, beautiful, dangerous, friendly—or maybe all four at once? It *is* possible with the right combination of name, avatar appearance, and animation/gesture set.

NOTE

FROM LINDEN LAB:
YOUR NAME SET IN STONE

While you can change your avatar's appearance as many times as you like, you cannot change your avatar's name. The name you choose to set up an account is the account, and the only way to reappear in SL under a new name is to open a new account.

CHOOSING YOUR SEX

First of all, remember this: in *Second Life*, you can change your sex every 10 minutes if you so desire. It doesn't involve any painful operations—just a few mouse clicks. You can be male, you can be female, you can be neither (by creating or choosing an avatar that's gender-neutral, such as the ready-made White Wolf from your Library). It's interesting to note that given all this freedom, most *SL* denizens choose to stay true to their real-life gender. Here are some numbers from an *SL* forum poll:

Male playing male—41.95%

Female playing female—40.05%

Male playing female—14.45%

Female playing male—3.55%

These numbers are very telling even when you assume the poll isn't very accurate. They show clearly that the majority of *SL* denizens make a conservative choice and stick to their real-life gender. At the same time, many *SL* people state that they treat their *SL* existence as the perfect opportunity for role play, that they switch sexes at the drop of a hat, and that everyone is free to choose whichever sex they fancy at any given moment (see the sidebar "Gender Bending"). So, where's the truth?

The truth, as always, lies in the middle. No one will mind if your avatar's of a different gender than *you* really are as long as they do not have a close personal relationship with you. As a certain disappointed female avatar said, "I wouldn't have minded if he told me he's really a guy within the first few weeks. But when he told me after six months, wow, it just blew me away. I just find him impossible to trust after that."

NOTE

ADDITIONAL INFO:
GENDER-BENDING

The default gender choice for your primary avatar is your real-life gender. If you go the other route, be prepared for unexpected twists and turns in your virtual friendships. The rules that apply there are the same as the rules in real life: friends don't like to be deceived.

Do not let this stop you from switching gender when you feel like it. But if you want to form a virtual friendship with someone, it's important that they know who you *really* are. The best way to handle this is simply to include some info about the real-life you in your *SL* Profile (Figure 4.2).

Figure 4.2: Let people know what you want them to know about the real-life you.

CHAPTER 4

INTRO

PART I

PART II

PART III

APPENDICES

FIRST CHOICES

RESIDENTS SPEAK:
SWITCHING AVATARS

"It's hard to say what motivates me to look the way I do in SL, I have so many looks to choose from. I have a firm belief in tasting everything on the buffet, and being picky like I am, I went for the best of the best. It is hard to tell what I'm going to be from one day to the next: a magnificent dragon, a bipedal wolf, a vampire, or a really good-looking human. That's the beauty of SL; you're not stuck in any single stereotypical role unless you choose to do that to yourself."

—Lupus Delacroix

"As Lupus noted, you can create as many avatars as you like. Save them as 'outfits' and include the gender and all body parts—then just wear the entire folder. There is no limit to what you can be; you can be Neo one minute and slip into your Donna Dominatrix avatar the next. If you do a search on SLBoutique or SLExchange for avatars, you will see the amazing range of what is out there and what you can make yourself.

"What motivates people to look a certain way is something I wouldn't even begin to speculate on. Ultimately, your avatar is your representative in-world and can run the entire range of your personality. It's your second life; be whomever and whatever you want to be."

—Isablan Neva

"I actually have several different avs; some I used for fun, others are utilitarian. Most of the time, I run around in a Luskwood Red Dragon av. Although, I also use a Ninja Weasel Studios Red Eastern Dragon av, and a mu Kingyo Gold av (giant fishy). I do have my old 'generic' av for times when I need to attach something, and a furry av won't do the job. All of my avs are modded, some of them heavily. Generally on my usual av, I wear a Maximillion in Plum suit from Silver Rose, a custom-made top hat (which sits at an angle and is oversized), and a pair of round-rim glasses with purple lenses."

—Khashai Steinbeck

CHANGING YOUR APPEARANCE

You'll most likely be struck by an overwhelming urge to work on your avatar's appearance the moment you enter *Second Life* (Figure 4.3). Be strong, and resist the temptation to begin tinkering with your looks right away.

There are several good reasons for postponing your avatar's appearance improvements for a little while. To begin with, you won't be guilty of crowding Orientation Island's arrival area. Next,

Figure 4.3: The number-one priority of almost every new SL denizen: changing their avatar's appearance.

just a few steps into Orientation Island, you'll have the first of many chances to acquire freebie avatars complete with clothes. And soon enough, you'll be leaving Orientation Island for Help Island, where you'll undoubtedly hit the freebie store for a selection of outfits and hair types. And after *that*, you'll hit the mainland, where hundreds and hundreds of stores offer avatar appearance enhancements of outstanding quality. You can acquire them for free or nearly free if you periodically check out *Second Life*'s Classifieds, SLExchange, and SLBoutique.

NOTE

ADDITIONAL INFO:
FREE DOWNLOADS

There's a range of free downloads that include avatar mannequins and animation files; templates for creating new avatar skin, hair, clothes, and eyes; and a selection of high-quality textures at

CHAPTER 4

INTRO

PART I

PART II

PART III

APPENDICES

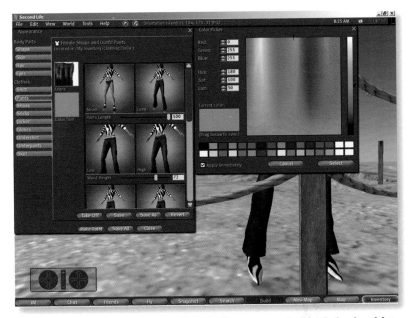

http://secondlife.com/community/downloads.php. *The downloads are accompanied by a concise manual. In addition, many SL creators offer free templates—you'll find numerous links to free template downloads in forum posts at* http://forums.secondlife.com/index.php. *Use the Search function to locate the templates you're interested in; for example, type "skin template" in the Search box.*

If you absolutely cannot bear the default avatar look, limit avatar appearance editing on Orientation Island to a few quick, simple changes (Figure 4.4). Doing anything more is a waste of time given the extra options that soon become available.

By now, you've probably gotten the idea that avatar appearance is a sum of several parts, and that these include more than the body parts from *SL*'s Appearance menu. The sections that

Figure 4.4: Switching the tint and texture of the default shirt and jeans takes just a couple of mouse clicks.

follow discuss each of these parts and offer polite suggestions of what to do with the parts you don't like. Naturally, we'll start with the body-part choices: Shape, Skin, Hair, and Eyes.

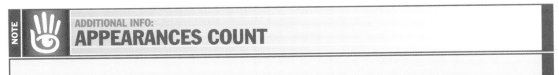

NOTE

ADDITIONAL INFO:
APPEARANCES COUNT

Opening the Appearance menu loads your avatar's current shape and outfit. Your Library contains several ready-made shape/outfit

combinations, and you'll be adding many more to your Inventory during your new existence. Switching avatar shape and outfit is as simple as dragging the appropriate folder from your Library or Inventory and onto the avatar. Don't forget to save your own unique shape/outfit combinations into your Inventory—and don't forget to delete the oldest/least used as your second life goes on.

RESIDENTS SPEAK:
AVATAR APPEARANCE

"I'm on the short side and trim. Always wanted to be bigger but genetics and metabolism declared otherwise (a few hundred people I know wish they had my metabolism). So my avatar is a bit tall and on the heavy side (but neither pudgy nor muscle-bound). He's Irish even if I'm not because I decided to port over my ID (Aodhan) from the last MMOG I was in. Irish name goes best with Irish surname.

"The cybernetic right arm was something I started fooling around with when I was new. I liked it and I just kept evolving it. It rarely fails to catch the attention of people I meet. I was initially planning to make a product version of it because it was attracting attention, but I decided not to because people liked that it gave me a unique look. In a world where any look can be made but where some looks are mass-produced, it's nice to know that one has something that is unique.

"I'm a techie-geek and proud of it. My look reflects that in all original equipment from the arm to the visor to the gadgety-looking belt."

—Aodhan McDunnough

"Here's a breakdown of what to consider:

"Skin: This is probably the most important aspect. A good skin can make or break an avatar's appearance. Demos are usually dirt-cheap, so stock up and experiment. Once you find a good design, then you'll have to decide skin tone and facial hair, as that overrides the default controls.

"Hair: Prim hair is a must. Finding good prim hair for men is hard. Women's hair outnumbers men's by about 1,000 to 1, it seems. And even when you do find men's hair, very often it's the same style. Nothing against long hair, mind you, but this far I've not been able to find hair that gives the GQ look, although the prim hair I have now is pretty close.

"Shape: Your shape will radically change how your skin looks, especially on the face. Professional shapes are usually better than what you can do yourself, but even then, its tough to find a shape that is everything you want.

"Eyes: Good eyes can add a nice touch.

"Animation override: The best avatar in the world will still look clunky if you use the default animation set.

"Clothing: As in real life, clothes mean a lot. There's a lot of garbage out there and some really nice things too. Don't be afraid to ask where people got their stuff. More often than not, other people are willing to help, and once in a while, you meet some cool people who turn into friends."

—Cannae Brentano

SHAPE

Shape (found under the Body Parts option) is the default option when you open the Appearance menu. Shape options are applied to nine categories, from Body to Eyes and Ears to Legs. Each category opens up a series of second-life-changing options, easily adjustable on a scale of 0 to 100 via a slider. You can save any combination of options as a separate male or female shape (with or without clothes/outfit) to your Inventory, then switch shape types at a moment's notice. If only changing this stuff in your first life were so easy!

The following sections discuss the options available in the order in which they appear in *Second Life*. This is done for ease of reference only and does not imply you should edit your avatar's appearance in the same order. On the contrary, editing avatar appearance is easier if you follow a different order. You should edit Body, then jump to Torso and Legs at the very bottom of the menu list, and only then proceed to edit Head options (second from the top). All such irregularities are highlighted in the sections below.

ADDITIONAL INFO:
RANDOM INSPIRATION

Make a point of clicking the Randomize button (at the bottom of the Appearance menu) a few times before you begin editing individual avatar body parts. You'll see clearly how changing proportions between body parts can result in a completely new look. What's more, many random avatars are very nicely put together, and you may want to use one of the randomly generated avatars as the base model when attempting to create your first unique shape.

The most powerful avatar appearance options are found under Body and Head. Adjustments to the values found there have a strong effect on your avatar's appearance; often, changing a single value results in a number of changes. Alterations to other appearance options are more predictable, affecting only a single body part or facial feature.

Finally, keep in mind that the suggestions below are just one take on what's involved in creating the most difficult avatar form you can possibly aim for: a natural-looking human being. Don't let that stop you from choosing whatever avatar you fancy, even if it's just a grayish bit of free-floating ectoplasm. What you want comes first whenever you make a choice in *Second Life*. Of course, it's making a choice that's difficult (Figure 4.5).

Figure 4.5: Exactly what I was looking for! Hmmm...well, almost, anyway.

INTRO
CHAPTER 1
CHAPTER 2
CHAPTER 3
CHAPTER 4
CHAPTER 5
CHAPTER 6
CHAPTER 7
CHAPTER 8
CHAPTER 9
CHAPTER 10
CHAPTER 11
CHAPTER 12
CHAPTER 13
APPENDICES

83

BODY

Under Body, you'll find the following slider-adjustable options:

- **Height.** The default is 80, and this translates roughly into six feet or 180 centimeters in real life. This is a safe middle-of-the-road value. Changing your height affects overall body shape, and you'll want to fiddle with the slider after you've done all the other adjustments and your avatar's shape still seems not quite right. Sometimes a shape that's just a bit off-kilter at 80 snaps into exactly the right proportions at 75.

- **Body Thickness.** The default value is a waif-like 20. While most *SL* denizens are unbelievably lithe and slender, rather the way we'd all like to be in real life, you might want to nudge the slider up a little—a value of 35 to 40 results in a more realistic body shape. Don't worry—your avatar will still appear attractively slim given all the other options.

- **Body Fat.** The default here's set at 0. Many *SL* denizens are more than happy to leave it at that. However, if you want to inject just a small dose of realism into your new existence, go for a value of 25 to 30—your avatar acquires a nice, solid aura, so to speak, that can make it a little more convincing.

The Shape options open by default when you enter the Appearance menu, and it's a safe bet you'll adjust them first. Make a point of returning to adjust them at least once before you finalize all the shapes that make up your new avatar. Adjusting the shape of your avatar's body often puts the final touch on its appearance.

> **NOTE**
>
> ADDITIONAL INFO:
> ## KNOW WHAT YOU WANT
>
> *Editing avatar appearance becomes much easier if you have a precise idea of what you want, and you refer to an existing image (photograph, drawing, illustration) while working. Also, it's a good idea to strip your avatar naked when editing selected Shape options (Body, Torso, and Legs) as well as Skin.*

HEAD

Here things get noticeably more complicated, as they should. Upon selecting Head, you'll face the following options:

 **Head Size.**
The default here is 70. The default is a meaningless, inoffensive choice, because the size of your head should harmonize with your Body Shape choices. If you're really tall, the default is too small; if you're short, it's too large. What's more, head size has to harmonize with the facial features you'll

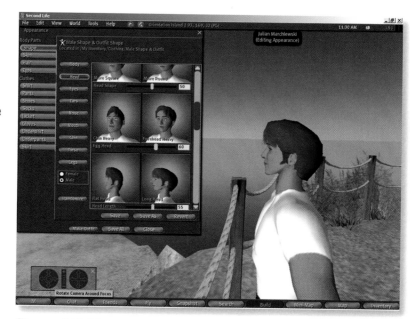

Figure 4.6: Use camera controls to view your avatar from different angles while editing its appearance.

choose. It's necessary to perform at least two head-size adjustments: one after setting Body Shape and another after you've gone through all Head submenu choices. Just like with Body Shape, quite often a final, slight adjustment of head size makes all other Head adjustments fit perfectly.

NOTE

✋ ADDITIONAL INFO:
CAMERA CONTROLS

Don't forget to activate and use camera controls (View menu) while editing your avatar's appearance! It's impossible to get things right otherwise (Figure 4.6).

INTRO
CHAPTER 1
CHAPTER 2
CHAPTER 3
CHAPTER 4
CHAPTER 5
CHAPTER 6
CHAPTER 7
CHAPTER 8
CHAPTER 9
CHAPTER 10
CHAPTER 11
CHAPTER 12
CHAPTER 13
APPENDICES

INTRO

PART I

PART II

PART III

APPENDICES

CHANGING YOUR APPEARANCE

Head Stretch. This is a very powerful option: adjustments here affect head shape, size, and a lot of facial features (for example, chin and nose shape). The default value is 20, and it's smart to leave it at that while working on your first avatar appearance. Once everything's done, use this option to fine-tune facial features and head shape. Of course, if you've always dreamed of having a head that resembles an eggplant stood on one end, go for it and slam the slider up to 100 right away.

Head Shape. The default here's a neutral 50. Making your avatar's head more square gives it a masculine air, more round—feminine. Note that any movement of the slider, up or down, results in perceived increase of head size. This is yet another powerful option that strongly affects facial features, especially lower jaw and chin shape.

Egg Head. This option dramatically affects head shape. The term "Egg Head" illustrates this option's two extremes: a head shaped like an egg standing on its pointy end, or like an egg standing on its blunt end. However, this describes only the straight-on view of your avatar's head; when you use the camera controls to view it from the side, you'll see that any movement of the slider results in big changes to your avatar's profile. Areas particularly affected are the back of the head, the forehead, and the chin/jaw. The default value of 75 is best suited for female avatars; if you're going for a classic male look, 50 to 60 is a good choice.

Head Length. Sweeping adjustments to the default 55 value are definitely not recommended—*unless* you want an avatar that looks like a character in a fantasy cartoon. Head Length makes a strong impact on facial features, too! Slight adjustments upward result in a more feminine appearance, and moving the slider down a few notches creates a more masculine look.

Face Shear. Moving the slider either way rotates one side of your face up and the other down: extremes make your avatar look, (when viewed straight on) as if it had been struck with partial face palsy. This is good for outlandish characters; otherwise, settle for small tweaks of three to six points on either side of the default 50 value. The default results in a face that is perfectly symmetrical, and thus a little bland; a slight skew to the features adds a certain attractive *je ne sais quoi* that injects extra character into a face.

Forehead Angle. This option is best left alone until you've chosen a hair type/ style that you're going to wear for a while. The default value of 37 is perhaps a little on the low side; adding a few points often results in a more natural look. Radical adjustments work great if you're after a fantasy look—for example,

definitely go the Vertical Forehead route when re-creating Frankenstein.

- **Brow Size.** Big, bony, protective protuberances above the eyes are usually associated with lower rungs of evolutionary development; probably that's why the default here is set at a highly civilized value of 13. Once again, this is an appearance option that's best left alone until you've got the hair (and eyes) you like and are likely to stick with for a while. Setting Brow Size at 0 gives your avatar's head a slightly ethereal air.

- **Upper Cheeks.** This is another option with a relatively low default. At 37, it lends your avatar's face a very civilized, sophisticated look; making the cheeks puffier results in a certain roughness. Increasing cheek puffiness by just a few points will give your avatar's face a more natural air, whereas decreasing it to 0 results in fashion-model sleekness.

- **Lower Cheeks.** This option is best left at the default 45 until you've completed work on your avatar's facial features. It tends to work best when applied as the final, finishing touch to the jaw and jowls.

- **Cheek Bones.** The default 38 value is a little low; adding up to a dozen points gives your avatar's face more character without a meaningful change in facial features.

NOTE

ADDITIONAL INFO:
SHAPE-SHIFTING

Don't spend too much time perfecting your avatar's features at the outset of your new existence. You'll be messing with them again the moment you acquire a custom avatar skin, as discussed later in this chapter. After a while, you're likely to have a number of different physical profiles saved in your Inventory. Second Life offers you great freedom: for example, if you like a certain hairstyle but it doesn't suit you, you can make yourself suit the hairstyle.

EYES

Eye-editing options pop up twice on the Appearance panel:

INTRO
CHAPTER 1
CHAPTER 2
CHAPTER 3
CHAPTER 4
CHAPTER 5
CHAPTER 6
CHAPTER 7
CHAPTER 8
CHAPTER 9
CHAPTER 10
CHAPTER 11
CHAPTER 12
CHAPTER 13
APPENDICES

🔹 In the Shape submenu, the Eyes button lets you adjust eye-detail options for your current avatar. These are the options discussed in this section.

🔹 In the main Body Parts menu, choosing the Eyes tab opens a submenu that lets you adjust the eye template, such as size of pupil, iris width and texture, and pupil/iris size. These options are discussed later on in this chapter.

Adjusting eye-detail options is much more straightforward than messing around with Body and Head, because the changes you make here affect the eye area only. However, they do impact your avatar's facial profile—use the camera controls to check it out.

The eye-detail options have no hidden implications or complex consequences like the ones encountered when editing Head options. Nevertheless, there are a few things you should keep in mind:

🔹 Eye Size and Eye Opening complement each other, so work those two sliders together. The relatively low default setting of 40 for Eye Size still has a strong *anime* feeling; try lowering it to 35 and increasing Eye Opening to 65 from the default 60.

🔹 Review Eye Depth after you've completed

Figure 4.7: The Eyes tab submenu lets you change your avatar's eye color as well as use alternate eye templates.

work on your avatar's nose and cheekbones, since these three facial features work together straight on as well as in profile.

🔹 If you're after a natural-looking face, use the Eye Bags and Puffy Lids sliders to

make your avatar's face more convincing; add a handful of points to the default values in each case.

🔲 The rather wild-looking Pop Eye option yields great results when used in moderation. Perfect symmetry is bland, so moving the slider either way by just a few points makes your avatar's face more interesting.

Remember that your Library contains extra eyes, so to speak. You'll find a pair of base (brown, blue) eye-color models in the Body Parts folder, and extra eye-color variations as part of the ready-made Shape/Outfit combinations in the Clothing folder. However, note that editing eye color and depth (darkness) is done through the *other* Eyes submenu—the one that opens when you click the Eyes tab under Body Parts (Figure 4.7). You'll find more details later in this chapter.

EARS

Editing your avatar's ears is even more straightforward than working on eye detail. Most of the time, you'll adjust ear options while viewing your avatar's profile; use camera controls to check on the effect of your changes straight on as well as from a three-quarters-front view. Also, note that although the Attached Earlobe images are correct, the Unattached and Attached labels are reversed.

NOSE

Editing your avatar's nose so that it combines character with a natural appearance is a complicated job. The editing options available here are straightforward and self-explanatory; however, adjusting one option almost invariably necessitates adjusting one or more other options. You'll certainly gain a new appreciation for real-life nose-job artists once you've attempted to edit your avatar's nose! Here are some suggestions that should make nose editing easier:

🔲 The nose is a prominent facial feature that must work well with other facial features. So edit other facial features first, including your avatar's mouth and chin—it makes determining the right nose shape and size much easier.

🔲 It's easier to work on a bigger nose. The default Nose Size is a cute, button-like 11 whose appearance straddles the line between fantasy and real life. You can safely increase nose size to 25 right away—that's the natural size for the

INTRO
CHAPTER 1
CHAPTER 2
CHAPTER 3
CHAPTER 4
CHAPTER 5
CHAPTER 6
CHAPTER 7
CHAPTER 8
CHAPTER 9
CHAPTER 10
CHAPTER 11
CHAPTER 12
CHAPTER 13
APPENDICES

default head, but it might be more if you've already edited head shape and size. In any case, it truly is much easier to work on a bigger nose, even if what you want is a small nose (see the "Nose Jobs" note).

> **NOTE**
>
> **ADDITIONAL INFO:**
> ## NOSE JOBS
>
> *Try increasing the nose size for shape-editing purposes, then size the shaped nose down—it will necessitate extra tweaks to some options, but should ensure a much easier time overall. Just remember to keep the size difference to no more than 10 points or so!*

- Nose and Nostril width as well as Nose Thickness and Nose Tip shape are very closely linked to mouth shape and size; tweak Mouth options as appropriate.

- When adjusting Upper and Lower Bridge, pay attention to how your changes work with the appearance of your avatar's brows and forehead.

Figure 4.8: Performing a good nose job will test your avatar-editing abilities.

- Using the camera controls often is key to doing the job right: all nose changes greatly impact your avatar's appearance from any viewing angle between two-thirds-back and full frontal.

You'll be spared a lot of effort if you go the fantasy-avatar route. A Pinocchio-like schnozzle is much easier to model than a natural-looking nose (Figure 4.8).

MOUTH

Shape your avatar's jaw and chin before starting to edit its mouth; you'll have a much easier time. The Mouth editing options are very straightforward, but focus almost exclusively on the lips, and there's more to the mouth than lips alone—the lips are just the final touch. As mentioned earlier, you'll also want to tweak Mouth options once you've finished working on your avatar's nose.

CHIN

Chin-editing options are powerful—changes there can necessitate a rethink of your avatar's head shape and size. Here's what you'll be dealing with:

- **Chin Angle.** On one end of the scale we have Mr. Lantern Jaw; on the other, the Chinless Wonder. The default setting of 52 is a little on the Chinless Wonder side, which isn't bad for female avatars. However, natural-looking male avatars require you to nudge the slider lower.

NOTE

ADDITIONAL INFO:
MOLDING YOUR CHIN

Although Chin Angle is the topmost option in the Chin submenu, editing Chin Angle is easiest when you've already finished shaping your avatar's jaw.

- **Jaw Shape.** This is one of the jaw-shaping adjustments that should precede finalizing Chin Angle. The default value of 55 results in a decidedly feminine chin and jaw, and you should add at least 20 points for a masculine look. However, note that this is true only if the other jaw-shaping settings are left at default. Changes in Chin Depth, Jaw Angle, Jowls, and Chin-Neck settings have a big impact on the Jaw Shape setting. You'll find yourself tweaking some of the options again and again after making changes elsewhere.

INTRO
CHAPTER 1
CHAPTER 2
CHAPTER 3
CHAPTER 4
CHAPTER 5
CHAPTER 6
CHAPTER 7
CHAPTER 8
CHAPTER 9
CHAPTER 10
CHAPTER 11
CHAPTER 12
CHAPTER 13
APPENDICES

4

INTRO

PART I

PART II

PART III

APPENDICES

CHANGING YOUR APPEARANCE

Chin Depth and Jaw Angle. These two options are grouped together because any adjustments to Chin Depth should be done in tandem with adjustments to Jaw Angle. A lower Jaw Angle naturally fits a deeper chin. The changes you make to these two settings have a strong impact on your avatar's appearance! Make sure you view your avatar's face from several angles following each setting change. The default settings of 42 for Chin Depth and 76 for Jaw Angle are on the feminine side; increase Chin Depth and decrease Jaw Angle for a more-masculine shape. Expect to readjust settings after any changes to Jowls and Chin-Neck.

Jaw Jut. This option should be handled very delicately unless you're after a comic effect. Slight deviations (literally a couple of points) from the default 50 value work fine—a tiny underbite can look good on a female avatar, and a similarly small overbite can be flattering on a male.

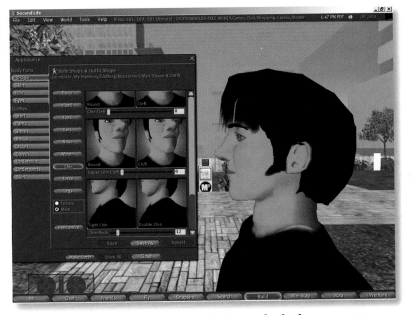

Figure 4.9: Getting your avatar's jaw to look the way you want it requires skill and patience.

Jowls. The default value of 17 results in a model-like, jowl-less look. Add points here for a more natural appearance, readjusting other Chin options as necessary.

Chin Cleft and Upper Chin Cleft. Adjustments here put the final touches on your avatar's chin; leave them till the very end. Making changes may necessitate rethinking your Mouth settings, particularly Lip Cleft and Lip Cleft Depth.

Chin-Neck. Any changes here are likely to impact Jaw Shape, Jaw Angle, and Jowls settings, and vice versa. Treat this option as part of the jaw-shaping package (Figure 4.9).

In summary, your avatar's chin has a powerful influence on your avatar's appearance. In real life, eyes and jaw shape are very important in projecting a personality type; in *Second Life*, jaw shape is extra-important because of technical considerations that, at the time of writing, limit eye-appearance impact.

TORSO

You should edit your avatar's torso right after you've finished adjusting Body options. The Torso options are very straightforward and do not require extra explanations. However, there are a few things to remember:

- Adjusting torso muscles also changes arm muscles—high settings have unfortunate visual effects.

- Neck Thickness and Neck Length should be finalized only once you've finished messing with your avatar's head.

- Torso-editing options collectively default to create the ideal torso: knockout busts for the females, broad shoulders and rippling muscles for men, etc. You may want to nudge the appropriate sliders a few points away from their default settings for a more realistic look.

- Arm Length and Hand Size are the two options you should start with. They are linked to Body choices as well as Leg Length and Foot Size. Torso Length should be proportionate to Leg Length.

- Love Handles and Belly Size are obviously best adjusted in tandem, and any adjustments here should be considered together with Body Thickness and Body Fat settings.

NOTE

ADDITIONAL INFO:
CANNIBALIZING AVATARS

Remember than any avatar can be cannibalized for body parts. You can switch body parts between avatars with ease or add custom body parts of your own.

INTRO
CHAPTER 1
CHAPTER 2
CHAPTER 3
CHAPTER 4
CHAPTER 5
CHAPTER 6
CHAPTER 7
CHAPTER 8
CHAPTER 9
CHAPTER 10
CHAPTER 11
CHAPTER 12
CHAPTER 13
APPENDICES

LEGS

Editing your avatar's legs includes setting their length and their shape. If you go to the trouble to take off your avatar's pants, you'll have an easier job. Note that Leg Length has a marked effect on Leg Shape, and that you can change leg appearance by adjusting Body Height, Body Fat, and Body Thickness values.

Leg-editing options include adjusting the size and shape of your avatar's hips, crotch, and buttocks. Adjustments in these three areas influence one another and may require quite a lot of tweaking following any significant change. Note that Body settings play a big part here, too.

Appropriately, at the very bottom of the Legs submenu you'll see a Foot Size option. Many *SL* people claim they get on very happily with a foot size of O, and it's true that a scaled-down foot makes footwear look better. It's up to you to strike the right balance between realism and beauty here. In real life, foot size corresponds to hand size, but this is *Second Life*, where most custom shoes are made to fit size-O feet.

SKIN

Clicking on the Skin tab on the Appearance panel brings up a list of options that are very straightforward and limited. They allow you to make basic changes to avatar skin appearance, such as change skin color (and not much more). The Face Detail and Body Detail submenus can be successfully used to create an older-looking avatar, but they won't make the skin more convincing (Figure 4.10).

Figure 4.10: Born into a virtual world a day ago and already showing age? Must be the pace of your second life.

Most *Second Life* residents agree that a custom avatar skin is a priority because of the dramatic effect it has on your avatar's appearance. Nice-looking skins can be obtained free of charge, and let's-have-virtual-sex-right-now skins can be had for the low four figures in Linden dollars. You may also attempt to create your own custom skin if you have the bent and the external application needed. You can download free skin templates, and *SL*-related forums are full of good, clear advice on what's involved in creating a new skin.

HAIR AND EYES

Avatar hair and eyes can alter your avatar's appearance. Unfortunately, most *SL* denizens seem to agree that trying to customize either through the Hair and Eyes tabs under Body Parts yields average-quality results at best. Yes, you can easily achieve a meaningful appearance change by adjusting basic values such as Color for both eyes and hair. However, any further attempts to mess with your hair are likely to end with much frustration, and taking eye changes beyond color and depth isn't possible without acquiring a new eye template, or an eye attachment that your avatar will wear over its default eyes. Some eye attachments come with scripts that add features such as simple animation (for example, blinking). If you want to have a stab at creating your own custom eyes, download the free eye template from http://secondlife.com/community/templates.php.

If you want your avatar to have good-looking hair, you'll definitely have to get a custom job. As mentioned earlier, the best-looking custom hair is built of individual prims and is worn as a head attachment. As you know by now, you can easily acquire decent prim hair for free, and great-looking custom hair is affordable, with prices ranging from a few hundred Linden dollars to the low four figures for hot new styles.

NOTE

ADDITIONAL INFO:
HAIRY CHOICES

When shopping for new hair, the three things to consider are the look, the price, and the number of prims involved. A hairstyle created using a large number of prims can have a negative effect on SL's performance on your computer because of increased lag whenever your new hair appears in the view. A master SL hairstylist always uses the minimum number of prims required to provide the intended effect.

INTRO
CHAPTER 1
CHAPTER 2
CHAPTER 3
CHAPTER 4
CHAPTER 5
CHAPTER 6
CHAPTER 7
CHAPTER 8
CHAPTER 9
CHAPTER 10
CHAPTER 11
CHAPTER 12
CHAPTER 13
APPENDICES

CLOTHES AND OTHER ATTACHMENTS

If you like clothes, *Second Life* will feel like heaven. You'll arrive with your Library containing several wardrobes' worth of clothing, and you'll add new outfits and individual clothing items while exploring Orientation and Help Islands. Within minutes of arriving on the mainland, your options to acquire good-looking clothes for free multiply like rabbits. You'll also see plenty of clothes (and other attractive things) offered at the symbolic price

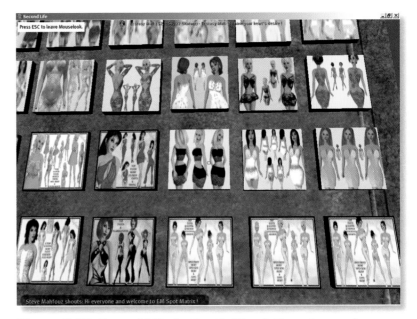

Figure 4.11: Second Life *is the thrifty clothes shopper's paradise.*

of L$1 (Figure 4.11). As pointed out elsewhere in this guide, even if you have zero Linden dollars and absolutely refuse to buy any, you can make a few Linden bucks instantly by engaging in such activities as sitting in a chair for L$3 per 15 minutes. In other words, *SL* lets you acquire a huge wardrobe for next to nothing in record time.

Making a few basic alterations to the ready-made Library clothes is relatively easy. The tabs under Clothes in the Appearance panel list standard clothing-item classes—Shirt, Pants, etc. The items your avatar is wearing at the time automatically become available for editing. In addition to sliders adjusting clothing details such as Sleeve Length or Pants Crotch, you can change the color/tint and texture of the selected clothing item:

- Clicking on the Fabric square opens a panel featuring the Library folder, which contains a special subfolder of fabric textures. Clicking a texture activates it.

- Clicking on the Color/Tint square opens a Color Picker panel. This lets you quickly pick a color by clicking a square, or create a custom color.

The clothing-editing options on the Appearance panel are great for simple alterations. However, if you want to design a clothing item from scratch, the plot thickens. As the *SL* template manual points out, it's not easy to design something in an external 2D application and subsequently make it fit a 3D object (your avatar).

You may also create clothing out of prims. However, even a relatively small and simple item such as a flexi miniskirt needs a number of carefully shaped prims. If you're interested in pursuing clothes design as a serious hobby or as a source of income, begin by signing up for at least a few of the tutorials and classes offered in *Second Life*. To see a list of the tutorials and classes currently on offer, open the Search panel and type "classes" or "tutorials" into the Search box.

NOTE

ADDITIONAL INFO:
TATTOOS AS CLOTHING

In Second Life, *tattoos fall into the clothing category. Tattoos can be worn as clothing items that are fully transparent except for the area covered by the tattoo. They also may be created in an external application and imported into* Second Life *as textures.*

Clothes have decisive impact on your avatar's appearance—the old saying that clothes make the man has never been more true than in the virtual world. Most likely, over half of the many thousands of items in your Inventory will consist of clothing, and 90% of that clothing won't ever be worn. There's a doctorate in sociology waiting for whoever draws the right conclusions.

Figure 4.12: Armed and dangerous? Not quite.

4

INTRO

PART I

PART II

PART III

APPENDICES

CHANGING YOUR APPEARANCE

Earlier in this chapter, Aodhan McDunnough described how he outfitted his avatar with a mechanical arm. While this is a somewhat extreme example, it illustrates the wide range of options you have for enhancing your avatar's appearance with an extra attachment. Appearance-enhancing attachments can include almost anything: you can wear a hat or a cap, lead a dog on a leash, or have a flying fish hovering over your head and attached by an invisible (i.e., fully transparent) thread. It's up to you to choose whatever you think suits your image (Figure 4.12).

Jewelry is another type of appearance-enhancing attachment. There's plenty of jewelry available, and it ranges from very simple to very elaborate: while everyone is talented enough to create a simple ring out of a single prim, few people are capable of making a multistone necklace whose jewels are scripted to display dazzling light effects. Note that jewelry can take many forms: animated, sparkling boot buckles and shoe laces are good examples.

AVATAR ANIMATIONS AND GESTURES

Avatar animations include every single move your avatar makes: ordinary walking, a gesture, dancing. Gestures are animations with extra content, such as sounds and/or special effects. Animations may be very simple (a hand wave, a nod) or very complex (a fencing system). They may be innocent or naughty, and some of the naughty ones are truly complicated.

Figure 4.13: I burn with shame.

Most *SL* residents who have been around for a while recognize the value of quality animations; a custom walk animation is high up on the list of avatar-appearance enhancements. However, you do not need to acquire a custom animation right

away to inject a little more life and charm into your avatar. You enter *Second Life* with a vast Library of gestures waiting to be used. All you need to do is activate the ones you like most by assigning them hotkeys, and display a sense of humor and good timing when you use them (Figure 4.13).

Avatar animations are most often created using an external application called Poser (there's also a free application called Avimator, though it isn't as sophisticated); they are much more complex than the simple animations you can apply to objects while remaining within the world. Subsequently, they are imported into *Second Life* and, if meant to replace a default animation, given an override script. Like most *SL* creations, custom animations can be obtained for free or for a symbolic price, but the flashiest animations can cost many thousands of Linden dollars.

NOTE

ADDITIONAL INFO:
BECOMING AN ANIMATOR

Creating custom animations isn't easy, which is why animators in **SL** *are both rare and well-paid. If you're interested, check out the Guide to Animations at* http://secondlife.com/knowledgebase/article.php?id=050.

Custom animations greatly enrich your virtual life because they enable your avatar to behave in a new way through custom moves or to participate in a new activity. However, you can greatly enhance your avatar's ability to socialize simply by using the animations or gestures from the Library. Accordingly, the next chapter takes a look at Library contents.

CHAPTER 5

USING YOUR LIBRARY

You already know that Library items and choices are a great help while working on your avatar's appearance. However, the Library is much more than that: its contents are your starting kit for creating a fulfilling second life, and many of the items it contains remain very useful throughout your *SL* existence.

The Library does not have its own onscreen button. It's just a folder in your Inventory, and it's accessed by clicking the Inventory button. That is why many new players, eager to get on with their new lives, fail to check out its contents. But you won't make that mistake, will you?

In this chapter, we'll discuss the Library in detail. You'll find out how it can get your new life off into a flying start, and which items remain uniquely useful no matter how long you've inhabited the *SL* metaverse.

CONTENTS

WHAT IS THE LIBRARY?

You can look at it this way: the Library is your starting Inventory, courtesy of Linden Lab. Every new *Second Life* resident receives the same set of items: a comprehensive starting kit that goes far beyond clothing. It includes a livable house (Atoll Hut) with an extra-small footprint for small land lots, a driveable vehicle (Kart), a popgun, and a wide range of landscaping items. New items are included in almost every *SL* update, so make sure to review your Library's contents regularly! It really pays—if you find it hard to believe, check out what some experienced Second Lifers have to say on the subject.

SIDEBAR

RESIDENTS SPEAK:
THE LIBRARY

"The Library is great—I use it more and more the longer I play. They occasionally add new things to it (for example, there are a number of full avatars there now which are much more interesting than the default Orientation Island avies), and it's a convenient place to find textures and other items useful in quickie landscaping and other kinds of builds.

"I've also made frequent use of the furniture; it's nice to be able to toss down some chairs or a bed for some role-playing without having to go shopping while in the middle of a scene."

—Wildefire Waldcott

"I use the Library quite a bit. The trees, of course, are the top item I use out of there. I'm a terraformer and landscaper and prefer the Linden trees over resident-made trees for their interaction with the wind and fewer prims. Even my waterfalls are made from Library parts."

—Ghoti Nyak

"I use a lot of the Linden plants for my terraforming and landscaping jobs. It's fantastic to have big, good-looking plants like the Plumeria bush and some of the trees, that fill a lot of space yet take up only one prim.

> *"I also use several of the library textures in my building work, and the scripts and stuff for waterfalls in the library have been very useful of late."*
>
> —Ceera Murakami

As mentioned in the previous chapter, you could have paid a few quick visits to the Library while editing your avatar's appearance—choosing a new texture or color automatically takes you to the Library folder, and the textures and colors contained therein. Later in this chapter, we'll look at the Library subfolders one by one, following the same order as the one in which they're displayed in *Second Life*. This should make in-game reference easier, and encourage you to use the Library often.

And use it often you should, right from the start. If you do, you'll feel like a veteran *SL* citizen even before you leave Help Island. Countless newbies will gape with slack-jawed amazement as you conjure up weapons, vehicles, and houses with effortless flicks of your wrist. The air shall ring with excited cries such as "Where did you get that gun?" and "How do you build this stuff so fast?" To which you'll reply, typing softly, "I got it from the Library."

NOTE

ADDITIONAL INFO:
MOVING ITEMS

You can move items between the Library and the Inventory. Open the folders, then just select and drag items from one location to the other. You can also give any item from either the Inventory or the Library to another SL denizen: to do so, select and drag the folder onto the recipient's avatar. However, some items are not transferable—find out by right-clicking on an item, and selecting Properties.

LIBRARY CONTENTS

As you must have gathered by now, there's more to the Library than meets the eye, especially at the hurried first glance thrown by a new, impatient resident of

INTRO
CHAPTER 1
CHAPTER 2
CHAPTER 3
CHAPTER 4
CHAPTER 5
CHAPTER 6
CHAPTER 7
CHAPTER 8
CHAPTER 9
CHAPTER 10
CHAPTER 11
CHAPTER 12
CHAPTER 13
APPENDICES

Second Life. The sections below list Library folders, and comment on their contents (Figure 5.1). Keep in mind that new Library items are added with almost every *SL* update!

Figure 5.1: There are many nice surprises waiting for you inside the Library folders.

BODY PARTS

You'll most likely access the Library's topmost folder while editing the appearance of your avatar, as described in Chapter 4. At the time of writing, the Body Parts folder contains these items and subfolders:

- **Hair—Men's.** There are seven instant hairstyle choices in this subfolder, including a rather wild afro. If you decide to use them, treat them as a starting point for creating your final stunning hairdo. Remember that you'll acquire new, better-looking hair shortly after starting your new existence. The Freebie Shop on Help Island will yield some, and soon after you move to the mainland you'll most likely get high-quality prim hair.

- **Hair—Women's.** This subfolder contains five instant hairstyles for female avatars. Keep in mind that you can and indeed should try applying male hairstyles to female avatars and vice versa—the results can be surprisingly good. At the time of writing, that's the way to give your female avie an instant afro. However, also keep in mind that, as mentioned earlier, you'll be acquiring better-looking hair shortly after your arrival in *Second Life.*

- **Creating Avatar Hair Textures.** This short document, discussed in the previous chapter, is a must-read if you're going to mess with your hair.

- **Eyes—Dark Brown.** This is an instant eye-color choice that should be treated as a starting point for determining your avatar's eye color.

- **Eyes—Gray.** Another starting point for determining your avatar's eye color.

- **Hair—Medium Brown.** This is probably the most natural-looking instant hairstyle choice at the time of writing; most likely, that's why it appears as a standalone item. It makes a good starting point for creating male and female hairstyles alike.

- **Shape—Thin.** This treasured Library item immediately endows your avatar with the svelte figure we all want to have in real life. It looks good, too, but remember that a cookie-cutter body is a cookie-cutter body, no matter how beautiful. As someone clever once put it, there's nothing as boring as perfection.

- **Skin—Lightly Tanned.** This choice gives your avatar the bronze skin tone favored by many movie stars. If you find it a little on the dark side, adjust it as described in Chapter 4.

The Body Parts folder is, predictably, most useful right at the start of your new life. As you spend more time in the *SL* metaverse, you'll inevitably acquire many more interesting options, starting with the Help Island freebies discussed in Chapter 3.

CLOTHING

Your avatar is born wearing a rather proletarian outfit: T-shirt, jeans, fire-sale flip-flops, plus standard underwear and socks. And as you know from the preceding chapters, the *Second Life* metaverse is a very fashion-oriented world, because literally everyone is a clothing—scratch that—a *costume* designer. It's never been as easy as it is in *Second Life*.

The Library comes with a thick Clothing subfolder, its size silently confirming the importance of looking good in *Second Life*. Inside the Clothing subfolder, you'll find enough stuff to fill several big real-life wardrobes, with new items added following almost every *SL* update:

INTRO
CHAPTER 1
CHAPTER 2
CHAPTER 3
CHAPTER 4
CHAPTER 5
CHAPTER 6
CHAPTER 7
CHAPTER 8
CHAPTER 9
CHAPTER 10
CHAPTER 11
CHAPTER 12
CHAPTER 13
APPENDICES

■ **Complete Outfits.** You'll see a long column of subfolders containing complete male and female outfits (City Chic, Goth, Harajuku, etc.). Hint: you can mix and match various items from different outfits, and save the results as a new outfit in your Inventory. Treat most

Figure 5.2: Customizing a complete outfit from the Library is the quickest way to look original.

of the complete outfits you'll find in the Clothing subfolder as the equivalent of real-life off-the-rack suits: you need to apply a little personal touch to make things look really good (Figure 5.2). Note that the More Outfits folder includes uniforms.

■ **Individual Clothing Items.** These include everything down to a spare set of underpants. This is important, since your carefree existence in *Second Life* means you don't really *have* to wear underpants, and with a little customization and imagination they may become an attractive trade item. Few people can resist entering a business dialogue when you open with, "Hey, I'm new and I'm poor. This stuff you make is so amazing I'd be willing to trade in my last set of underwear to have some of that."

The Clothing folder contains a lot of stuff, and upon examining its contents you should do what you'd do if you were suddenly given trunkloads of new clothes. Choose what you're likely to wear, and move it into your Inventory: select and drag items between the Library and Inventory folders, and save complete outfits as new Inventory subfolders.

GESTURES

This Library folder usually gets little interest from new *SL* residents. This is a big oversight: entertaining gestures can do more for your avatar's memorability than a top-of-the-line designer outfit purchased for many Linden dollars. It's been noted in Chapter 4, but to drive it home let's have it again: the impression you make on people you meet in *Second Life* depends on what you do, not only by what you look like. Creating and activating a personal Gesture folder is among your priorities.

There is also a Gesture subfolder in your Inventory; however, it contains just two subfolders—Common Gestures and Male Gestures if your avatar is male, Female if it is female. There are four Gesture subfolders in the Library: Common, Female, Male, and Other Gestures. Regardless of your sexual preferences, do not let yourself be limited by your avatar's sex when selecting gestures. A female making a male gesture can be very entertaining and memorable, and the same applies to a male making a female gesture. So if you want *SL* people to remember you, it's truly worth your while to assemble your very own gesture set from the Library choices right at the start of your existence. Here's what you'll find in the Library's Gestures subfolders:

- **Common Gestures.** This subfolder contains a set of gestures meant for avatars of either sex. There are some very nice animations in there, in spite of the "Common" moniker, so take the time to look through them all. As explained in Chapter 4, the timing of a gesture gives it a new meaning: for example, the "count" gesture works great when you want to emphasize a point in conversation. This folder also contains the three gestures needed for playing the popular "rock, paper, scissors" game.

- **Male Gestures.** This set of "standard" and slightly bland gestures includes a male voice where appropriate. Some of the animations are identical to those in the Female Gestures subfolder. This is perhaps the least exciting gesture subfolder in the Library, at least if you use them for the intended gender.

- **Female Gestures.** This set of "standard" gestures includes a female voice where appropriate. Again, the gestures within seem slightly bland when employed by an avatar of the intended sex, but gain in originality when used by males. You'll crack people up if you are a big, well-muscled guy who unexpectedly says "Get lost" in a high-pitched, female voice.

- **Other Gestures.** Make sure you check out this subfolder in detail: some of the animations within are very entertaining. "Embarrassed," "nya," and "shrug" are good examples of gestures that work equally well for avatars of both sexes.

INTRO
CHAPTER 1
CHAPTER 2
CHAPTER 3
CHAPTER 4
CHAPTER 5
CHAPTER 6
CHAPTER 7
CHAPTER 8
CHAPTER 9
CHAPTER 10
CHAPTER 11
CHAPTER 12
CHAPTER 13
APPENDICES

ADDITIONAL INFO:
UTILIZING YOUR INVENTORY EARLY ON

Remember that when you begin your new life, the Library has much more to offer than the Inventory does. The little folder at the end of the Inventory list looks unimportant to many fresh SL inhabitants, so making use of its contents can instantly make you stand out from the crowd.

LANDMARKS AND NOTECARDS

These two Library subfolders are most useful at the start of your new existence. The Landmark folder contains just a single landmark: the Welcome Area on the *SL* mainland. The Welcome Area is where you should go upon leaving Help Island; as explained in Chapter 3, it is the right spot to pick up information on ongoing *SL* events. It is also a very good spot to pick up, er, make new friends. Many new *SL* denizens hang around there for a while, eager to show off their new selves (Figure 5.3).

Figure 5.3: Some people will go to great lengths (and heights) to make sure they're noticed.

The Library's Notecard folder contains just four items that are *not* included in the Inventory's Notecard subfolder. Three of these are pretty important, and you would be wise to keep them:

HELP! This notecard contains answers to many of the questions new denizens have about *Second Life.* It's worth your while to check out the contents even if you don't want to read it (there's a lot of stuff in there!). The topics covered in this notecard will instantly make you aware of the multitude of options available to you in your new existence. Read the titles of the featured Beginner's Guides to various aspects of *Second Life* (such as owning land), and check out the step-by-step instructions for selected *SL* activities. Purchasing and owning land, removing items from a box, and making movies in *Second Life*—these are just some of the issues covered in the Library's HELP! notecard. Obviously, this notecard's a keeper.

Community Standards. This notecard explains what you can and cannot do in *Second Life.* The *Second Life* metaverse can continue to exist only if its inhabitants follow certain rules. These are explained in the Community Standards notecard. They are very reasonable; the only denizens likely to find them oppressive are those who are consumed by hunger for sex and violence. If you happen to be one of them, remember that mutual consensus rules in *SL.* Join or assemble a group of like-minded people in a defined area who play by your kind of rules, as explained in Chapter 2.

Media Player Help. This notecard discusses activating streaming media so that you can play music and movies on your land. Music and movies draw people, which can be useful (see Chapter 2 for details). It most likely will be a while before you turn into a media mogul, so keep this card for future reference.

Welcome Note. This ultra-short note tells you how to obtain extra notecards discussing selected aspects of *Second Life.* These extra notecards will appear in the Notecard subfolder in your Inventory.

You may drag the three keeper notecards into your Inventory's Notecard folder so you have all your notecards collected in one place.

OBJECTS

This is one of the most interesting among the Library folders. It contains plenty of subfolders and individual items that you'll find useful and entertaining throughout your *Second Life* existence. Its contents swell following almost every *SL* update, so check the folder often! Here's a descriptive list of the goodies that are available at the time of writing:

INTRO
CHAPTER 1
CHAPTER 2
CHAPTER 3
CHAPTER 4
CHAPTER 5
CHAPTER 6
CHAPTER 7
CHAPTER 8
CHAPTER 9
CHAPTER 10
CHAPTER 11
CHAPTER 12
CHAPTER 13
APPENDICES

INTRO
PART I
PART II
PART III
APPENDICES
LIBRARY CONTENTS

Atoll Continent Stuff. This modestly titled subfolder contains an atoll hut–style home complete with accessories (footbridge, walkway, etc.). As you know from Chapter 3, you can pick up a free house on Help Island—a design much classier than the modest atoll hut. But one thing about the atoll hut is unbeatable: it has a tiny footprint, making it a very good choice on the small, pay-no-upkeep building lots, aka First Land. When you have only 512 square meters to play with, the atoll hut's small space requirements can make it a very attractive choice.

Business. This subfolder contains a Resident Store Kit. You can set up your own store in a blink of an eye—the kit comes with a notecard containing what's probably the simplest set of instructions ever written for erecting a small commercial building.

Dominos. This subfolder contains a single, large domino block that can be copied endlessly. See the "What Can You Do with Library Objects?" sidebar to find out how other users play with dominos.

Household. Here you'll find another freebie starter home—a small, single-room cabin—plus a builder's tape measure, and the basic furnishings for your new home (bed, lamp, coffee table, rug, etc.). Other interesting items in this folder include a dead parrot waiting for a script to bring her to life … or to face whatever fate you devise.

Landscaping. This is yet another very useful folder. Contents include quite pretty freestanding and potted plants (Figure 5.4), an assortment of ornamental rocks, and decorative items such as latticework.

Orientation stations with notecards. This folder contains the interactive signs and orientation stations you pass by right after you start your second life. These signs and stations are demo pieces; treat them as starting points for your own interactive signs. Note that you can right-click on a sign and choose Open from the pop-up pie menu—this will reveal object contents, such as attached sound effects and scripts. If you've missed your chance to obtain Male or Female Outfit #3 at the start, right-click the Outfit #3 signs and choose Open from the pie menu. You'll be given the option to wear each sign's clothing content, and/or copy it to your Inventory.

Telehubs. Telehubs can be used as arrival points for teleporting *SL* denizens. This folder offers three models: the invisible telehub, the small telehub, and the big Linden telehub (which has sentimental value for long-term *SL* citizens—a long, long time ago, residents could not teleport at will, and were forced to

use telehubs). Telehubs are useful when you want to direct traffic on land you own. Use invisible and small telehubs for low-volume traffic (home, small business) and the big model for high-volume traffic (large commercial establishments, events).

Figure 5.4: Some of the plants included in the Library's Landscaping folder are little works of art.

- **Trees, plants, and grasses.** This Library folder is extremely useful throughout your second life. A lot of the flora it contains looks superior to most user-made items; as mentioned earlier, it's even used by professional *SL* landscapers. You'll really appreciate the contents of this folder when you acquire your starter land and are in a hurry to make it look good.

- **Walkways.** There are five types of walkways on offer here. Click and drag the icon for the selected type repeatedly to lay down the walkway of your choice, piece by piece.

NOTE

ADDITIONAL INFO:
LIBRARY OBJECTS AND SCRIPTING

Library objects are extremely useful if you're planning to create items. Editing Library objects is a great exercise in building and texturing. The scripts in the scripted items can be copied to newly created objects, and most can also be modified. Adding or deleting a couple of script lines is always easier than writing everything from scratch!

INTRO
CHAPTER 1
CHAPTER 2
CHAPTER 3
CHAPTER 4
CHAPTER 5
CHAPTER 6
CHAPTER 7
CHAPTER 8
CHAPTER 9
CHAPTER 10
CHAPTER 11
CHAPTER 12
CHAPTER 13
APPENDICES

The Walkways subfolder is followed by a series of individual objects that provide tons of fun. You must check them out, even if you don't look at anything else! Many new denizens don't, and they are the ones who will be staring at you and asking, "Where did you get that gun?"

SIDEBAR

RESIDENTS SPEAK:
WHAT CAN YOU DO WITH LIBRARY OBJECTS?

"The Library popgun is fun to shoot each other with. The popgun is good when you are learning scripting. It serves as an example of how to rez an object from another one.

"The beach ball is fun to play with. It has a good script for beginning scripters also. The basic chair is good to use as a model when you are learning to build. It has another good basic script, a sit script. The dice and fireworks have good beginner's scripts in them.

"The dominoes—who could forget the dominoes? Thousands of dominoes stacked in a delightfully tempting manner, and they set themselves back up automatically. For fun, make an object that pushes dominoes, so when you find a set of dominoes, turn on your domino pusher, plough into the dominoes, and watch them fly away at high velocity.

"There's some things in the Landscaping folder that a person might find useful setting up a small home. Everyone starting out needs a pink flamingo.

"The gesture folders are pretty nice to have. In case anyone doesn't know it, you can activate an entire folder of gestures such as the Common Gestures by dragging the folder onto your av.

"There's now some Linden Telehubs in there, quaint reminders of the days of yore. Whatever yore is.

"Some of the orientation stations are in there in case one gets nostalgic for Orientation Island and can't be bothered to go to the fairly new public Orientation Island.

—SuezanneC Baskerville

THE FUN STUFF

For many *SL* denizens, the standalone items in the Objects folder will be worth more than a freebie custom house complete with furniture (Figure 5.5). All of them come with operating instructions, which are accessed by right-clicking the chosen object and selecting Open from the pie menu. This will let you view the object's contents, which usually include a notecard with instructions.

Figure 5.5: A car! A gun! That's every real guy's get-rich-quick kit, no?

The following is a descriptive list of the standalone items in the Library's Objects folder at the time of writing:

- **Kart 1.0.** This is your freebie *SL* starter vehicle: a smart little go-cart in bright red. It goes pretty fast, too. To go for a drive, drag the Kart icon onto the ground, right-click on it to open the pie menu, and click on Drive. If you can't be bothered to read the Kart notecard, keep in mind that movement is activated by the arrow and WASD keys.

- **Media Player.** This item contains the media player and its script. Drag the Media Player icon from your Library and onto building-permitted ground, then right-click the elegant oblong box that appears to view its contents. They consist of the media player proper—a nifty flat screen—and the script. There is *no* notecard with operating instructions; click on the script to find operating info inside, inserted as comments to the script code.

- **Popgun.** For many players, this is the best freebie Library item of them all. Drag the Popgun icon onto your avatar, and the gun will appear in your right hand.

INTRO
CHAPTER 1
CHAPTER 2
CHAPTER 3
CHAPTER 4
CHAPTER 5
CHAPTER 6
CHAPTER 7
CHAPTER 8
CHAPTER 9
CHAPTER 10
CHAPTER 11
CHAPTER 12
CHAPTER 13
APPENDICES

NOTE

ADDITIONAL INFO:
FIRING A POPGUN

To fire your new gun, follow the onscreen instructions: first, switch to Mouselook and zoom into first-person view. Moving the mouse aims the gun, left-clicking fires sickly green orbs at your target. They're powerful enough to knock someone back, and a series of hits can move the targeted avatar a fair distance. There is no injury involved.

Basic Chair. This is a very useful item for more than obvious reasons. The chair comes with a Sit Down script attached, and this script can be copied as-is to furniture you make yourself.

Beach Ball. Big, colorful, and bouncy, the beach ball comes with a piece of script that features extensive comments: it's almost like a little script-writing tutorial. As usual, access the contents by dragging the object icon onto the ground, right-clicking on it, and choosing Open from the pop-up pie menu.

Celtic Sword. What do you know: Library offerings even include a wicked-looking hand-to-hand-combat weapon. However, there isn't much sense in walking around with a sword in your hand if you can't hit people with it, and hitting people involves making appropriate gestures and scripting appropriate, complicated effects. You may wait with bated breath for an update that includes all this stuff; you can try to buy appropriate scripts (at the time of writing, a couple can be had for free), or—in a pinch—you can use appropriate Library gestures. For example, playing Pointme from the Common Gestures subfolder while holding the sword results in an animation that looks like a rather elegant, if unhurried, block against an enemy sword thrust.

Dice. Drag the Dice icon to the ground, then switch to Mouselook and click on the dice to roll them.

Firework Launcher. The firework launcher comes with an inexhaustible supply of rockets and operating instructions. The launch animation and sound effects are very well done and deserve to be copied (hint, hint).

Hand Lamp, Party Hat. An old-fashioned hand lamp and a conical party hat round off the list of standalone Objects-folder items. The hand lamp doesn't have to be attached to your hand; it can be put anywhere to function as an ordinary lamp

(and actually looks very appropriate in a cabin home). To put the hand lamp upright, right-click on it, choose Edit from the pie menu, and use the Rotate function.

The standalone objects in the Objects folder are a great help when you begin creating your own items and building things. As mentioned earlier, it's always easiest to begin by modifying existing stuff instead of building from scratch, and the vast majority of the Library items can be modified and copied any way you like (Figure 5.6).

In addition to the items in the Objects folder, the content of the Photo Album folder qualifies as Fun Stuff. However, at the time of writing it contains only a single snapshot depicting a nice sunset.

Figure 5.6: Modifying Library objects is a great way to learn building and scripting.

THE BUILDING AND SCRIPTING STUFF

The last three Library folders are especially important to everyone who wants to get creative in *Second Life*. After you've explored a little, you're bound to try your hand at bringing new items into existence by modifying existing items, and building new ones from scratch. This involves making things look and sound the way you want them to, and eventually adding scripted animations.

The Library offers you plenty to work with:

🔹 **Scripts.** This folder contains three useful scripts. As you might guess, Anim Smooth smooths out animations; HoverText Clock turns an object into a clock

INTRO
CHAPTER 1
CHAPTER 2
CHAPTER 3
CHAPTER 4
CHAPTER 5
CHAPTER 6
CHAPTER 7
CHAPTER 8
CHAPTER 9
CHAPTER 10
CHAPTER 11
CHAPTER 12
CHAPTER 13
APPENDICES

by making it display Pacific standard time; Rotation Script is extremely versatile and can be included in a wide variety of objects. For example, right-click on the hand lamp that you've just rotated upright with the Edit panel's Rotate function; then click on the New Script button and paste the Rotation Script contents inside the New Script file (delete any existing content; the New Script file always contains the code for creating a New Script file). Save, exit, and watch the hand lamp turn round and round. There—you've just scripted an object to behave in a certain way.

Sounds. This folder contains a subfolder titled Gestures. Its contents include male and female sounds, and sound bites designed to go with specific avatar gestures, but of course they have more uses than that. If you've ever wanted a dog that speaks with a human voice, for example, use some of the sound bites from the Gestures folder. Simply upload custom-made sound bites, and who knows—maybe you'll be the first *SL* citizen to breed talking police dogs? "Hands up!" he barked, and all that.

Textures. The final folder in the Library is also its biggest: it contains an awesome number of textures, plus Avatar Body and Clothing templates. You'll use these templates and selected textures in Hair and Fabric folders frequently while editing your avatar's appearance. Take the time to review all the other choices, because there are quite a few, and new ones are added often. Naturally, many textures can be used for purposes other than the ones intended, with great success. For example, Atoll Wood Plank can be used whenever you want a nice wood plank texture, Sand or Mulch look good on carpets and rugs, and Asphalt (from the Building subfolder) may be used to imitate thick-grain leather texture. There are so many choices, and so many different tastes, that the best way to find what works for you is to experiment, and attend one of the tutorials mentioned in Chapter 3.

NOTE

ADDITIONAL INFO:
DOWNLOADING FREE TEXTURES

Don't forget to download the free textures available at http://secondlife.com/community/textures.php. *They're of high quality and useful even if you aren't into building and texturing as such (Figure 5.7).*

As you can see, the Library folders are a veritable treasure trove. Whether you're trying to get your SL existence off to a quick start or looking for ways and means of improving your building and scripting skills, the Library's invaluable. It provides a huge

selection of ready-to-use items, as well as countless examples to emulate while learning to create exciting new stuff in *Second Life*. However, as you live your new life, the Library's importance and size will be eclipsed by your Inventory's.

The next chapter discusses the Inventory and its role in your virtual life. It also explains how it differs from the Library and provides advice on Inventory management.

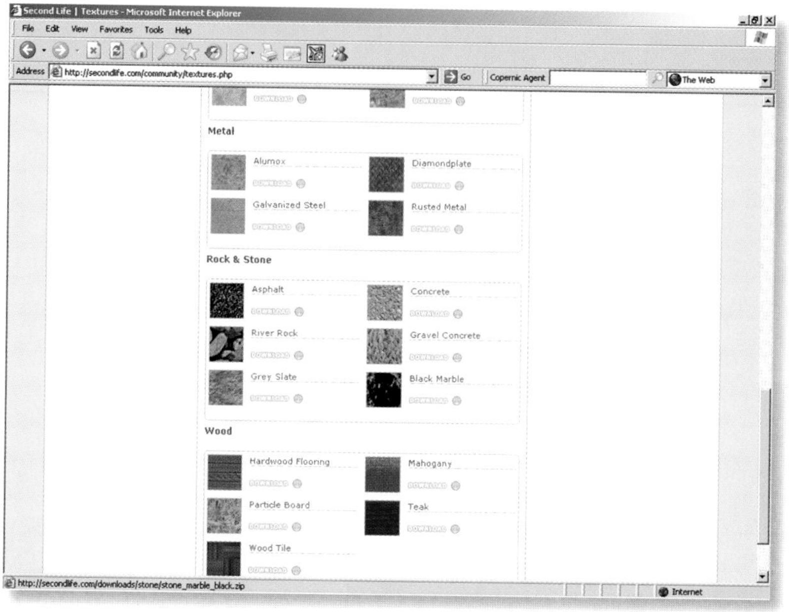

Figure 5.7: Black marble, too! Just what I wanted for my, erm, bedroom.

INTRO
CHAPTER 1
CHAPTER 2
CHAPTER 3
CHAPTER 4
CHAPTER 5
CHAPTER 6
CHAPTER 7
CHAPTER 8
CHAPTER 9
CHAPTER 10
CHAPTER 11
CHAPTER 12
CHAPTER 13
APPENDICES

CHAPTER 6

MANAGING YOUR INVENTORY

The Inventory is very many things. It is your own, unique collection of *Second Life* items ranging from complete houses and spaceships to socks and bubble gum. It is also a pet that grows into a monster. If anyone ever wanted clear proof that humans are insanely acquisitive by nature, the *SL* Inventory is that proof. A long time ago, when *Second Life* was in its infancy, there was a cap on the number of items you could have in your Inventory: 255. Now that there's no limit, most *SL* denizens quickly accumulate many thousands of objects. It's easy to let your Inventory get out of control, and once it does, more and more of your new life will be spent looking for stuff instead of enjoying yourself. Sound familiar?

If you're new to *Second Life* and are frowning with disbelief, consider this: *SL* is a world in which you carry everything you own—house, car, 50 wardrobes of clothing, and so on—on your person. And if you're also running a business, and/or constantly creating new unique items... let's just say keeping track of all the items in your Inventory isn't easy. It's in your best interest to have as little as possible (for most *SL* denizens, "as little as possible" means fewer than 5,000 items).

In this chapter, I'll take a close look at the *SL* Inventory and discuss how to manage it effectively. You'll find out how to organize Inventory folders, and keep them under control even though they're multiplying like rabbits. You'll also learn how to store stuff in locations other than your Inventory. In short, this chapter is an Inventory master plan that should make your new existence more carefree and enjoyable.

CONTENTS

INTRO
PART I
PART II
PART III
APPENDICES
THE INVENTORY VS. THE LIBRARY

THE INVENTORY VS .THE LIBRARY

When you begin *Second Life*, your Inventory seems to be an underdeveloped offspring of the Library. The few folders in the Inventory correspond to Library folders with the same names, but they are mostly empty, or at best have just part of their Library equivalents' content. There is no warning of your Inventory's imminent mutation into something resembling a garage sale thrown by a freshly bankrupted and slightly deranged millionaire. This moment of peace is ideal for taking a look at the important differences between the Inventory and the Library.

The Library, as you might guess, is public: it's shared by everyone. Your Inventory is your own, and no one else's. Of course, initially your Inventory is identical to everyone else's, but it quickly becomes as unique as the choices you make in *Second Life*.

You cannot delete or modify the contents of your Library, but you can do as you please with the Inventory (there are exceptions, discussed later in this chapter). Note that when you use a Library item, it is automatically copied into the appropriate folder in your Inventory. These copies are prime candidates for the trash can during your periodical Inventory cleanouts. Your number-one Inventory-management rule is to never keep two copies of an item in the same Inventory. Stick to this rule from the start, and you'll save yourself lots of time. Otherwise you might spend most of your new existence looking for stuff hidden among thousands of other items!

NOTE

ADDITIONAL INFO:
PARTING WITH YOUR CREATIONS

Don't get overly sentimental about your own creations. Don't keep everything you've made just because you made it. The very next object you make will be exclusively yours too, and most likely better than what you created earlier. If you want a private museum of your work, store it outside your Inventory.

Of course, no matter how hard you try, you'll always have a ton of stuff in your Inventory. As you know from Chapter 3, your Inventory will start to grow almost

as soon as you arrive on Orientation Island—that's even before you get to Help Island and begin filling your Inventory with all the cool freebie items available there. If you don't monitor your Inventory from the very start, you'll be overwhelmed before you know it. An important Inventory-management rule is to organize Inventory contents right at the start of your new existence (Figure 6.1).

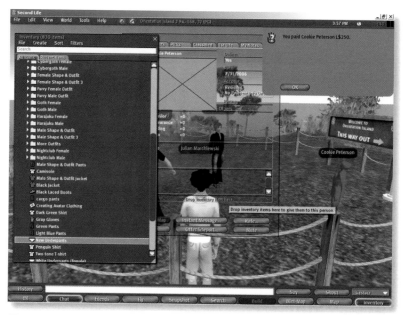

Figure 6.1: To trash or to stash? That's the big question you'll be asking yourself again and again in Second Life.

ORGANIZING YOUR INVENTORY

One of the first things you should put into your Inventory is some order. Trash unwanted items and reorganize your Inventory before you depart Help Island for the *SL* mainland. It's best to get a handle on things right away!

 NOTE

ADDITIONAL INFO:
KEEPING YOUR INVENTORY UNDER CONTROL

When you open your Inventory, a line at the very top will tell you how many items it contains. If you do not work on keeping the Inventory under control with beady-eyed zeal, the number displayed will reach four figures before you leave Help Island and will grow to five figures soon after you arrive on the mainland.

FOLDER RULES

First of all, take a good look at your existing Inventory folders. You'll notice some of them feature little icons. Any Inventory folders marked with icons cannot be moved, deleted, or even renamed; they're part of the Inventory setup. So, to begin with, move all your unmarked folders inside the icon-marked folders. Naturally, use logic: put clothing items into the Clothing folder, textures into the Textures folder, animations into Animations, hair into Body Parts, and so on.

NOTE

ADDITIONAL INFO:
FOLDER-MANAGEMENT OPTIONS

Double-click to open and close folders. Right-click on a folder to open a menu that shows a list of folder-management options. If the menu that appears is blank, the selected folder is part of the Inventory setup and cannot be manipulated in any way.

Once you've done that, open each folder in turn, and organize its contents. For example, you might want to create a Hair subfolder within the Body Parts folder for all the different hair types and styles you'll have by the time you leave Help Island.

Clothing also merits special attention, as always. It's a good idea to group clothing items into outfits, creating a subfolder for each complete outfit. Any remaining clothing

Figure 6.2: Keep the number of folders in your Inventory as low as possible, but not at the expense of your comfort.

items can be organized the way you organize things in real life, except that you'll be

using folders instead of closets and drawers for your shirts, pants, socks, etc. While you're at it, ask yourself whether you'll really, really wear a particular item. If you proceed on the "what I own can't hurt me" principle, you'll quickly find out that indeed it can. Don't forget to check out the Inventory-management advice from longtime *SL* residents in the sidebar.

The bonus of keeping a lean, well-organized Inventory (Figure 6.2) is extra time. You won't have to wait long for your Inventory to load, and you'll find stuff much faster. You'll be doing a bit of good for the *SL* community, too: huge Inventories cause slowdowns for everyone in the *SL* world.

SIDEBAR

RESIDENTS SPEAK:
MANAGING INVENTORY CONTENTS

"Subfolders are your friend. Making your own folders to keep 'important' stuff and your 'single copy' objects really helps keep things organized."

—DolphPun Somme

"I think of it the same way I think of organizing my hard drive. General folder, more specific subfolder, specific subfolders...i.e., clothing, casual, shoes. Or building materials, textures, exterior textures, brick. I spend around 30 minutes of every session cleaning up, naming, and moving around Inventory items.

"Something I just discovered last night in terms of clothing: activate the debug menu (ctrl-alt-D) and then go to the bottom of it and select Clothing. A list of everything you have that's defined by the system as clothing appears and can be put on/removed via the list. It's a good way to find the undershirt under the shirt under the jacket that you think you might have on."

—Rakkasa Lewellen

INTRO
CHAPTER 1
CHAPTER 2
CHAPTER 3
CHAPTER 4
CHAPTER 5
CHAPTER 6
CHAPTER 7
CHAPTER 8
CHAPTER 9
CHAPTER 10
CHAPTER 11
CHAPTER 12
CHAPTER 13
APPENDICES

CREATING AND USING STORAGE PRIMS

You can also realize your dream of a lean, mean Inventory by putting Inventory items inside prims. This has its advantages and disadvantages. You can remove the storage

INTRO

PART I

PART II

PART III

APPENDICES

ORGANIZING YOUR INVENTORY

prim from your Inventory and store it elsewhere; on the other hand, you cannot store folders inside a prim. If you attempt to move a folder into a prim, you'll move the folder's contents but not the folder itself. Upon opening the storage prim, you'll see all of the folder's items in exactly the same order as they were in the folder.

Another snag is that you won't see what's inside the storage prim until you open it. Give your storage prims names that will help you remember their contents. For example, if you're going to store an outfit consisting of a number of items, you might want to name the prim after the outfit—that's the way most *SL* old-timers handle things.

Here's the procedure for creating and using a storage prim:

1. Make sure you're on land that allows building: the top menu bar will show the No Build icon if it's not allowed.

2. Create a prim—any prim. Size and shape don't matter; you're free to make it anything you like. My personal favorites are mysterious black cubes, and steel-plate cylinders. They simply look cool.

3. Name the prim right away (under the General tab in the Edit menu). As mentioned earlier, give it a name that's illustrative of its contents.

4. Open your Inventory, and right-click on the item or items you want to put inside the prim to check their properties. As a rule, don't mix items that can be copied with items that cannot. Create a separate storage prim (or folder, if you don't want to mess with prims) for noncopyable items. The prim containing no-copy items will be particularly valuable, so keep it in your avatar's Inventory (Figure 6.3).

5. Click and drag the folder/items from your Inventory and onto the storage prim. You'll see the cursor change to a little white folder marked with a plus sign; release the mouse button to drop the transferred item into the prim. Occasionally, you may run into trouble when transferring entire folders: you'll see the universal red circle with a slash through it to indicate your action is forbidden. Try opening the affected folder and transferring the items within one by one; that's how they'll be stored inside the prim, anyway.

6. Right-click on the prim to bring up the pie menu. You should see an active Open option. Click on it to view prim contents, and note the buttons at the bottom of the Contents menu that let you instantly copy all stored items into your Inventory (assuming they're replicable). You may also view the prim's contents by choosing Edit from the pie menu and selecting the Contents tab.

7. Decide whether you want to keep the storage prim's contents private: select the appropriate check boxes in the Edit menu (General tab).

As you can see, storing items in prims is a simple process, and very popular among *SL* citizens. However, there are also more-elegant solutions, such as special security boxes. If your building and scripting abilities don't allow for making

Figure 6.3: Twenty pairs of pants, ten pairs of shoes, a dozen shirts—all packed uncreased into a tiny metal cylinder! Only in Second Life.

one of those, you can purchase them at stores such as the THiNC store mentioned in the "Storing Inventory Contents" sidebar later in this chapter. They're not expensive—to give you an idea of what you get for what money, here is a selection of THiNC offerings and their prices at the time of writing:

Inventory Box Organizer—L$215 (copyable). This stores all types of items, from clothes to landmarks, with the exception of scripts. It allows you to browse through contents and quickly locate the items you want. The name you give to the organizer is displayed on the box, which lets you store numerous boxes inside one main organizer without identification problems. This organizer has full privacy and security features; only the owner can access functions. Sleep Mode changes the organizer's appearance: buttons and text disappear, and it looks like a standard trunk.

Multi-Texture Organizer—L$650 (copyable). This organizer lets you store, browse, and manage stored textures through a nine-panel display. All functions are owner-accessed only. Privacy and security features include Sleep Mode. A cheaper model, the Single Texture Organizer for L$115 (copyable), provides the same functions but features a single-panel display for browsing and texture management.

INTRO
CHAPTER 1
CHAPTER 2
CHAPTER 3
CHAPTER 4
CHAPTER 5
CHAPTER 6
CHAPTER 7
CHAPTER 8
CHAPTER 9
CHAPTER 10
CHAPTER 11
CHAPTER 12
CHAPTER 13
APPENDICES

INTRO

PART I

PART II

PART III

APPENDICES

ORGANIZING YOUR INVENTORY

THiNC Book 2.0—L$75 (single version). This versatile book can be used as a photo album, a novel, or a catalog. It comes with a full set of animations and sound effects (book opening, book closing, pages being turned). Transferable and fully modifiable by the owner.

THiNC Printing Press—L$895 (single version). This lets you produce unlimited, exact copies of the THiNC Book 2.0 for unlimited distribution. Each published book has copy and transfer rights modifiable by the owner (publisher).

The THiNC store is one of many that specialize in offering great Inventory-management aids. There is a wide variety on offer, and who wants to keep *SL* snapshots in a boring folder named Photo Album when they can be stored and viewed on a copyable TV set? Consider spending a few hundred Linden bucks on Inventory-management tools; you'll likely find they're your best investment.

SIDEBAR

RESIDENTS SPEAK:
INVENTORY MANAGEMENT

"Use the search box at the top of the Inventory panel to quickly locate Inventory items by associated keywords. For example, typing 'WORN' into the search box returns a list of all the items your avatar is currently wearing, along with their Inventory locations. The keyword you enter into the search box acts as a filter regardless of whether it's an item name or property. For instance, if you enter 'NO MODIFY' you'll see a list of all Inventory items that cannot be modified, while entering 'HAIR' will display a list of all the hair in your Inventory.

"To run a check on Inventory items acquired [since] your last online session, select the Recent Items tab on the Inventory panel. Note also that you can sort all Inventory folders and items by name or by date of acquisition.

"When you want to rearrange your Inventory, select New Window from the File menu to open a mirror Inventory panel—it's easier to keep track of what you're doing when you have two identical Inventory panels side by side. Drag the Inventory items and folders you want to move to their new locations in the mirror Inventory panel.

"Also, there are online resources you can use to improve your Inventory-management skills. Visit http://secondlife.com/knowledgebase/article.php?id=074 *for tips on Inventory filters, and read Willow*

NOTE

FROM LINDEN LAB:
TRANSFERRING FOLDERS TO AN OBJECT'S INVENTORY

When a folder is dropped into the inventory of an object, all of the folder's items are transferred individually to the object. Note that scripts transferred using this process are deactivated (each script must be dragged separately, or selected using Shift and/or Control-clicking and dragged as a mass selection). A UUID number is automatically attached to items without unique names (the UUID, or Universal Unique Identifier, is the 128-bit unique number assigned to every asset in Second Life).

CHAPTER 6

MANAGING MULTIPLE INVENTORIES

Real life abounds in paradoxes, and so does *Second Life.* You've just learned that you should strive to keep your Inventory as small as possible; now you'll find out why you should have *two* Inventories: sadly, no technology is perfect, and occasionally Inventories become corrupted. To put it bluntly, you can lose everything you own in *Second Life* because of a few rogue electrons somewhere, just like you can lose everything you own in real life because the weather and/or earthquake gods have a hangover.

After making sure your Inventory contains absolutely no trash (remember to empty that trash can regularly!), copy it. You can copy everything except for nonreplicable items into a single prim and store it on your property, rented or owned.

INTRO
CHAPTER 1
CHAPTER 2
CHAPTER 3
CHAPTER 4
CHAPTER 5
CHAPTER 6
CHAPTER 7
CHAPTER 8
CHAPTER 9
CHAPTER 10
CHAPTER 11
CHAPTER 12
CHAPTER 13
APPENDICES

127

INTRO

PART I

PART II

PART III

APPENDICES

MANAGING MULTIPLE
INVENTORIES

> NOTE
>
> ADDITIONAL INFO:
> ## THE 16-SQUARE-METER PLOT
>
> *There are always plenty of tiny 16-square-meter plots available for sale or rental; they let you store up to three prims (Figure 6.4). How much stuff you store within those prims is, of course, your private business.*

If you have a free account that does not allow you to own land, try renting. You should be able to negotiate rental of a prim storage lot for less than L$250 a week, and probably less than L$100. There's also another solution—not very elegant, but effective. This is to create an alternate avatar, and back up your Inventory by copying it to the alternate avatar's.

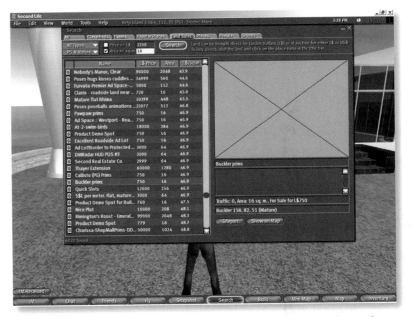

Figure 6.4: A 16-square-meter plot is perfect for storing prims.

CREATING AN ALTER EGO FOR INVENTORY BACKUP

To begin with, you must create a new character. The obvious route is to open a new free account and create a mule without land-owning privileges. However, remember it may actually be worth your while to create a second Premium account. As explained in Chapter 2, this gives you two shots at buying First Land at the rock-bottom price of one Linden dollar per square meter. You can buy two First Land parcels side by side and join them to create a bigger parcel, or you can sell one parcel and keep the other—as noted in Chapter 2, practically all First Land can be sold immediately at a healthy profit.

Having created an alter ego, move it to the mainland and transfer all the replicable items you really, really don't want to lose to the alternate avatar's Inventory. Of course, you can do it via a storage prim—just make sure your alternate avatar has the rights to open the prim and to copy its contents into its own Inventory! However, you can also effect a direct Inventory-to-Inventory folder and item transfer using the Search function:

1. Click the Search button on the main game menu, and select the People tab.

2. Type in your alternate character's name, and make sure the Online box is *not* checked.

3. Click the Search button next to the name you typed in. This opens your alternate character's Profile panel on its default 2nd Life tab. You'll see a Give Item slot near the bottom of the panel.

4. Drag and drop Inventory folders and/or items into the slot, one by one. A blue info panel will tell you about your alter ego's offline status and state that the items will be saved for delivery.

5. When you log on as your alter ego, you'll see a blue info panel asking whether you want to accept the items; and after you accept them, you'll find them in your Inventory (Figure 6.5). Note that, at the time of writing, transferring an Inventory item via the Profile panel to someone who is *online* isn't confirmed until the recipient accepts delivery.

Figure 6.5: If another SL denizen gives you something while you're offline, you'll get a message as soon as you return to Second Life.

CHAPTER

INTRO

PART I

PART II

PART III

APPENDICES

MANAGING MULTIPLE
INVENTORIES

SIDEBAR

RESIDENTS SPEAK:
STORING INVENTORY CONTENTS

"It is possible to put items in prim boxes to reduce Inventory clutter, and reduce the complexity of your Inventory.

"Once you have made one of these storage collections, you can store one copy of the box in-world, or you can give a copy to a friend (or an alt) to keep in their inventory in case yours gets corrupted. I highly advise doing that, as inventories are just collections of data records in the asset server database, and Linden Lab is not responsible for restoring lost content!

"The downside is, you can't search Inventory to find any of those items unless you look inside the contents of each box and see what's there! Ever open a box that's been stored for years? Ever been surprised that you even owned half the stuff in there? You can repeat this as much as needed. Have a prim called ZZZ—The Attic and store all the other boxes in that.

"Warning: If you want to store no-copy stuff this way, such as purchased clothes that you don't wear very often, make sure the storage box has been named before you put the first no-copy item into the box! I advise keeping the no-copy stored items separate from the copy-permitted ones, because while there is a no-copy item in a storage box, the entire box's contents can't be duplicated."

—Ceera Murakami

"I will tell you my secret to my perfect Inventory system. First of all, every matching outfit gets its own prim box, and is labeled according to what that outfit is. Then I put the prim boxes into the copyable, no-transfer organizer boxes from THiNC. Why are the THiNC boxes so wonderful? They have arrows on them that let you browse through the contents, and quickly retrieve what you want.

"My 4,500+ textures are organized by type. The THiNC copyable, no-transfer machines let me pull out a fresh one for, say, castle-type textures and store all my castle textures in there. All my tile textures go into another one, and so on.

"My entire Inventory is organized this way, and it is mainly because of the Library that my Inventory is at 2,000—yes, you read it right; my Inventory ➡

is at 2k and I grumble over it constantly. I try to keep it as low as possible so I do not get any Inventory lag."

—Tyci Kenzo

THE FIVE GOLDEN RULES OF INVENTORY MANAGEMENT

In summary, getting a firm grip on your Inventory right from the start is a major—some might say *the* major—factor in enjoying your new life to the max. It frees you from the drudgery afflicting real life, in which the tyranny of material things makes people go postal. To maximize your chances of freedom and eternal happiness in *Second Life*, here are the five main Inventory-management points:

1. Organize Inventory contents before you leave Help Island for the mainland, and don't keep two copies of the same, replicable item in your Inventory. As discussed earlier on in this chapter, this includes all the items in your Library folder.

2. The subfolders are your friends. Don't keep miscellaneous items rattling around in the main Inventory folders.

3. Don't carry stuff you aren't likely to use in the near future. Trash everything you probably won't use, and store seldom-used items inside storage prims. Store the storage prims outside your Inventory, except for the single prim containing nonreplicable items.

4. Make a backup copy of your Inventory. Put it in a storage prim outside your Inventory, or copy folders and items into an alternate character's inventory.

5. Make a point of emptying the trash can at the conclusion of every *SL* session. The items in the trash can take up as much space as they did in their original folders. There always should be some trash to delete at the conclusion of a session; if there isn't, you're either an Inventory-management genius, or rather hopeless.

Accumulating enough of your own stuff to fill a large museum is easier than you may think. A large part of *SL* activity revolves around creating new in-world objects—not surprising, considering that the *SL* world as such has been mostly built by *SL* denizens. Accordingly, the next chapter discusses building new things.

CHAPTER 7

BUILDING

Unlike in other virtual environments, nearly
everything you see within *Second Life* is
actually created within *Second Life* itself—not
by the company that runs the world, but by its
users. You don't need a lot of special software
or training to build things in *SL*; you only need
a *Second Life* account. Building is fun and easy,
like playing with Lego bricks. In this chapter,
we'll discuss how these simple building blocks
can be used to construct everything from
houses to vehicles.

CONTENTS

THE BASICS

The following sections will introduce you to the basic terminology behind building in *Second Life*.

PRIMS

In *Second Life*'s 3D graphics, a primitive, or "prim," is a basic three-dimensional geometric object. The terms "prim" refers to a single unit of the "matter" that makes up all *Second Life* objects. Prims are the irreducible building blocks of *Second Life*—the unsplittable atoms that make up the things of the world.

In *Second Life*, a prim is one of several 3D shapes: a box, a cylinder, a prism, a sphere, a torus, a tube, or a ring. In addition to these, there are two specialty object types that are not made up of primitives: grass and trees. These last two are obviously not basic shapes, but they're built into *Second Life*, and therefore are treated like ordinary prims.

OBJECTS

Objects are linked groups of individual prims. Objects can contain anywhere from 1 to 255 prims. Yes, this means a single prim is an object in its own right.

PARAMETRIC MODELING

Unlike most 3D software, *SL*'s building tools use parametric models. Parametric modeling reduces the amount of data traveling between your computer and the *Second Life* server because it describes objects using a few simple parameters rather than explicitly describing every part of every object like other modeling techniques do.

Prims in *SL* exist as a two-dimensional shape extruded along a path. What does this mean? Consider a square; it's a two-dimensional shape, existing on a

plane. Imagine if you could stretch this shape upward into the third dimension, forming first a squat box, then a cube, then a taller column. That's what parametric modeling does.

MODELS

In the world of 3D graphics, a model is a 3D representation of an object, whether or not it represents something that exists in the real world. Models are constructed out of many two-dimensional polygons grouped together.

Prims in *Second Life* are models, though they're not very complex. However, their simplicity is what allows them to be so flexible for builders.

The grass and tree prim types are examples of more-complex 3D models. As mentioned earlier, they're not primitives in the classical 3D-graphics sense but are treated like other prims within *Second Life*. Another example is the avatar model, though you can't use it like you can a prim. These more-complex models have been added to fill out the sorts of builds that *Second Life* residents enjoy. Without them, the world would be a far blockier and less organic place.

MESHES

The term "mesh" comes from the pattern of triangles that typically comprise a 3D model. For example, the avatar object in *SL* is a mesh. (So, for that matter, are *SL* primitives, but within *SL* designers refer to prims simply as *prims*.)

REZZING OBJECTS

To create a prim or object is to "rez" it. This term refers to Disney's 1982 film *Tron*, in which the anthropomorphic inhabitants of a computer are forced to play video games until they "de-rez," or die.

GETTING STARTED

If you've used other 3D modeling software in the past, adjusting to *Second Life's* system might take a minute or two. It's a little different. There's no mesh-import functionality. Everything within *Second Life* is made up of primitives, and they can't be deformed as freely as they can in professional 3D software like Maya or LightWave. The trade-off, as mentioned earlier, is that these limits allow object data to be streamed from the server very quickly—there simply isn't a lot of data to send.

If you've never used graphics or modeling software before, that's OK. Most residents pick up *Second Life's* building tools fairly quickly. Don't be discouraged if you don't get the hang of it right off, though. Some new builders need to try several approaches before they find one that works. If you feel you need more guidance after reading this chapter, try attending a building class.

REZZING YOUR FIRST PRIM

First, right-click on the ground or on another object (but not the sky or an avatar!).

Right-clicking will display a pie menu, from which you can select Create (Figure 7.1). This will open the Build tools window

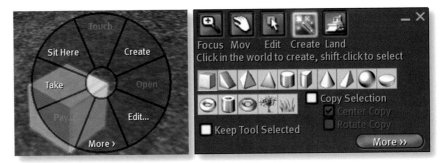

Figure 7.1: The pie menu when you're clicking on an object

Figure 7.2: The Build window's Create tab

(you can also open it simply by pressing the B key), which you'll use to create and edit objects. It'll also put you into Create mode. Now all you have to do is choose which prim you want to create, click the position at which you'd like to create it, and voilà—you now have a prim (Figure 7.2).

EDITING YOUR PRIM

You can edit a prim right after creating it. Upon its creation, you'll automatically switch into Edit mode. If you deselect your prim after creating it, just click it again while in Edit mode, and you'll be editing it again. If your Build window has closed altogether, right-click/Control-click your object and select Edit; you'll be back editing it once more.

OBJECT HANDLES

The most basic and flexible way to manipulate your prims and objects is through the use of their object handles. These are just what they sound like: things you can grab to manipulate your objects. When editing your object, you'll notice several red, green, and blue cones and triangles attached to it. These are your object handles, color-coded according to the following axes and real-world directions:

- **X:** east/west (red)

- **Y:** north/south (green)

- **Z:** up/down (blue)

When you hover your cursor over an object handle, the object handle will brighten. This tells you that you can select it. You can click and drag it around. Depending on which object handle it is, it will do different things.

MOVE HANDLES

In normal Edit mode, you'll see the Move handles. The three intersecting lines allow you to drag the object along a given axis. This axis can be relative to the rest of the world or to the object itself. The triangular planes allow you to move an object on two axes at once, treating the object as if its axes were three two-dimensional planes.

INTRO
CHAPTER 1
CHAPTER 2
CHAPTER 3
CHAPTER 4
CHAPTER 5
CHAPTER 6
CHAPTER 7
CHAPTER 8
CHAPTER 9
CHAPTER 10
CHAPTER 11
CHAPTER 12
CHAPTER 13
APPENDICES

137

ROTATE HANDLES

Holding down the Control key allows you to enter Rotate mode, which replaces the object handles with a sphere inside three circles. Clicking and dragging the sphere allows you to manipulate the object's rotation in all three dimensions at once, while clicking and dragging one of the circles rotates the object on that axis alone.

STRETCH HANDLES

Holding down Control and Shift puts you into Stretch mode. This places a white object handle on the eight corners of your object, as well as a colored one on each of the six sides. (Remember—even if your object isn't a cube, the editing tools still treat it like a box.) By clicking and dragging the side handles, you'll stretch the entire object along the associated axis, making it wider or narrower, taller or shorter. By clicking and dragging the corner handles, you'll stretch the entire object proportionately.

If the Stretch Both Sides check box in the Build window's Edit mode is checked, your object will remain in one location; dragging a handle will just scale the object as if it were pulled from both the handle you're clicking on and the one on the opposite side or corner.

In the case of linked objects, you won't be able to stretch the object along one axis, but you will be able to scale it and to stretch individual prims in the object.

BUILD WINDOW

Now that you're editing your prim, you'll want to extend the Build window by clicking the More button to access the other editing options. These are the heart of the building tools.

GENERAL TAB

The General tab (Figure 7.3) contains the following options:

Name: It's a good idea to name your unique objects according to what they are. That way, you can easily identify them in your inventory. "Front Door" and "Roof" are acceptable names, but you can be more descriptive: "My Brick House - Red

Door" will let you know both what the object is and what project you used it in. Either way, an inventory full of things named "Object" is not fun to search through!

Description: You can store extra information about your objects in this field. You can't search your inventory for objects' descriptions, but the Description field lets you know more-specific information about an object.

Creator: This is the account that created the prim. No matter how much you modify the prim, it will still have the original creator's name in this field. In a linked object, only the root prim's creator will show up as the creator.

Owner: Who currently owns this object? Remember, an object's current owner is frequently different than its creator.

Group: This doesn't have to do with linked objects, but rather with the resident group to which an object is set. By default, the group is the one the object's owner belonged to when the object was rezzed. To change the group, click the Set button and pick one of your groups. This is a useful way to filter objects on your land. If only members of a certain group can keep prims there, you won't need to worry about other people leaving their prims on your land.

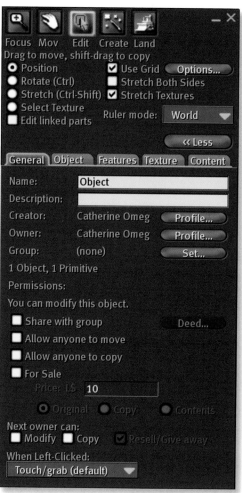

Figure 7.3. The Build window's General tab

OBJECT TAB

The left side of the Object tab is always the same. The right half of the tab changes, depending on the type of prim being edited. Different primitives use different parameters.

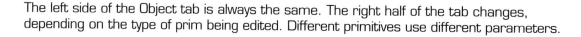

INTRO
CHAPTER 1
CHAPTER 2
CHAPTER 3
CHAPTER 4
CHAPTER 5
CHAPTER 6
CHAPTER 7
CHAPTER 8
CHAPTER 9
CHAPTER 10
CHAPTER 11
CHAPTER 12
CHAPTER 13
APPENDICES

Locked: You can lock your objects in place within the region, stopping anyone who has modify permissions from repositioning or editing them. The Select Only Movable Objects option under the Tools menu allows you to select a group of prims without selecting locked objects. This can be useful for ensuring you don't link the wrong prims together.

Physical: This toggles how your object will interact with *Second Life*'s physics engine. Making an object physical will allow it to be kicked (like a ball), dropped off buildings, and so on. Physical objects have their uses, but you won't need to use them much (which is good, since they add to lag). They can be fun to play with, though!

Temporary: Setting this and then re-rezzing the object will cause that object to disappear after about 60 seconds. This isn't very useful for building, but it's a good feature for scripters.

Phantom: This setting allows you to designate whether physical objects or avatars will penetrate the prim. A phantom object can be walked through or driven through or have a ball tossed through it. When you link phantom prims together, the resulting linked object will take on the property of the root prim. If the root prim is phantom, the whole object will be phantom as well.

Position: Objects within a region can be positioned anywhere from 0 to 255m on the X and Y axes, and up to 512m on the Z axis.

Size: Prims in *Second Life* can be as large as 10m and small as 0.01m (1cm) on any axis. Though many builders find it restrictive, the 10m limit ensures prims can't stick through into other regions.

Rotation: Objects can be rotated between 0 and 360 degrees on any of their three axes. Prims can be rotated along multiple axes and will retain their rotation when re-rezzed from your inventory

Material: The Material setting allows you to swap between the preset collision particles and sounds you hear when your avatar hits an object. You can choose between several settings—Stone, Metal, Glass, Wood, Flesh, Plastic, and Rubber—each with its own collision properties.

FEATURES TAB

The Features tab (Figure 7.4) combines the control for two special editing features: Flexible Path and Lighting. These allow you to achieve some of the most realistic and stunning effects in *Second Life*.

FLEXIBLE PATH

Flexible prims, popularly known as flexiprims, are a purely client-side effect. This means that they don't appear to be flexible from the server's perspective, because they don't interact with anything on the server. Of course, everyone viewing flexiprims will see them as flexible, though not necessarily flexing in the exact same position (Figure 7.5).

Figure 7.5: Flexible prims

Figure 7.4: The Features tab

Because they describe a kind of behavior rather than just a shape or a color, the effects of the flexible path settings are not easily documented. Rather, they require a bit of experimentation to get the hang of them. Don't be frustrated if it doesn't make a lot of sense at first.

INTRO

PART I

PART II

PART III

APPENDICES

EDITING YOUR PRIM

SIDEBAR

RESIDENTS SPEAK:
USING FLEXIPRIMS

"Flexiprims have allowed me to take digital clothing to a whole other level from both a creative standpoint and an experiential standpoint for my customers. They allow hems to float and with their various physical settings, I can simulate both heavier materials and more diaphanous materials like chiffon and silk.

I have used flexiprims for everything from ribbons on cuffs or dress bows to the ruffles on a blouse; they're staples in every skirt and dress I make. I've even made flexi cowls and draped fabric on outfits. I use them wherever the RL counterpart components to an outfit would have loose, hanging, draped, or skirted material."

—*Ginny Talamasca*

LIGHTING

Second Life supports emissive OpenGL lighting. What does this mean? Simple: you can set a prim as a light source and illuminate other objects around it.

You can have up to eight light sources per scene, and your *Second Life* viewer will draw only the ones closest to your avatar. Use light sources sparingly, as lights will flicker when they come into and out of view. Lighting effects can be controlled with the following options:

Color: The color of the light emitted by your prim.

Intensity: Your light's brightness, anywhere from 0.0 to 1.0.

Radius: The radius of your light source's effects.

Falloff: How sharply the edge of your light source stops.

TEXTURE TAB

The Texture tab allows you to set the color, texture, and shininess of an object. We'll discuss advanced texturing techniques later in this chapter.

CONTENT TAB

In the previous chapter, you learned about your avatar's inventory. Like avatars, objects have inventories where you can place any inventory items. Putting things in an object's inventory is most useful when you're dealing with scripts, but we'll talk about that more in Chapter 8.

DUPLICATING PRIMS

You can duplicate an object by editing it and using the key command Control-D. If you don't have copy permissions for the object, you won't be able to duplicate it.

DELETING PRIMS

You can delete multiple prims by selecting them all and pressing Delete on your keyboard, but there's no way to undo a deletion. Deleted prims are erased permanently from the server, so be careful when deleting more than one prim at a time.

CHAPTER 7
USING THE CAMERA

Second Life's camera is far more flexible than the cameras you'll find in most 3D software or games. With just a few keys and your mouse, you can reposition it anywhere, zooming in on details or rotating around the scene from a hundred meters away.

The easiest way to use the camera is with the following keyboard commands and the mouse.

- **Zoom:** Alt + left-click

- **Orbit:** Control-Alt + left-click

- **Pan:** Control-Shift-Alt + left-click

When in Focus mode (accessible from the Tools menu), the camera acts as though the Alt key is already being held down. You can click on objects to zoom, Control-click to orbit, and Control-Shift-click to pan (Figure 7.6).

Figure 7.6: The Build window's Focus mode

RESIDENTS SPEAK:
LEARNING THE CAMERA

"It's absolutely necessary to learn and understand how to use the camera if you want to build. Once you teach someone how to use the camera to help in their building, you can see that one of the problems limiting them most has just gone away. Their frustration diminishes and their imagination runs wild.

Most seem to be able to handle the camera once they're taught how to handle it, but many skip that lesson on Orientation Island."

—Mera Pixel

CHAPTER 7

LINKING PRIMS

You can link together multiple prims into a single object. This allows you to move and manipulate the combined object easily.

To link a group of prims, simply select all the prims you want to link by clicking on them individually while holding down your keyboard's Shift key, or click on the ground or sky while in Edit mode and drag a box out to encompass all the prims you wish to link (Figure 7.7).

LINKING PRIMS

You may have trouble selecting or linking your prims for a few reasons:

- You may be selecting other people's prims as well. Try checking Select Only My Objects on the Tools menu, or pan your camera around to get a better angle.

- You may be missing some of your prims if you're selecting them individually with Shift-select rather than selecting them by dragging a selection box around them.

- If you have several prims selected already, you may be forgetting to hold down Shift when you click on the next one.

- You're trying to link prims that are too far apart. Prims cannot be linked together if they're beyond a certain distance (which scales according to the sizes of the prims involved). This means you can link two large prims over a greater distance than two very small ones—the maximum distance is proportionate to the prims' size.

When you've selected all the prims you wish to link, link them by selecting Link from the Tools menu or using the keyboard command Control-L (Figure 7.8).

See how the highlight changed on your collection of prims? This means that it's now a linked object. The last prim you selected is now highlighted in yellow, indicating that it's become the parent (or root) prim. The prims highlighted in white are called the child prims. They're all now part of the same object. By deselecting

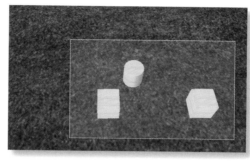

Figure 7.7: Multiple prims selected in a selection box

Select Tool	⟩
Select Only My Objects	
Select Only Movable Objects	
X Select By Surrounding	
X Show Hidden Selection	
Show Light Radius for Selection	
Show Selection Beam	
X Snap to Grid	G
Snap Object XY to Grid	Shift-X
Use Selection for Grid	Shift-G
Grid Options...	Ctrl-Shift-B
Link	Ctrl-L
Unlink	Ctrl-Shift-L
Stop All Animations	
Focus on Selection	H
Zoom to Selection	Shift-H
Take	
Take Copy	
Save Object Back to My Inventory	
Save Object Back to Object Contents	
Show Script Warning/Error Window	
Recompile Scripts in Selection	
Reset Scripts in Selection	
Set Scripts to Running in Selection	
Set Scripts to Not Running in Selection	

Figure 7.8: The Menu bar with the Tools menu open and Link selected

the object and then reselecting it, you can see that all the prims are still highlighted in yellow and white. You can move the entire object around just as if it were a single prim (Figure 7.9).

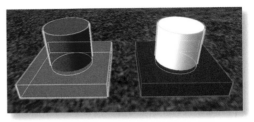

Figure 7.9: Comparison of the selection halo on linked and unlinked prims

UNLINKING LINKED OBJECTS

To unlink a linked object, select it then choose Tools > Unlink, or use Control-Shift-L.

> **NOTE**
>
> **ADDITIONAL INFO:**
> ## UNLINKING PHYSICAL OBJECTS
>
> *Be forewarned! If you attempt to unlink a physical object, its component prims will stay physical when you unlink them. If this happens, the prims may explode in all directions when you deselect them. Make sure you uncheck the Physical check box in the Object tab of the Build window before unlinking.*

To easily remove a single prim from a linked object, do the following:

1. Select the object.

2. Unlink it as described earlier, but keep the group of unlinked prims selected.

3. Holding down the Shift key, click the prim you wish to remove from the group; this will deselect it.

4. Relink the selected prims. They will link back together in the same link order as before, minus the prim you just removed from the original linked object. You're now free to move the newly relinked object and the extra prim independently. You can also unlink multiple prims at the same time by clicking more than one prim in step 3.

WORKING WITH LINKED OBJECTS

Positioning and rotating any object works the same, no matter how many prims it contains. However, scaling linked objects is a little different than scaling an ordinary prim. Edit the object and drag its object handles to make it bigger and smaller. You'll be able to scale the entire object proportionately, but you won't be able to stretch it along the X, Y, or Z axis.

NOTE

ADDITIONAL INFO:
SHRINKING A PRIM IN A LINKED OBJECT

You won't be able to shrink a prim in a linked object beyond the minimum dimension allowed on any axis (1cm). This means that a more-complex object may not shrink as small as you'd prefer. Try unlinking that single prim and repositioning and scaling it individually.

Unfortunately, there's no way to scale a linked object without the mouse. You can't just type in the new scale like you can with an individual prim.

When the Stretch Both Sides check box is checked, you can scale the object in place, and it will grow or contract in all three dimensions. Despite what the name implies, you still won't be able to stretch it along the X, Y, or Z axis, though. You can only make linked objects bigger or smaller (Figure 7.10).

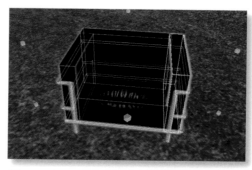

Figure 7.10: Scaling a linked object

ADDING PRIMS TO A LINKED OBJECT

Prims and linked objects can be linked to an existing object just as a group of individual prims can be linked together. Simply select the prims or linked objects and click Tools > Link from your menu bar, or use the key command Control-L.

Remember that the last prim selected will become the root in the new linked object. If the last object you selected was a linked object, its root prim will become the root for the new linked object.

INTRO
CHAPTER 1
CHAPTER 2
CHAPTER 3
CHAPTER 4
CHAPTER 5
CHAPTER 6
CHAPTER 7
CHAPTER 8
CHAPTER 9
CHAPTER 10
CHAPTER 11
CHAPTER 12
CHAPTER 13
APPENDICES

WORKING WITH INDIVIDUAL PRIMS IN A LINKED OBJECT

Sometimes you'll want to manipulate individual prims within a linked object. To do so, check the Edit Linked Parts check box in the Build window's Edit mode. This will let you edit each prim in a linked object as if it were a separate prim without having to unlink them first (Figure 7.11).

Remember that each prim in your linked object is still a separate prim. It has its own parameters and properties, as well as its own inventory. When editing individual prims in a linked object, remember that your prims are still constrained by the limits of linked objects. You won't be able to scale or reposition a prim beyond the limits at which you would be able to link it normally (Figure 7.12).

Figure 7.11: The Edit Linked Parts check box

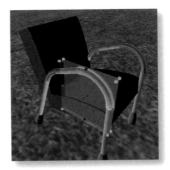

Figure 7.12: Scaling a single prim within a linked object

USING THE GRID

The Lindens use the term "grid" to describe all of *Second Life* (or alternately, the Main and Teen grids) because of the grid pattern that the different regions make up on the map. In building terms, the grid is an alignment tool to allow you to more easily position prims within a region. Each region within *Second Life* is a 256m x 256m square. (Obviously, there's a third dimension of hundreds of meters of space above this as well, but *SL* follows a two-dimensional map layout.)

Sometimes you'll find that Snap-to-Grid doesn't work as well as you get farther away from the region's origin point, <0,0,0>. When using Snap-to-Grid high up in the

air or toward the northeastern corner of the region, you'll still see prims lining up, but they won't be aligned precisely anymore. When we're dealing with decimals, (as we are when building) the larger the number, the less precise it is. The reason for this lies in how *Second Life* stores positioning data for prims.

This isn't a big deal in practical terms, but some builders are frustrated by it. If you're really obsessive-compulsive about your grid positioning, try to limit your precision building to locations near the region's origin point, its southwest corner.

SNAPPING TO THE GRID

The Use Grid feature allows you to easily align your objects to points on the grid. This is handy because it allows builders to create and duplicate objects quickly without having to line up prims—they snap into place automatically.

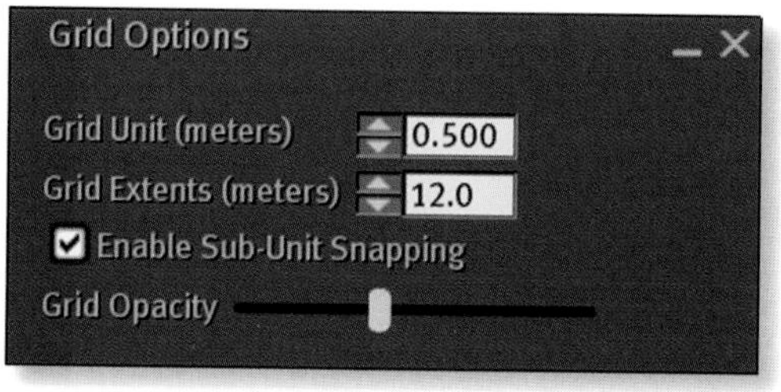

Figure 7.13: The Grid Options window

To activate the grid, select the Use Grid check box in the Build window's Edit mode (it should be checked by default). By clicking the Options button next to it, you can open the Grid Options menu (Figure 7.13), in which you can change various properties of the grid:

Grid Unit (meters). Setting the grid unit allows you to snap objects to a smaller grid. When building large structures like houses, many builders opt for a grid line every 0.25 or 0.125 meter. This allows you to drag very large prims into place easily while having the flexibility to line up 0.25m prims precisely. Because measurements in *Second Life* use the metric system, some builders opt for a 0.1m grid. It's up to you to decide what you like best.

Grid Extents (meters). This is how far from the center of the object the grid appears. Changing it from its default setting of 12 meters is rarely necessary.

Enable Sub-Unit Snapping. Check this box to snap to smaller grid divisions when the camera is zoomed in. This feature depends heavily on the camera, and an object's position within the region, and may not divide accurately. For best results, use Sub-Unit Snapping only when you're editing objects close to the region's origin.

Grid Opacity. This slider allows you to set the transparency of the grid displayed when moving, rotating, or scaling a prim or object. Remember—you'll be able to

INTRO
CHAPTER 1
CHAPTER 2
CHAPTER 3
CHAPTER 4
CHAPTER 5
CHAPTER 6
CHAPTER 7
CHAPTER 8
CHAPTER 9
CHAPTER 10
CHAPTER 11
CHAPTER 12
CHAPTER 13
APPENDICES

see the grid only while you're manipulating an object using its object handles. Most builders prefer a low to medium opacity.

For detail work (especially small objects such as attachments), Use Grid becomes ungainly. When it becomes a hindrance, turn it off.

COLLABORATING WITH OTHER RESIDENTS

One of the best features of *Second Life* is the way it allows you to collaborate with other residents. Together, you can work on bigger and more complex projects, build on each other's strengths, and make things that you might not be able to on your own. However, collaborating with other residents can be difficult, and not just when it comes to playing well with others.

There are four options for collaborative building. This section discusses the advantages and disadvantages of each.

MODIFY RIGHTS

The best way to build collaboratively is to grant another resident modify rights to your objects. Essentially, you're allowing them to edit all your objects. To grant someone modify rights, they must first be on your Friends list. It's not enough to simply have their calling card; they must appear in the Friends window. Open it by selecting Friends on the toolbar (if you have it turned off, turn it on under View > Toolbar) or by the keyboard command Control-Shift-F.

To grant someone else permission to edit your objects, select their name in your Friends list, and select Grant Modify Rights. You'll see a dialog box asking you to confirm this, and after clicking Yes, you'll see the words "granted rights" next to the person's name in your Friends list.

Once you grant someone modify rights, they'll be able to edit anything you own, anywhere in the world. If you don't trust them with everything of yours, consider collaborating with them using an alternate account.

To *revoke* a resident's modify rights, select the person's name in your Friends

list and click Revoke Modify Rights. When removing someone from your Friends list altogether, their modify rights will be revoked automatically.

When granting modify rights, the other person will see the chat message "You have been granted the privilege to modify [your avatar name]'s objects."

After the initial message, though, the only way to see if someone has granted *you* modify rights is to attempt to edit their objects.

GROUP LAND

When building with other people, it can be a good idea to form a group and deed land to that group. By then setting all your objects to the same group, any group member can edit those objects; you can return nongroup objects, or even prohibit other people's objects from existing on your group's land. Setting land to group ownership also allows you to own 10% more on the same land tier.

Group land will let you collaborate with other users on larger builds, but to actually link your objects together you'll need to transfer ownership to one person and have that person link the objects. To do that, you have to play with asset permissions, which we'll explore next.

ASSET PERMISSIONS

Asset permissions are set in the General tab of the Build window. They define how future owners of the object (or copies of that object) may use it. Permissions are relatively straightforward to use. When collaborating with other builders, make sure that permissions are granted on all prims, textures, and inventory items, or your fellow designers won't be able to link them together.

GROUP DEEDING

Deeding an object transfers ownership of that object to a group—which means it may not work properly if it's a scripted object. Many scripts rely upon the object being owned by a single owner. These scripts will fail to varying degrees if they're deeded to a group. It's also an imperfect process. You're generally better off not deeding objects

INTRO
CHAPTER 1
CHAPTER 2
CHAPTER 3
CHAPTER 4
CHAPTER 5
CHAPTER 6
CHAPTER 7
CHAPTER 8
CHAPTER 9
CHAPTER 10
CHAPTER 11
CHAPTER 12
CHAPTER 13
APPENDICES

to a group itself, but instead granting modify permissions to each group member. This keeps the transfer-of-ownership rate to a minimum and allows you to more easily control your prims' permissions.

ATTACHMENTS

Attachments are what they sound like: objects that can be attached to your avatar. These range from handheld tools, props, or weapons to jewelry and even hair and shoes.

Unlike normal prims, attachments are always phantom, no matter what you do. This means that they'll intersect your avatar, each other, and other objects that are unattached to you. This can pose some problems when making attachments that are likely to intersect, so you'll often need to work around the limits. You'll see more avatars with shorter prim-based hairstyles than with long hair for just this reason—long prim hair frequently intersects the back and tends to look weird.

MAKING ATTACHMENTS

For the most part, you'll be working with very small prims, at least compared to those you'd use to build a house or a castle. Because *Second Life* prevents you from making a prim less than 1cm in any dimension, you'll often need to use the Cut and Dimple tools. Cut allows you to slice a section out of your prim, like cutting a slice of pie. Dimple is limited to the sphere primitive and allows you to create a dimple in the top of the sphere.

Holding the avatar still is very important when working with attachments. Ordinarily, your avatar is moving at least a little, and even small movements can make it difficult to position your attachments correctly.

A good tool for immobilizing your avatar is Rickard Roentgen's R-Type Pedestal, available at Rickard's store in the Midnight City region. It allows you to hold your avatar's arms and legs in a stationary position so that you can construct and edit attachments without having to worry about your avatar's pose shifting.

When working with small objects like earrings or body jewelry, you may find that they become "buried" within your avatar. You can get around this in a couple ways.

The best way is to link your attachment's prims together, then add a larger prim (not overly large; a 0.125m cube should suffice) to the existing object as a child prim. By ensuring the larger prim isn't the root of the resulting linked object, you can use the larger prim as a temporary handle and delete it later without having to worry that you're deleting the prim that determines the object's position. This will allow you to attach the object to your avatar and move it around by the "handle" prim. After it's where you want it, detach the attachment, rez it on the ground, unlink the handle from the rest of the attachment, take the now handleless object into your inventory, and wear it again. It will reattach to its original attachment point, and in the correct position.

Another option is to use Debug mode to temporarily turn off avatar rendering on your computer. You'll be able to zoom in on and edit your attachments without your avatar blocking them.

To do this, ensure that the Client and Server menu options are available to the right of the Help menu at the top of your window. If they're not active, turn Debug mode on with Control-Shift-Alt-D. Next, select Client > Rendering > Types > Character. When you've positioned your attachment well outside your avatar's body, you can turn avatar rendering back on so you can see what you're doing.

SIDEBAR

RESIDENTS SPEAK:
ATTACHMENTS' PRIM COUNTS

"Attachments really can be built without regard to prim count. Oh, sure, you'll get the complainers and the Hoochie Hair Haters, but if the customer wears the item, it does not count against the land's prim count. But I will say that you can really cut prim usage with textures!"

—*Wynx Whiplash*

You may encounter some problems with some attachment points. When attaching an object, it is positioned relative to your avatar's skeleton—yes, your avatar really has a skeleton!—not its skin. This can lead to attachments that appear to be floating through your avatar, rather than embedded within it.

INTRO
CHAPTER 1
CHAPTER 2
CHAPTER 3
CHAPTER 4
CHAPTER 5
CHAPTER 6
CHAPTER 7
CHAPTER 8
CHAPTER 9
CHAPTER 10
CHAPTER 11
CHAPTER 12
CHAPTER 13
APPENDICES

LANDSCAPING

There's more to building in *Second Life* than simply manipulating prims. Many residents enjoy landscaping their plots. You can create plant prims only on land that you own, or on group land if you're an officer, but the results can be impressive.

Besides the usual primitives, *Second Life* allows you to use several predefined tree models as primitives. Beyond the two dozen or so types, your options for creating plant life are somewhat limited, however.

In *Second Life* parlance, trees are plants that are affected by wind, whereas grass is a complex model of individual tufts that adhere to the ground surface beneath them. A grass prim will always stay at ground level, no matter how high you attempt to position it.

Even though they look like grass, the Beach Grass and Eelgrass models are actually classified as "tree" prims and will sway in the breeze. Don't be confused by their names!

The specific type and dimensions of a grass or tree model is chosen randomly when you create a new one. This is to give the impression of randomness but can result in odd-looking forests, should you choose to keep the assortment you create. The variety of trees available ranges from palm trees to snow-covered pines. Fortunately, all the plant models exist in your Inventory's Library folder, under Library > Objects > Trees, Plants and Grasses.

Creating a tree through the Build tools causes it to be rezzed with its base at ground level. It doesn't matter if you create it up in the air; the tree will still appear down on the ground. To avoid this, try rezzing trees that already exist within your inventory—from your Library folder, for instance.

To give the effect of a more natural scene, you'll want to rotate and scale trees if you use a bunch of identical tree types clustered together. Introducing a little variety is key. It helps to give the illusion of nature.

NOTE

ADDITIONAL INFO:
USING SCRIPTED PLANT REZZERS

By using scripted plant rezzers, you can take a few different trees and other plant objects and automatically cover your land with foliage to your tastes.

CHAPTER 7

TEXTURING

Creating untextured primitives is the bulk of what is considered "building" in *Second Life*, but to produce truly stunning content, you'll need to rely on textures. Textures are ordinary image files applied to the sides of objects. They can range from simple patterns used as wallpaper in your virtual house to meticulously hand-drawn clothing. In this section, we'll discuss how to manipulate textures, as well as some ideas for creating your own.

To start, open the Texture tab on your Build window (Figure 7.14).

TEXTURE

Clicking the Texture box opens the Texture Picker window. The Texture Picker is one part texture previewer and one part special Inventory filter. The inventory half of the Texture Picker works just like your normal inventory, but with a filter applied to allow you to see all the textures and screenshots in your inventory, no matter where they are. Just select them from the Texture Picker's Inventory pane; they'll appear in the texture-preview pane of the Texture Picker.

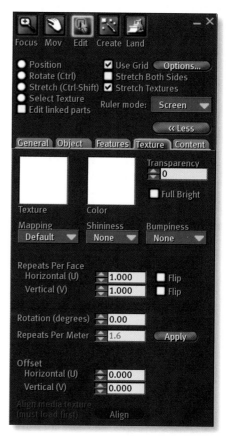

Figure 7.14: The Texture tab

INTRO
CHAPTER 1
CHAPTER 2
CHAPTER 3
CHAPTER 4
CHAPTER 5
CHAPTER 6
CHAPTER 7
CHAPTER 8
CHAPTER 9
CHAPTER 10
CHAPTER 11
CHAPTER 12
CHAPTER 13
APPENDICES

If the 160x160-pixel texture previewer is too small, double-click on any texture within the Texture Picker's Inventory panel and open the texture as you would in your normal inventory.

Once you've selected the texture you want, click Select, or if you have the Apply Immediately box checked, just close the window.

Figure 7.15: The Texture Picker window in Eyedropper mode

Another selection tool is the Eyedropper. When you click on the Eyedropper icon, the mouse pointer changes to allow you to click on any texture face on any object you have edit permissions for; you can then copy the texture to the Texture Picker. This allows you to apply the texture you just grabbed to your selected faces (Figure 7.15).

ADDITIONAL INFO:
AN ALTERNATIVE

If you don't want to use the Texture Picker, you can always drag a texture directly from an open Inventory window onto the Texture box of the Texture tab.

COLOR

Clicking the Color box opens the Color Picker. It allows you to select the color you wish to apply to your selected faces.

You'll notice two multicolored areas: the narrow Tint/Shade Picker on the right, and the large square Hue/Saturation/Luminosity Picker to its left. By clicking and dragging your cursor to different positions on these areas, you can quickly select a color. Another option is to manually enter red/green/blue (RGB) values that you've selected from graphics software such as Adobe Photoshop. When working with textures, you may already have some color scheme in mind.

If you're having trouble choosing a color or getting the balance just right, try clicking one of the two dozen or so preset boxes at the bottom of the Color Picker

window. Doing so will automatically load the selected color and give you a good starting point. You can also simply click Select to close the Color Picker, and use the preset as your new color.

If you'd like to save a color you've picked, click and drag the Current Color box to the preset squares in the lower section of the window. The four boxes at the bottom right of the Color Picker are blank, but you can replace any of the preset colors with your own custom ones.

NOTE

ADDITIONAL INFO:
THINK TWICE

Once you change your presets, you won't be able to get them back without uninstalling and reinstalling SL, so before you replace your presets with custom ones, be sure you never want the original preset colors again!

Like the Texture Picker, the Color Picker (Figure 7.16) allows you to use the Eyedropper tool. The only difference between the Eyedropper tool in the two Pickers is that you don't need edit permissions to grab a color from another resident's objects. This can be particularly handy when collaborating with other residents.

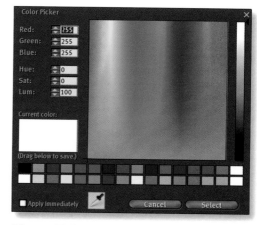

Figure 7.16: The Color Picker window

TRANSPARENCY

By setting the transparency of a prim, you can easily produce translucent windows and effects for all kinds of objects, from waterfalls to light bulbs to crystals to bottles. You can't set an object to more than 90% transparency using the Build tools—that would make it too difficult to find. However, you *can* set it completely invisible by using scripts, which are discussed in Chapter 8.

INTRO
CHAPTER 1
CHAPTER 2
CHAPTER 3
CHAPTER 4
CHAPTER 5
CHAPTER 6
CHAPTER 7
CHAPTER 8
CHAPTER 9
CHAPTER 10
CHAPTER 11
CHAPTER 12
CHAPTER 13
APPENDICES

CHAPTER 7

INTRO

PART I

PART II

PART III

APPENDICES

TEXTURING

FULL BRIGHT

This setting allows you to declare a face immune to the effects of lighting and shadows. It will appear completely unshaded from all angles and will stand out brightly at night. Because of this, Full Bright can be a handy feature to use when making things like signs or boxes in a store. Remember that you can have a Full Bright prim emit light by choosing Light on the Features tab. This lets you create things such as light bulbs or neon signs—light-emitting objects that are completely illuminated, as they would be in the real world (Figure 7.17).

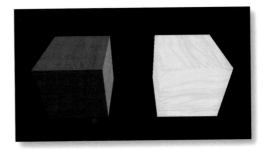

Figure 7.17: A Full Bright cube next to a normal cube

TEXTURING SPECIFICS

When making more than the most basic objects, you'll almost certainly want different textures for different faces. This is most easily done by using the Select Texture option on the top of the Edit tab of the Build menu.

Dragging a texture out of your inventory and onto a prim's face will apply the texture to only that face. To apply it to all faces on the destination prim, hold down the Shift key when you release the texture. For safety reasons, there's no way to apply a texture to all prims in an object this way; Undo doesn't work when dragging and dropping textures!

CLOTHING

Clothing in *Second Life* is created in the same way as a normal object is textured: by wrapping a two-dimensional image around a three-dimensional shape. Unlike with normal textures, however, you can't just upload any old texture and hope it fits. Specific parts of a clothing or skin texture correspond to locations on your avatar. The creation process is called UV mapping, and the textures used are UV maps.

As mentioned previously, 3D modeling uses the X, Y, and Z coordinates to determine the position of an object; UV maps are so named because they add two

further dimensions: U and V. U corresponds to the right/left on the image that is wrapped around the model, and V corresponds to the image's up/down.

Linden Lab has created a set of templates you can use to make your own textures, but most designers use far more detailed and accurate templates created by Chip Midnight or Robin Wood. All three sets of templates are included on the CD in this book, along with an in-depth guide to using use them.

The most popular software for texture creation is Adobe Photoshop, though many people also use JASC/Corel's Paint Shop Pro, Corel Photo-Paint, or the free image-editing software GIMP. Advanced users may even use 3D-rendering software such as LightWave or Maya to assist in creating clothing.

SIDEBAR

RESIDENTS SPEAK:
PICKING THE RIGHT TOOLS FOR THE JOB

"For making textures, I use Photoshop CS2 and Eye Candy. Photoshop is my life. I have used it since version 2 and I probably only know how to use half of it, but I use it for everything. Especially because I like fur and scales as opposed to the flat look of an untextured prim. I will add that I am an avid user of Abobe Illustrator and use that for quite a bit of detail work too."

—*Wynx Whiplash*

"I employ a 'mutt' software system of Photoshop CS2 and LightWave. I use that for both mesh and prim work. I use objects and applied UV-maps in LightWave to work with primitives. But my system is imperfect. I do a lot of blending in Photoshop to reduce the seaming between mesh and prims."

—*Ginny Talamasca*

"I do all my textures in Corel Photo-Paint—I think it's a superior tool to Photoshop, especially when handling layers and alpha transparencies, at a fraction of the price. I think it's also a much more intuitive tool to learn, especially for novice users."

—*Francis Chung*

RESIDENTS SPEAK:
BAKING LIGHT EFFECTS INTO YOUR TEXTURES

"Producing realistic shadows and lighting effects in real time is not possible for today's hardware. The process called ray tracing, which produces realistic shadows, is just too slow and would make Second Life *impossible to enjoy. To compensate, I "bake" shadows and lighting right into the textures for all my builds. I do this by painting the shadows and light, or using third-party rendering tools like Maya to create a dramatic scene. If I have a stool in one of my sets, I simply draw the shadow of the stool under it and the visual effect can be stunning."*

—*Aimee Weber*

CHAPTER 7

UPLOADING TEXTURES

To get your textures into *Second Life*, you'll need to upload them from your server to the *Second Life* servers. *Second Life* accepts textures in the Targa (.TGA), Windows Bitmap (.BMP), and JPEG (.JPG/.JPEG) file formats. If the texture you wish to upload is in another format, you'll need to convert it first.

Textures are sized according to a "powers of two" rule. For ideal results, your textures should be 32, 64, 128, 256, 512, or 1024 pixels wide or tall. Your textures don't need to be square, but most are because a square is the best shape for most applications. This means you could have a 512x256-pixel texture, for example. Don't worry about fitting the pixels on a prim, though! You can scale a texture to fit any prim, or even show a small fraction of the entire texture.

Because of the "powers of two" rule, a 640x480 image will automatically be resized to 512x512 when uploading. Textures will be rounded up or down to the nearest power of two and may look distorted when viewed in the Texture Upload window or placed on a prim that doesn't maintain the original texture's proportions.

The term used to describe an image's proportions is *aspect ratio*. It is a comparison of an image's width and height. For instance, normal televisions and computer monitors use a 4:3 aspect ratio. This means that the width of the picture is 1.333 times the height.

When uploading a photo texture to share with your friends as a billboard, stretch a prim to be 4m across and 3m high, then stick the texture on the side. No matter the resolution of the uploaded image, *Second Life* will rescale the texture to appear at its original resolution.

TEXTURE UPLOAD WINDOW

To upload a texture, select File > Upload Image. This will open an OS-native File Picker that will look like any other Open File window on your computer. You will have to pay L$10 to upload a texture. (This restriction is intended to discourage residents from filling up the *Second Life* servers with extraneous textures.) The window contains the following options:

Name: This is the name of the texture as it will appear in your inventory.

Description: The Description field is handy for including additional information about the texture, but the texture itself must be viewed to see the description.

Preview Image As: The Preview Image drop-down allows you to change the preview mode, selecting between Image, Hair, Female Head, Female Upper Body, Female Lower Body, Male Head, Male Upper Body, Male Lower Body, and Skirt. Depending on which option you choose, you will see a flat image (in the case of the Image option) or a three-dimensional body part with your texture wrapped around it.

Although *Second Life* uses the same avatar model regardless of which gender you choose, skin and clothing textures will stretch differently based on how the avatar itself is stretched. If you're designing a piece of clothing to be worn by a specific gender, you'll want to make sure it looks good on that gender.

Once you're sure the image looks how you want it to, press the Upload button. It may take a minute or so to upload your texture, depending on how busy *Second Life* is at the time.

If your texture doesn't look exactly how you pictured it when you actually view it in the *Second Life* world, don't be discouraged. Most designers have to upload several versions before they're totally satisfied.

INTRO

CHAPTER 1

CHAPTER 2

CHAPTER 3

CHAPTER 4

CHAPTER 5

CHAPTER 6

CHAPTER 7

CHAPTER 8

CHAPTER 9

CHAPTER 10

CHAPTER 11

CHAPTER 12

CHAPTER 13

APPENDICES

CHAPTER 8

USING THE LINDEN SCRIPTING LANGUAGE

It is time to look under the hood and dive headfirst into the world of the Linden Scripting Language (LSL). It lets you add behaviors and interactivity to objects inside *Second Life*. Scripting is just another word for programming, so in learning about LSL you will end up learning about programming as well. Do not be afraid, though—between this chapter and the many resources available both online and in-world, you'll be up and scripting in no time. You do not need to write scripts to have fun in *Second Life*, but scripting drives the magic, from vehicles and guns to vendors and HTTP requests.

This chapter walks you through creating your first script and covers the LSL syntax and more-advanced language features. It also teaches you how LSL scripts can sense and communicate with the rest of *SL*, and how LSL can apply physical forces and move scripted objects onto your screen as heads-up display (HUD) attachments. Finally, it covers the many resources available for when you want to learn more.

CONTENTS

THE ORIGINS OF LSL

So, where did LSL come from? When *Second Life* was still called *LindenWorld* and had small space ships and eyeballs flying around instead of avatars, it did not have a scripting language. Instead, anything created in-world was built via static creations and physics. Thanks to rigid body dynamics, objects in *Second Life* act more or less like real-world objects, colliding with each other, falling under the effect of gravity, etc. This enabled a wide variety of creations, but many types were missing.

Take airplanes, for example. In a few more years (thanks to Moore's Law) we will be able to simulate a wing in real time, solving the many complex equations needed to properly model the interactions of the wing, turbulence, fluid flow, Bernoulli's Principle, etc. However, computers are not yet powerful enough to do that. So full simulation is not the answer. Instead, LSL allows residents to create content that can't be simulated currently within *SL*'s physics system.

Technically, the scripting language that you will be playing with is LSL2, as the language added to *LindenWorld* in August of 2002 was LSL. However, since only a few early alpha users ever had to build using the original LSL, the current language is simply referred to as LSL. The current language is far more powerful and easier to use than the original, so be glad that you never had to play with the first one!

YOUR FIRST SCRIPT

OK, so you are ready to take the first step. Great! Fire up *Second Life* and go somewhere you can build, such as a sandbox or land you own. Create a box on the ground and select it. Select the Content tab of the Build window and click on the New Script button. The Script Editing window will pop open with the default "Hello, Avatar!" script (Figure 8.1). We'll break down the script in a moment, but for now click the Save button on the lower right of the window. Two lines will appear in the bottom of the window—first "Compile successful, saving..." and then "Save complete." The box then chats "Hello, Avatar!" at you. If you close the Build window and right-click on the box, the script will respond with "Touched."

Congratulations! You have created your first script within *Second Life*! So, what have you done?

Let's break down the script. Right-click the box to pull up the pie menu and select Edit. Again, click on the Content tab. The box will now contain one item, called New Script. Double-clicking on New Script will reopen the Script Editing window. Now we can look at the script:

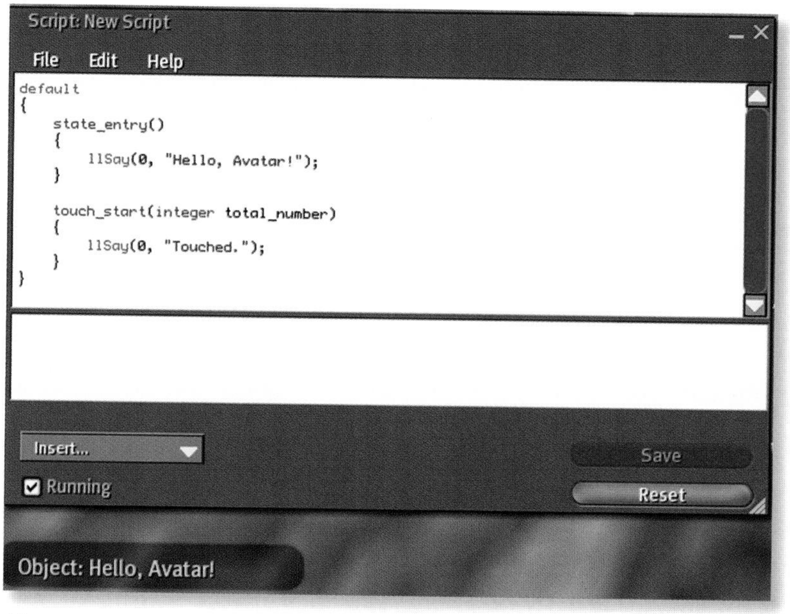

Figure 8.1: The "Hello, Avatar!" script

```
default
{
    state_entry()
    {
        llSay(0, "Hello, Avatar!");
    }

    touch_start(integer total_number)
    {
    llSay(0, "Touched.");
    }
}
```

Even if you've programmed before, few of the keywords will be familiar you to you, so let's break them down one at a time.

The keyword `default` indicates which state the LSL program will begin executing in. You will learn what states are and that LSL programs can have multiple states later in this chapter, but for now you need only know that every LSL program must have at least one state and that it is labeled `default`.

The curly braces, { and }, that follow `default` encapsulate the event handlers within that state—in this case `state_entry` and `touch_start`. The `state_entry` event is triggered whenever execution enters that state, so in our example as soon as you clicked Save to upload the script to the simulator and attach it to the object,

the LSL program began to execute and entered the default state. This triggered the `state_entry` event, meaning that any code sitting within the `state_entry` was run.

In our example, the only code was the library function `llSay`. `llSay` allows a script to chat text, much like an avatar, onto a channel of its choosing. Channel 0 is the channel that all avatars chat onto and listen to, so by saying "Hello, Avatar!" onto channel 0, the script ensures that any avatars nearby can hear it. What `llSay` does is controlled by the arguments within the parenthesis that follow `llSay`, in this case the integer 0 and the string `Hello, Avatar`. We'll talk about arguments more later.

Of course, what if you forget what the arguments for `llSay` are? One option is to visit the LSL Wiki (`http://lslwiki.com/lslwiki/wakka.php?wakka=HomePage`) or search "llSay" on Google. Fortunately, there is an even easier way, which is to hover your cursor over the word "llSay" in the Script Editor window. This will pop up the following tooltip and remind you what `llSay` does and is looking for:

```
llSay(integer channel, string msg)
Say msg on channel
```

The second event handler is `touch_start`. Recall that when we clicked on the box, it chatted "Touched." in response? This is what the `touch_start` event handler does. It is triggered when an avatar begins clicking on the object. Again, the only code that exists within the event handler is the `llSay` library function, which we covered a moment ago.

Now let's start making this script our own. If you don't have the Script Editor up, open it by selecting the box, going to the Contents tab, and double-clicking on New Script. Clicking anywhere within the window allows you to edit the text of the script, so go ahead and change "Avatar" in "Hello, Avatar!" to your name. For me, that would be, "Hello, Cory!" As soon as you change the text, the Save button lights up to indicate that the script in the text window does not match the script that has been loaded up to your box. Click the Save button to recompile and save the script.

You should see the same sequence of "Compile successful, saving..." and then "Save complete." displayed in the bottom of the editor and then the box should chat your name at you. Well done!

But what if you wanted to go back to "Hello, Avatar!"? Fortunately, the text editor supports both undo and redo. Click in the text-editor window and hit Control-Z to undo your change. You'll see your name replaced by the text "Avatar" and the Save button lights up since the script has again changed. If you want to redo the changes, use Control-Y.

Remember that until you hit Save, your changes exist only in the text editor and haven't actually been uploaded into *Second Life*. When working on really complicated or critical scripts, it is often a good idea to use a text editor outside of *SL* and then cut and paste the text into *SL*, since that way you'll always have backups. The LSL Wiki has a list of external editors that have syntax highlighting for LSL (`http://lslwiki.com/lslwiki/wakka.php?wakka=AlternativeEditors`).

It is also important to realize that once you have added a script to an object, the script will remain on the object, even if you derez and rez the object into and out of your inventory. If you want to remove the script permanently, the best way is to delete it from the object's inventory.

To fully understand the connection between the text you type and what actually runs on *Second Life*, you need to dig a little deeper into LSL.

DEEPER INTO LSL

Now we'll focus on compilation, uploading, and execution (Figure 8.2). LSL is a scripting language that runs server-side, on a piece of software called the simulator. The simulator does just what it's name implies—it simulates the virtual world of *Second Life*. Each simulator runs everything for 16 acres of virtual land—buildings, physics, and of course, scripts. While you manipulate the script text in a form that is somewhat easy to

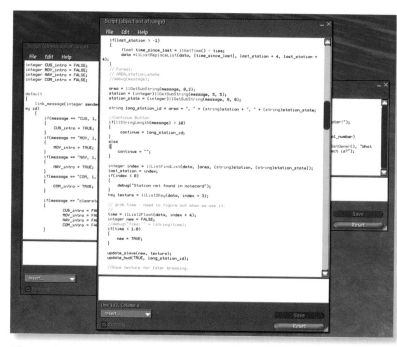

Figure 8.2: A bunch of more-advanced scripts

8

INTRO

PART I

PART II

PART III

APPENDICES

DEEPER INTO LSL

read, the actual code that runs on the simulator is compiled. A compiler is a piece of software that takes the text version of the script and converts it into something that can actually run. In the case of LSL, the compiler exists within the *Second Life* viewer itself. In the future, it is likely that the compiler will move from the viewer into the *Second Life* simulators, but where the code is compiled isn't very important. What matters is that the text is converted into a form that can run on the simulators.

Compilers also serve the function of detecting errors in the code you've just written. Although compilers can't detect all errors, it can detect common mistakes like syntax errors (Figure 8.3). Let's return to our "Hello, Avatar!" script. We can introduce a syntax error in many ways, but one example would be to remove the trailing brace, }, from the end

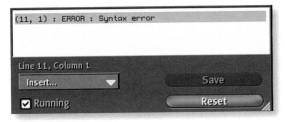

Figure 8.3: ERROR: Syntax Error

of the `state_entry` event. Since we have modified the text, the Save button lights up; click on it to attempt to compile the text. Rather than the "Compile successful, saving..." and then "Save complete." we've become accustomed to, we instead see "(7, 4) : ERROR : Syntax error" and the cursor moves to the first letter of the `touch_start` event.

What does all this mean? The "(7, 4)" tells us that the error is at or near row 7, column 4 of the script, which we also know because the cursor has been positioned there. The "Syntax error" tells us that we've probably made a relatively simple typing error. If we examine our script, we see that the braces don't match. The compiler, upon reaching the `touch_start` event, was expecting a trailing brace, so it flagged this as an error and stopped compiling the script.

Notice something else. If you exit the Build tool and click on the box, it fails to respond with "Touched." When a script fails to compile, *Second Life* stops executing the script on the target object. This is to reduce confusion and prevent broken or mismatched scripts from continuing to operate with *Second Life*. Simply add the trailing brace back in and save the change to both fix the error and to recompile the script.

When a script properly compiles, it generates LSL bytecode. Bytecode is a simple form that is relatively easy to execute. In the future, LSL may compile to a different form for execution, but that won't change how you write scripts. It will simply change how *Second Life* handles things under the hood. Why would we be contemplating these types of changes? Performance, primarily. LSL currently executes quite slowly, so we will continue to make changes to improve what you can do within LSL.

Either way, once the compiled code is on a simulator, it can actually be executed. Execution is simply the process of checking to see whether the script needs to do anything. In our example script, when an avatar clicks on the box, *Second Life* checks to see if any `touch` event handlers exist. Since one does (`touch_start`), the code within the handler executes. Once that code is complete, the script goes to sleep until it needs to do something else.

This process of doing work only when required is key to both how LSL is structured and to writing good LSL scripts. It requires you to understand states and events, however. We'll discuss states first. As was covered earlier, all LSL scripts need to have at least one state, denoted by the `default` keyword. A state is a collection of code between the opening and closing braces of the state. In its simplest form, a script has a single state and all of its code lives there.

For example, imagine that you are creating a script to manage a very simple door that you touch to open or close. Using states can clarify what your code does:

```
// default state is closed
default
{
    touch_start(integer tnum)
    {
        // insert code to open the door here
        // . . .
        state open;
    }
}

state open
{
    touch_start(integer tnum)
    {
        // insert code to close the door here
        // . . .
        state default;
    }
}
```

Note that this is different from the traditional way of writing this, where you would maintain whether the door was open or closed in a global variable, something like this:

```
// default state is closed
integer is_closed = TRUE;

default
{
    touch_start(integer tnum)
    {
        if (is_closed == TRUE)
        {
            // insert code to open the door here
```

INTRO
CHAPTER 1
CHAPTER 2
CHAPTER 3
CHAPTER 4
CHAPTER 5
CHAPTER 6
CHAPTER 7
CHAPTER 8
CHAPTER 9
CHAPTER 10
CHAPTER 11
CHAPTER 12
CHAPTER 13
APPENDICES

```
        // . . .
        is_closed = FALSE;
    }
    else
    {
        // insert code to close the door here
        // . . .
        is_closed = TRUE;
    }
  }
}
```

In this simple case, it may look like the global variable option is easier, but when other behavior also has to change between the open and closed state, splitting the code into multiple states is much simpler than having to wrap everything in if statements.

These code samples illustrate some other basics of LSL syntax. First, the "//" denotes a comment. A comment allows you add text to your script to remind you of why you wrote the code a particular way, to lay groundwork for later coding (such as "insert code to open the door here"), or to make it easier for someone else to follow your work. Note that only the text to the right of the "//" is part of the comment, allowing comments to be added to a line that contains code. For example, in the line

```
state open // this is entered when the door opens
```

"// this is entered when the door opens" is the comment.

Second, we introduce global variables and the variable type "integer." Global variables, like is_closed, are available anywhere in the code. They are similar to global variables in other programming languages, such as C, and they can be any of the types available to LSL (see the section "What Are Types?"). LSL is a statically and strongly typed language, meaning that variables are given types when created and generally require typecasting to convert between types.

SIDEBAR

FROM LINDEN LAB:
AN ANIMATION OVERVIEW

Animations are the personality of an avatar. They're the finishing touches after you've gotten your hair, outfit, and body just right. Sure, you could use the standard animations to get your point across, but with patience, software, and a bit of luck, you can bring your favorite real-world movements into your Second Life experience.

The first thing needed is software to create the animation outside of Second Life. There are several free options; for example, Avimator, Slat, DAZ Studio, Blender, and QAvimator, as well as commercial software like Poser, Maya, and Posemaker. Each system has its own advantages, but all make superb animations. SL uses the BVH motion format, so be sure to export this way.

The jargon related to animations is the same regardless of the software. A key frame is a frame in the animation sequence with a specified joint location, and the program will fill in all the frames between key frames to create a smooth motion. A spline is the set of equations the program uses to generate this smooth motion; if you find that your animation is moving past the key frame or in other odd ways, breaking the spline on the key frames often fixes the problem. Inverse kinematics (IK) is an option that allows you to move the entire arm or leg by moving the hand or foot along the three axes, but if you turn this option on and off, it is important to check your key-frame splines again. Playing with IK can create amazing motions, but it can also have difficult-to-predict consequences, so always save before changing the IK settings.

Now that you have the software, check that the avatar loaded into it is compatible with SL. SL cannot accept information from finger, toe, genitalia, or facial joints, so you may have to use an imported or outdated avatar. You can also edit the key frames after creating the animation to delete the information from these joints.

Let's animate! All joints used in your animation must be in a different position between the first frame and the second frame. The second frame is the first frame you will see in SL, and a good first frame often twists the avatar into a ball. If you want to exclude a body part from the animation so that only part of the SL movements are overridden, the excluded joints should be in the same position in both the first and second frames.

In the second frame, the avatar should be in the starting pose for the animation. Depending on your software, each joint can be dragged by the mouse into position or selected and then moved through parameter dials.

The next key frames will be the different poses your avatar will move through to complete the animation. Remember that humans rarely coordinate moves precisely, so when moving your avatar from one pose

to another, set different body parts to arrive in the target pose a few seconds within one another.

There are a few different ways you can end your animation. The most common way is with the same pose as the second frame (allowing for a seamless loop to be uploaded), or in a unique pose from which the avatar will shift back into normal SL animations. You may also create an animation with a beginning animation, a section with matching key frames at each end that can be used as a loop, and a leading-out animation. If you plan on creating this type of animation, write down the numbers the loop begins and ends at.

Once you have your animation done, export it as a BVH motion and log into SL. SL's uploading process allows you to finish customizing the animation. Here you set a priority level for your animation. The higher the number, the higher the priority. The default animations are a two, so to completely override the SL default, upload a three or four.

Timing your loop can make or break an animation. Avoid a jerky animation with a bit of math. Each end of the looped section should have the exact same key frame, and dividing the key-frame number by the total number of frames will give you the in and out percents within a degree or two. Preview the animation a few times from different in and out percents to check the loop, and don't be afraid to make the matching key frames into two or three static frames to give yourself more leeway.

Hand poses and facial expressions can be set at this stage, and beyond that, ease-in and ease-out settings define how fast your avatar will transition between animations. Now you can upload and begin testing your animation. The test server is a great place to practice. There you won't have to spend your hard earned Lindens getting that hand motion just right.

There are some limits. Subtle movements aren't always picked up by SL, and animations are limited to 30 seconds. While you can upload an animation with 60 frames per second, users will likely only see between 15 and 20 frames per second, so animations are often best in this range. Full-body movements must come from the hip joint, not the body joint, and smaller- or larger-than-normal avatars will require custom animations to maintain the motion. The fastest way to get used

to the quirks of the system is to dive right in and start testing it out for yourself. In no time, your avatar will be able to do your favorite dance move or develop a signature walk or strut as unique as the rest of you.

—Kiari Lefay and Leslie Havens

WHAT ARE TYPES?

A type determines what kind of data can be stored and LSL supports seven distinct types:

INTEGER

An integer is a whole number between –2,147,483,648 and 2,147,483,647. The following are some examples of integers in use:

```
integer int = -23; // in the language C, integers are called int. Don't be
    confused by this!
integer foo = 235632;
integer blar = 0;
```

FLOAT

This is a floating point (or decimal) number with seven significant figures that can be positive or negative. The largest positive or smallest negative number that can be represented is +/– 3.4028235E38, while the smallest positive or largest negative number that can be represented is +/– 1.17549351E-38. Examples of floats are as follows:

```
float e = 2.718128; // the decimal point indicates that this is a float
float f = 0.f; // a trialing ".f" can also be used
float one = 1; // even though the literal "1" is an integer, this assignment
    will work.
integer i_one = ˉ1; // note: if (one == i_one) is a BAD idea! More on this
    later.
```

INTRO
CHAPTER 1
CHAPTER 2
CHAPTER 3
CHAPTER 4
CHAPTER 5
CHAPTER 6
CHAPTER 7
CHAPTER 8
CHAPTER 9
CHAPTER 10
CHAPTER 11
CHAPTER 12
CHAPTER 13
APPENDICES

INTRO

PART I

PART II

PART III

APPENDICES

DEEPER INTO LSL

STRING

A string is a collection of characters, such as the following:

```
string name = "Exposition Linden";
string character = "c"; // single characters in LSL are just string
string number = "1"; // note: "1" != 1
```

VECTOR

A vector is three floats representing x, y, and z components. A vector is generally used as a position, velocity, acceleration, or color. All three values can be set simultaneously, or they can be set as individuals:

```
vector pos = <123.3, 54.f, 32>; // vectors will promote entries into floats
vector vel;
vel.x = 12.f; // this is much
vel.y = 23.f; // slower than initializing via a
vel.z = 36.f; // vector!!
```

LIST

Since LSL doesn't have arrays or structures, the primary method for storing collections of data is lists. All the other data types may be placed in lists (but a list can't be placed in a list). There are many different ways to work with lists; this chapter will cover some of them, and the LSL Wiki (http://lslwiki.com/lslwiki/wakka.php?wakka=list) has excellent examples. More on lists later.

ROTATION

A rotation is four floats representing the x, y, z, and s components of a quaternion rotation. Although quaternions are extremely complicated and often confusing, LSL allows them to be used without your having to master the underlying theory. We'll talk more on rotations later, and you can check out http://lslwiki.com/lslwiki/wakka.php?wakka=rotation. Here are some sample rotations:

```
rotation rot = <0.f, 0.f, 0.f, 1.f>; // Rotations in LSL are internally
    normalized
rotation rot = <32, 2, -9, 128>; // even if your initialization is not
```

KEY

A UUID, or Universally Unique Identifier, is used to identify many objects within *Second Life*. Like rotations, keys allow you to use UUIDs without having to write a lot of code to support them. We'll go over details later, but you can also consult `http://lslwiki.com/lslwiki/wakka.php?wakka=key`.

```
// you almost never need to initialize keys with literals like this.
key object_id = "00000000-0000-0000-0000-000000000000";
```

Typecasting is used when variables of different types are assigned to each other. LSL supports two implicit conversions: integer to float and string to key. These allow the following statements to work correctly:

```
float my_float = 4; // although you really should write this as 4.f
// data between " and " can be either a string or a key.
key object_id = "00000000-0000-0000-0000-000000000000";
```

For any other conversions, explicit typecasting is needed. Like C, a typecast is the type you wish to cast to inside parentheses:

```
integer bad_pi = (integer)3.1425926; // bad_pi == 3
float good_pi = (float)"3.1415926"; // good_pi == 3.1415926
```

Now let's discuss the `if` statements. The `if` statement is the simplest of the conditional, or flow control, statements in LSL. If the code within the parentheses evaluates to `TRUE`, then the code within the braces is executed. The `if` statement is only type of expression in LSL for flow control. Flow control allows you to make decisions about whether pieces of code are executed (for more detail, consult `http://lslwiki.com/lslwiki/wakka.php?wakka=FlowControl`). LSL's flow-control statements are as follows:

```
integer expression = TRUE; // TRUE is an integer constant in LSL. TRUE == 1
if (expression)
{
    // do something if expression == TRUE
}
else
{
    // do something else if expression == FALSE
}

if (expression)
    // do something in one line
else
    // do something else in one line

while(expression)
```

INTRO
CHAPTER 1
CHAPTER 2
CHAPTER 3
CHAPTER 4
CHAPTER 5
CHAPTER 6
CHAPTER 7
CHAPTER 8
CHAPTER 9
CHAPTER 10
CHAPTER 11
CHAPTER 12
CHAPTER 13
APPENDICES

```
    {
        // do something until expression == FALSE.  FALSE == 0
    }

    do
    {
        // do something until expression == FALSE.  FALSE == 0
    } while(expression);

    integer i; // an iterator

    for (i = 0; i < 100; i++)
    {
        // do something 100 times, where i starts at 0 and counts up to 99
            // this code will exit when i == 100

        }


        @again; // this is a label
    // this code will be executed forever
    jump again; // move execution to the @again label
```

There are two additional flow-control mechanisms. The first is the `state` transition, which we already covered. The second is the `return` command, which we will cover in the section "Advanced Language Features."

In all of the flow-control examples, the decision of which path to take was determined by the value of an expression. In LSL, an expression is a combination of operators and functions. Functions will be explained in more detail in the "Advanced Language Features" section. Operators are divided into several broad categories. As with other categories, the LSL Wiki covers this in great detail (`http://lslwiki.com/lslwiki/wakka.php?wakka=operators`).

OPERATOR TYPES

UNARY

Unary operators are arithmetic operators that modify one value, as in the following example:

```
    integer  count = 1; // create a new integer variable and assign it the value
        of 1
        count++; // the "++" operator adds 1 to "count" and assigns the result to
        "count"
    llSay(0, (string)count); // says "2"  -- note the type conversion
```

BINARY

Binary operators are arithmetic operators that act on two values to produce a third, as shown here:

```
integer a = 5;
integer b = 2;
integer c = a % b; // compute a modulo b, so c = 1
```

BOOLEAN

Boolean operators always generate TRUE (1) or FALSE (0) results:

```
integer a = 5;
integer b = 2;
integer c = a != b; // "!=" returns TRUE if its arguments are not the same.
```

BITWISE

Bitwise operators act on the bitfields that make up integers. Here are some examples:

```
integer a = 5; // 0x101 in binary
integer b = 2; // 0x010
integer c = a | b; // a or b = 0x111, so c = 7
```

ASSIGNMENT

Finally we have the assignment operators, which take the result of an expression and assign it to a variable. In addition, LSL supports several variants of the assignment operator that perform an arithmetic operation along with assignment, as in the following example:

```
integer a = 5; // assigns 5 to a
a += 5; // adds 5 to a, then assigns the result, so a = 10
```

INTRO
CHAPTER 1
CHAPTER 2
CHAPTER 3
CHAPTER 4
CHAPTER 5
CHAPTER 6
CHAPTER 7
CHAPTER 8
CHAPTER 9
CHAPTER 10
CHAPTER 11
CHAPTER 12
CHAPTER 13
APPENDICES

ADVANCED LANGUAGE FEATURES

Like other languages that share C-like syntax, blocks and scope are fundamental to understanding how to write good code in LSL. Generally speaking, in LSL a code block is any code set off by braces within a global function or an event handler, as shown here:

```
string GlobalString = "Hi!";   // this global variable is
                               // visible anywhere
                               // in the LSL program

integer factorial(integer n)   // this is a user-defined
                               // function more on them
                               // below

{                              // this brace begins the code
                               // associated with
                               // the function factorial

    string local = "Bye!";     // a local variable is
                               // visible in the block it is
                               // created in and any new
                               // blocks created within that
                               // block

    llSay(0, GlobalString);    // global variables can be
                               // used anywhere in the LSL
                               // program

    llSay(0, local);           // local is available anywhere
                               // inside the factorial

    if (n < 3)
    {          // the if statement creates another code block

        float pi = 3.14;       // pi is only available
                               // inside the if block

        llSay(0, local);       // local is available
                               // anywhere inside factorial
                               // including inside new
                               // blocks created within it

        llSay(0, (string)pi);  // this works since we're
                               // still inside the block

        return n;              // the return statement
                               // jumps back to the calling
                               // function or event handler

    }          // end of the if block
    else       // the else clause creates another block
    {
```

```
        float e = 2.71828;     // e is only available inside
                               // the else block

        llSay(0, (string)pi);  // ERROR!! We aren't in the
                               // block that made pi
                               // so this is an error!

        return n*factorial(n - 1);   // this is recursion,
                                     // more later

    }            // end of the else block

    llSay(0, local);           // local is available
                               // anywhere inside factorial

}            // end of the factorial block

default
{        // states create scope in the sense that they
         // determine which event handlers will
         // be called

    state_entry()
    {            // this starts a block in state_entry()

    integer num = 1;   // the variable do_something
                       // is a local

    if (num)
            num = 4;   // even though there are no braces,
                       // this line is actually a code block

    llSay(0, GlobalString); // global variables may
                            //be used anywhere in the
                            // LSL program
      llSay(0, (string)factorial(num));
                        // user-defined functions may be
                        // called form any event handler.
                        // This will say "24".
    }            // end of the state_entry block
}          // end of the default state
```

There is a lot going on in the simple example program. Although it is a rather silly bit of code, it shows where blocks begin and end, and introduces the idea of scope. For variables and functions, scope defines when they may be called or used. Within LSL, there are two levels of scope: global and local.

Global scope applies to user-defined functions and global variables. Both global variables and user-defined functions may be used anywhere in an LSL program; thus they are considered to be "globally accessible" and therefore of global scope. In the preceding example, the function `factorial` and the string `GlobalString` are globals.

Local scope applies to variables created within code blocks (there are no local functions in LSL). As the example shows, functions, event handlers, and flow control create blocks, and these blocks may have further blocks nested within them. The

INTRO
CHAPTER 1
CHAPTER 2
CHAPTER 3
CHAPTER 4
CHAPTER 5
CHAPTER 6
CHAPTER 7
CHAPTER 8
CHAPTER 9
CHAPTER 10
CHAPTER 11
CHAPTER 12
CHAPTER 13
APPENDICES

scope for a local variable is the code block it was created within, as well as any new blocks created within that block. Consider this example:

```
{                       // a code block
    integer true = TRUE;
    list foo = ["I", "am", "a", "list"];    // a local list
    if (true)
    {                   // a new code block

        foo = [];       // we can still see foo,
                        //so assigning an empty
                        // list to it

    }
}
```

Note that these scope rules can allow some really bad coding habits, like in the following example:

```
{
    float pi = 3.14;
    if (pi)                 // if a floating point value
                            // is used in an
                            // expression, it is FALSE
                            // if it is exactly
                            // equal to 0.f,
                            // and TRUE for any other value
                            // This is a bad habit,
                            // since floating point
                            // values are often near to 0.f
                            // but not exactly
                            // equal to 0.f.

    {                       // start of if code block
        integer pi = 3;     // this local pi has the same name
                            // as pi from
                            // the earlier scope and
                            // is said to "shadow"
                            // the other variable.

        llSay(0, (string)pi);       // Which pi will be used?

    }                               // end of the if block
    else
    {               // start of the else block
        string pi = "3.1415";       // Ack!  Another pi
        llSay(0, (string)pi);       // Now which pi will be
                                    // used?

    }
}
```

Please do not ever write code like this! Although it compiles and (if you are very fortunate) may even work, it will cause you—or anyone you share your code with—headaches and confusion.

Now that you understand scope, let us turn to functions. In the last section we introduced global functions, the first of the two types of functions in *Second Life*. The second type, library functions, will be discussed shortly.

User-defined functions allow you to create blocks of code that perform a specific task or calculation. They are placed above the default state, either before or after global variables, and are written as follows:

```
type   function_name(type parameter1, type parameter2, . . .)
{
   // do something in here
}
```

The type is the function's return type, which means that if you want the function to return a value after it is called, you need to specify the type. For example, if you wanted to take the absolute value of a float, you could write the following function:

```
float fabs(float num)
{
   if (num > 0.f)       // already a positive number, just return it
      return num;    // the return command returns the value of
            // the expression that follows it
   else
      return -num;   // the negation operator returns the -1*num
}
```

This would be used as follows:

```
float negone = -1.f;
float posone = fabs(negone);     // passes -1.f to fabs, returns 1.f
llSay(0, (string)posone);   // will say "1.f"
```

Notice that `fabs` takes one parameter of type float. Functions can have any number of parameters (including zero). So, the following are all legal formats for naming a function:

```
do_something()
string do_something_else()
vector do_something_too(string target)
list do_something_now(integer number, rotation rot1, rotation rot2)
```

Two important features of LSL functions are that their parameters are passed by value and they support recursion. To understand the concept of pass by value, look at the following function:

```
integer add_one(integer n)
{
n = n + 1;
```

INTRO
CHAPTER 1
CHAPTER 2
CHAPTER 3
CHAPTER 4
CHAPTER 5
CHAPTER 6
CHAPTER 7
CHAPTER 8
CHAPTER 9
CHAPTER 10
CHAPTER 11
CHAPTER 12
CHAPTER 13
APPENDICES

```
return n;
}
integer number = 10;
number = add_one(number);
```

So, what is the value in number? As you would hope, the value is 11. This is because when number is passed into add_one, it is passed in as its value, 10. Thus, any operations on n within the function are acting on a local copy, not on the variable number. Generally, this is what you want to have happen, but it means that in order for your function to return a value, you have to use the return command. If you had written add_one as follows, the number would still be 10:

```
add_one(integer n)
{
n = n + 1;
}

integer number = 10;
add_one(number);
```

User-defined functions are covered in considerable detail at http://lslwiki.com/lslwiki/wakka.php?wakka=UserDefine dFunction.

The second type of function in LSL is library functions (Figure 8.4). They are built-in functions that are there to perform common tasks or to provide functionality that would be difficult to write in LSL directly. More than 300 functions are built into LSL, and more are being added regularly.) For a comprehensive description of all of the functions, check out http://lslwiki.com/lslwiki/wakka.php?wakka=functions.) It is important to recognize that LSL functions operate just like the user-defined functions. They are available within any event handler or user-generated function, their arguments are passed by value, and they may or may not return a value. One additional aspect is that some of them have a delay value associated with them. This delay exists to protect *Second Life* from certain types of abuse.

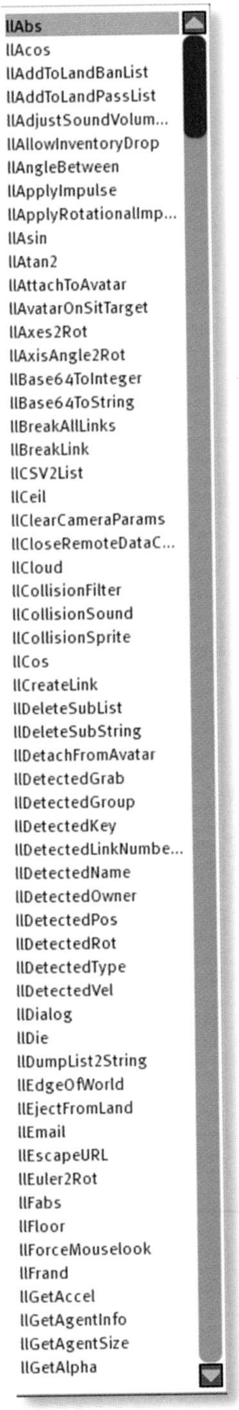

Figure 8.4: Library-function list

CONNECTING TO THE WORLD

LSL's real power is in its ability to allow an object to communicate and interact with the rest of the world. To cover everything you can do with it would require a separate book, but the following should get you started.

CHAT

In our first example, we showed that an object can chat to the rest of the world using the llSay function. This is handy for communicating to people near the object, and it can also be useful for local object-to-object communication.

```
default
{
    state_entry()
    {
        llListen(0, "", llGetOwner(), "");
    }

    listen(integer channel, string name, key id, string message)
    {
    llSay(0, message);
    }
}
```

The preceding script is a simple chat repeater that illustrates the basics of scripted chat. All it does is repeat everything the object's owner says. When the script starts, llListen sets up the listen event so that the object can listen for chat. llListen lets you filter what you want to listen for by chat channel, name, UUID, and message.

```
integer llListen(integer channel, string name, key id, string message)
```

In the example, the script listens on channel 0, which is the public chat channel that all avatars chat on. There are a few billion chat channels so that objects can chat to each other without fear of message collision. The name and message parameters are left blank in this case so the script will listen for all names and messages. llGetOwner returns the UUID of the owner, so in this case the script ends up listening for public chat made by the script's owner.

INTRO
CHAPTER 1
CHAPTER 2
CHAPTER 3
CHAPTER 4
CHAPTER 5
CHAPTER 6
CHAPTER 7
CHAPTER 8
CHAPTER 9
CHAPTER 10
CHAPTER 11
CHAPTER 12
CHAPTER 13
APPENDICES

183

When the script "hears" something that matches the requirements set in llListen, the listen event will be triggered. In this case we just pass the message that was heard to llSay.

Chat sent with llSay can be heard in a radius of 20 meters; alternatively, chat can be sent with llWhisper (10 meters) or llShout (100 meters).

Because there are times when you want to use chat but keep it private, there is also llOwnerSay—a special chat that only the object's owner can hear.

IM

There are times when you want to send a message to someone who is not within Whisper, Say, or Shout radius, or you want to keep your message private. The easiest way to do this is through an instant message (IM). IMs can be "heard" anywhere in *Second Life*, but only by the intended recipient. To send an IM, you need to know the intended recipient's UUID.

```
llInstantMessage(key uuid, string message)
```

If the resident is offline, the message will be saved until they log in next. Objects cannot IM other objects.

SENSORS

Sensors allow you to gather information about avatars and objects near your object. Setting up a sensor is somewhat like setting up a listen for chat. When llSensor is called, the parameters filter out the results, and if there are any matches a sensor event is called. The major difference is that whereas llListen is continuous, llSensor is a single request. The following script is an example using a sensor.

```
Default
{
    state_entry()
{
    //Set up a repeating sensor, that once a second looks for any
    //avatars within a sphere with a 20 meter radius.
llSensorRepeat("", "", AGENT, 20.0, PI, 1.0);
}

sensor(integer detected)  //A sensor returns the first 16 items detected.
```

```
    {
        // Say the names of everyone the sensor detects
        for(i=0;i<detected;i++)
    {
    llSay(0, llDetectedName(i));
    }
            }


            }
```

PAY

Scripts can also give and take
L$ (Figure 8.5). This is handy
for creating vendors, gambling
games, and more. In order for
an object to accept money, the
script must have a `money` event:

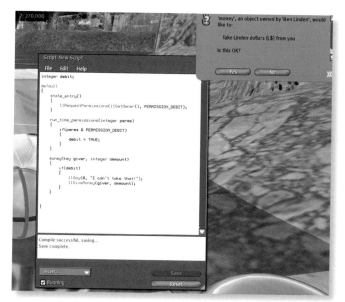

Figure 8.5: Giving and taking money

```
default
{
    money(key giver, integer amount)
{
    llSay(0, "Thanks for the " + (string)amount + "L$ donation!");
}

}
```

Giving money via a scripted object is a bit more complicated. The script needs to
request permission from the object's owner to debit L$ from their account.

```
default
{
    state_entry()
{
    llRequestPermissions(llGetOwner(), PERMISSION_DEBIT);
}

touch_start(integer number_touching)
{
    llGiveMoney(llDetectedKey(0), 1);
}
}
```

The preceding script gives L$1 to whomever clicks on the object that's using `llGiveMoney`. This script will not work unless when the `llRequestPermissions` function is called, the owner grants permission to let the object give money.

INVENTORY

An object has an inventory (Figure 8.6)—this is where the script lives, but it can also contain most of the things a resident's Inventory can. The script can give, take, and use inventory. For instance, a gun would need `llRezObject` to shoot a bullet. A vendor would use `llGiveInventory` to give a single item, or `llGiveInventoryList` to give a folder.

The following is an example of a drop box that shows how to give and take inventory;

```
default
{
    state_entry()
{
    //Allows anyone to drop inventory
    llAllowInventoryDrop(TRUE);
}

touch_start(integer number_touched)
{
    //Only the owner can take it out.
    if(llDetectedKey(0) == llGetOwner)
{
    //Make a list of all the objects in the inventory
    list contents = [];
integer I;
    for(i=0;i<llGetInventoryNumber(INVENTORY_OBJECT);i++)
    {
        contents += llGetInventoryName(INVENTORY_OBJECT, i);
    }
```

Figure 8.6: Object inventory

```
        //Give all the objects in a folder
        llGiveInventoryList(llGetOwner(), "Drop Box", contents);
    }


    }
```

PHYSICS AND MORE

Second Life has a server-side physics simulation, which means objects will fall, bounce, and collide correctly. A script can change how the built-in physics affect an object.

By default, an object in *Second Life* is "pinned." This means that if you lift it up and let go, it will not fall down. To make it fall, you can set its status to physical:

```
default
{
    state_entry()
    {
        llSetStatus(STATUS_PHYSICS, TRUE);
    }
}
```

An object can also change its collision status by becoming "phantom" with the llSetStatus function:

```
llSetStatus(STATUS_PHANTOM, TRUE);
```

APPLYING FORCES

By changing the forces on a physical object, you can control how it moves. There are several ways to do this; the easiest way is to use llSetForce or llApplyImpulse. These work just like your high-school physics class taught you: a force is a continuous push, and an impulse is a single, instant push. A simple example:

```
default
{
    touch_start(integer touched)
    {
        // bounces the object up in the air.
        llApplyImpulse(<0,0,100>, FALSE);
    }
}
```

INTRO
CHAPTER 1
CHAPTER 2
CHAPTER 3
CHAPTER 4
CHAPTER 5
CHAPTER 6
CHAPTER 7
CHAPTER 8
CHAPTER 9
CHAPTER 10
CHAPTER 11
CHAPTER 12
CHAPTER 13
APPENDICES

VEHICLES

For more control, there is a suite of functions that let you change over 20 parameters to alter every aspect of how a physical object moves, from buoyancy to friction (Figure 8.7). The vehicle code is much more complex but correspondingly more powerful. For more information, check out the vehicle page at `http://lslwiki.com/lslwiki/wakka.php?wakka=vehicles`.

Figure 8.7: A scripted airplane in flight

CONTROLS AND DISPLAYS

You probably don't want to interact with an object via text and clicks alone. Flying a jet across a sim will be tough if you have to type "up" over and over again. Likewise, no one wants to watch your slide show if it is just text describing the pictures you put inside.

TAKING CONTROL

A scripted object can take over the normal movement controls from an avatar. This makes it easy to create guns that shoot when you click the mouse, or a car that drives when you use the arrow keys.

A script needs to request permission to take over the controls from the avatar. In the special case of attachments and vehicles, permission is granted automatically, but the script still needs to make the request.

The following example is a portion of a very basic gun script:

```
default
{
    // If we attach the gun, request permissions; if we detach, release
    control.
    attach(key attachedAgent)
    {
            if (attachedAgent != NULL_KEY)
            {
llRequestPermissions(llGetOwner(), PERMISSION_TAKE_CONTROLS);
            }
```

```
        else
        {
            llReleaseControls();
        }
        }

        // When permission is granted, the run_time_permissions event is triggered
        // Use this as a cue to take controls.
        run_time_permissions(integer permissions)
        {
            if (permissions == PERMISSION_TAKE_CONTROLS)
            {
    //We want to take the left mouse button in mouselook.
                llTakeControls(CONTROL_ML_LBUTTON, TRUE, FALSE);
            }
        }


        control(key name, integer levels, integer edges)
        {
            // After taking controls, if those controls are used, take the
        appropriate action.
            if (  ((edges & CONTROL_ML_LBUTTON) == CONTROL_ML_LBUTTON)
                &&((levels & CONTROL_ML_LBUTTON) == CONTROL_ML_LBUTTON) )
            {
                //  If left mouse button is pressed, fire
                fire();
            }
        }
    }
}
```

DISPLAY

Scripts can also control the appearance of an object. Probably the most used example
of this is changing textures for things like slide shows. To change a texture, it is easiest
to use a texture in the object's inventory. If you have a bunch of great snapshots, you
can drop them into a box with the following script to watch them display:

```
integer i;

default
{
    state_entry()
    {
        // Change image every 10 seconds
        llSetTimerEvent(10.0);
    }

    timer()
    {

        if(i<llGetInventoryNumber(INVENTORY_TEXTURE))
        {
            i++;

        }
```

8

CHAPTER
INTRO
PART I
PART II
PART III
APPENDICES

HOW TO LEARN MORE

```
else
{
    i = 0;
}
// set the texture on the "0" face of the object.
llSetTexture(llGetInventoryName(INVENTORY_TEXTURE, i), 0);
}
}
```

CHAPTER 8

HOW TO LEARN MORE

If this brief introduction to LSL has left your head spinning, don't worry! If you haven't programmed before, the promise and power of adding code—of adding behavior—to objects in *Second Life* can be overwhelming. Even if you are an experienced software developer, the quirks and unique aspects of LSL can take a while to wrap your brain around, but once you do you will have opened up entirely new worlds of possibilities. No matter what, you're going to be hungry for more—more knowledge, more examples, more people to learn with. Fortunately all of these exist, both within *Second Life* and on the Web.

Let's begin inside *Second Life*. The Event Calendar is a great place to start looking for help about LSL. Every week there are many classes on LSL, ranging from Scripting 101 to Advanced Vehicles. Not only do these classes provide concrete information on the mechanics of scripting in *Second Life*, but they also can connect you to the community of scripters within the world. By meeting the other students and instructors, you can build a strong network of friends and fellow scripters to question, to collaborate with, and to find new challenges.

There are many different communities of scripters within *Second Life*, from the professional content developers doing large real-world projects to the beginners gathering to play in the sandboxes. You are certain to find one that matches your skills and interests. Like other forms of creation within *Second Life*, scripting is the most fun when done with others, so use the time when you're learning LSL to meet other people and groups.

Classes in *Second Life* are only one resource for learning about scripting. Two *Second Life* forums exist as resources for scripters; The Scripting Library forum (http://forums.secondlife.com/forumdisplay.php?f=15) acts as a repository for various scripts, new ideas, and the basic building blocks every scripter would otherwise have to reinvent. The Scripting Tips forum (http://forums.secondlife.com/forumdisplay.php?f=54) allows scripters to share knowledge on a daily basis.

Both forums see daily contributions by a many scripters, and both are worth reading and contributing to. They will connect you to other scripters rapidly.

A more specialized support option is the *Second Life* Scripters mailing list (`http://secondlife.com/community/mailinglists.php`). It tends to cover very specific questions about or problems with LSL, often before they show up on either the forums or the LSL Wiki. The mailing list is a good place to lurk as an intermediate scripter, but really it's best used by expert scripters looking to connect with other advanced scripters. However, like mailing lists in general, it isn't the best resource for general searches or broad questions. Fortunately, another option exists.

That resource is the LSL Wiki (`http://lslwiki.com/lslwiki/`), a wonderful resource for all things *Second Life*. Beyond the most comprehensive documentation of all LSL functions (`http://lslwiki.com/lslwiki/wakka.php?wakka=functions`), it also calls out known bugs (`http://lslwiki.com/lslwiki/wakka.php?wakka=KnownBugs`) and gotchas (`http://lslwiki.com/lslwiki/wakka.php?wakka=annoyances`). Moreover, it has numerous tutorials (`http://lslwiki.com/lslwiki/wakka.php?wakka=LSLTutorials`) and links to many of the scripting groups, mentors, and teachers (`http://lslwiki.com/lslwiki/wakka.php?wakka=ScriptingMentors`) in *Second Life*. Most importantly, the LSL Wiki is a wiki, so it is constantly being added to, always being updated by the *Second Life* community. As you begin to learn about LSL, you should become familiar with the LSL Wiki and contribute to it yourself. It is yet another way to meet other scripters and to become part of the LSL community within *Second Life*.

A final resource for LSL is the *Second Life* Education Wiki (`http://www.simteach.com/wiki/index.php?title=Second_Life_Education_Wiki`). The *Second Life* Education Wiki provides up-to-date information on the education and research projects going on in *Second Life*. Educators and researchers provide both a resource to scripters and a market for specialized scripts and builds. Campus:*Second Life* (`http://www.simteach.com/wiki/index.php?title=Campus:Second_Life`), as well as other university and education builds within *SL*, often brings groups into contact with LSL, either because their students are exploring LSL or because of specialized needs. As you become more confident with LSL, you will find educators to be some of the most collaborative and open scripters in *Second Life*. If you are looking for interesting and unusual projects to apply your budding scripting skills to, look no further than the Education Wiki.

Of course, no book can keep up with the resources constantly appearing on the Web in support of LSL, so new options will have appeared by the time this book is on shelves. Seek them out!

INTRO

CHAPTER 1

CHAPTER 2

CHAPTER 3

CHAPTER 4

CHAPTER 5

CHAPTER 6

CHAPTER 7

CHAPTER 8

CHAPTER 9

CHAPTER 10

CHAPTER 11

CHAPTER 12

CHAPTER 13

APPENDICES

PART III

SUCCESS IN SECOND LIFE

CHAPTER 9

WHO ARE YOU?

What is best about *Second Life*? If you've made it this far, you know the answer: it is the chance to be whomever you want to be. Practically all the restraints and limitations of real life are absent. The virtual world lets you look the way you've always wanted to look via your *SL* alter ego—your avatar. It lets you play, it lets you work, it lets you fly. Apart from the few rules that apply when you're outside your virtual home (see Chapter 1), you're free to pursue the dreams you cannot realize in real life.

This chapter discusses some of the choices you can make in *Second Life*—there are almost as many as there are *SL* residents. It describes aspects of a virtual existence as seen through the eyes of residents. Their virtual lives are a good cross-section of what goes on in *Second Life* and should provide you with both entertainment and food for thought. The voices featured are those of the residents themselves—real-life people who have agreed to share their experiences and observations. There is a twist: the first three avatars featured all belong to Michael Rymaszewski—the writer talking to you right now. The observations of Michael Control, Frank Freelunch, and Delia Ellsberg provide a general idea of what life is like in *Second Life*; the other residents provide different perspectives.

CONTENTS

LOOKS, LIFESTYLE, AND CAREER

Most of the choices you make in the virtual world impact your looks, lifestyle, or career. However, the boundaries of those topics are drawn differently from the way they are defined in the real world:

- Your avatar's appearance can be completely changed within a couple of seconds with a single mouse swipe; all it involves is dragging a new shape and outfit folder onto your avatar. What's more, you can do this as often as you like.

- In the real world, lifestyle is strongly influenced by income. That's not as true in *Second Life*. Every *SL* resident is rich enough to live pretty much the way they want and to do pretty much whatever they want. In this context, the notion of lifestyle acquires a different meaning: it mostly applies to how you spend your time in the virtual world.

- A virtual career works the same way it does in the real world, with one exception: everything happens much faster. The *SL* notion of full-time work illustrates this well—in the virtual world, full-time means eight to ten hours a week instead of 35 and up. Things are sped up to the max when it comes to building new stuff: an experienced builder can build a family house from scratch (including furniture, decorations, and streaming music) in less time than it takes to fill out an application for a building permit in real life.

One of the biggest differences between real and virtual life, however, is the amount of control you have over your existence. Virtual life offers you total control of everything—you even choose when to enter the world and when to leave, an ability that's sadly lacking in real life. You are truly the master of your destiny.

MICHAEL CONTROL

I've always wanted to be Everyman. I'm a professional writer in real life, and writers aren't average people—that's why they're writers, for better or for worse. And if, like me, you're stuck with distinctive looks (not necessarily in the fortunate sense), this yearning to merge into the masses can grow to obsessive proportions.

Second Life gave me that option: a ready-made, cookie-cutter, aesthetically pleasing avatar. I made a few adjustments mainly because I spent a lot of time fooling around with avatar-appearance tools. Lesson one—if you want to be Mr. Incognito in *Second Life,* stick with the default avatar and make just a few changes. If you don't make *any* changes, you *will* get noticed, as in "Who is that noob who still hasn't sussed out you can change your avatar's appearance?"

Although given Premium-member privileges by the generous folk at Linden Lab, I wanted to experience *SL* the way a shipwrecked sailor experiences an uninhabited island: no help from the outside world in the form of generous cash transfers, and no purchasing anything—everything I wore or owned was to be made by myself. To this end, I practically memorized the building tutorials and parked myself in an empty sandbox. After a few hours, I was able to quickly build uncomplicated objects with simple animations (I ruthlessly copied the existing scripts that fit instead of scripting from scratch). It made me feel very proud, and then a woman appeared—a very beautiful woman equipped with a pair of wings that would be the envy of most angels. In the space of maybe five minutes, she built a beautiful double bed, complete with elaborately decorated headboard and footboard. She didn't invite me to try it out, and I slunk away, feeling very small. So this was what being an Everyman was about! Not so nice when you're looking for action.

Fortunately, this incident let me discover something I overlooked at the outset of my virtual life: you don't have to do a thing if you don't enjoy it. You can have almost anything your heart desires for free, or possibly for one Linden dollar. The only exception is when you want a virtual place of your own, regardless of whether you buy or rent. Personally, I didn't feel the need for that—for me, one of the most exhilarating things about *Second Life* is that you don't need the things you need in real life. You don't need a home and it never rains—in fact, you can set the sun to shine the way you like most.

FRANK FREELUNCH

Well, I had an advantage: this Michael Control guy shared his wisdom with me before I even stepped into *Second Life.* Among the things I heard was that everyone's sooo good-looking it almost hurts to watch.

INTRO
CHAPTER 1
CHAPTER 2
CHAPTER 3
CHAPTER 4
CHAPTER 5
CHAPTER 6
CHAPTER 7
CHAPTER 8
CHAPTER 9
CHAPTER 10
CHAPTER 11
CHAPTER 12
CHAPTER 13
APPENDICES

INTRO

PART I

PART II

PART III

APPENDICES

WHO ARE YOU?

I didn't want to be a hunk, though; I took the other route. Some fooling around with the avatar appearance tools, and presto!—I was your friendly construction worker from the bar that sells cheap beer. The standard white T-shirt, jeans, beer belly, shaved head; I threw in a pleasant but definitely low-IQ face for full effect. First observation: I was the only ugly guy in the whole virtual world. That got me noticed! But other people were kind of nonplussed, and whenever I talked to someone there was this unspoken question hovering in the air: "That's what you look like in real life, right?"

Being a construction worker, I decided to do some construction work. I got my little First Land parcel and set about building a house. First I had to level the land and you know, it's not that easy—I guess that's why you see so many plots for sale that are advertised as flat and green and cost many times more than the original price. The thing to do is to first get a small area exactly right—flat and as high as you want it. Once I got one corner of my plot right, it was easy to work from there. When I was half done, I split for a beer break—you can get beer in *Second Life*, and you can get a fridge, too, so that it stays cool. Then when I got back to work, something caught my eye. I looked up and there was this beautiful house that wasn't there before, floating maybe a hundred feet above the neighboring land parcel. So I said a few words to myself and went to get another beer.

My favorite activity in *SL*? Playing games. I got hooked on the *Space Invaders* on Help Island—it was a fave of mine in the real world when I was a kid. So once I was done with building, I hit the games emporiums for a little fun. You have to pay to play most of the games, but almost every game place has camping chairs and money trees. You play for a while, and if you run out of money you just relax for a bit on one of those paying chairs, maybe also pick up some cash from the money tree if you're lucky. (There are money tree scavengers around who go from tree to tree picking up free money, and most times the trees are picked clean.)

I also like sightseeing, so I wandered around a lot and visited various places. The place I liked most? Well, you'll be surprised. It wasn't an exotic island or a Japanese village; it was that part of the mainland they call Grignano. They have a streetcar service there, and it wasn't until I sat down inside it after waiting at the stop that I felt at home in the virtual world. You should walk or drive or ride the streetcar in *SL* instead of teleporting or flying—it makes the whole experience seem much more real.

DELIA ELLSBERG

I wanted to see what it was like to be a chick in *Second Life*. Not a virtual *woman*, but the nice, girl next door who's popular with everyone. A lot of guys choose avatars of the opposite sex, and I wanted to see why.

I found out why right away. When you enter *SL* as a woman, you're young and beautiful, with a body many models would kill for. I was hit on for the first time maybe five minutes after I arrived—I was still standing in the arrival area. Despite my positive reception, I hated the original color of my hair and switched to jet black. When I tried out the freebie clothes from Help Island and found I didn't like them much—nice, but not me—I just dyed my jeans a different color, did some work on my face, put on some makeup, and made myself a nice-looking long-sleeved zebra-striped T-shirt and a pair of stilettos to match. I can tell you, making a pair of shoes that look good with the tools you get is a drag; no matter what you do, the heel is always ugly. There are lots of good shoes for women on the mainland, though—guys don't have even a third of the choices, by comparison. Just keep your feet size O: they look cute and most shoes are made to fit that size.

Anyway, to get back on track: those two guys I know—Michael Control and that fatso Frank Freelunch—complained no one ever wanted to talk to them. I know why. A guy has to look real sharp in *SL* to get attention. It's completely different if you're a girl. I told you I got hit on even before I got off the arrival area on Orientation Island. Well, after I got the zebra shirt and high heels and generally made things nicer, I got hit on several times with each venture into the world. Guys just bend over for you in *SL*—that's my experience. Example: I wanted to switch my First Land for a plot owned by a local business king who advertised he'd buy any First Land for a good price. Cool guy, him—hair in a topknot, samurai pants, naked tattooed chest—and he gave me 10% more than advertised for my plot.

I never had any problem getting help from anyone, either, and Control and Freelunch moaned about people not giving them the time of day. Well, what do they expect? If you're a guy and you're reading this, get this into your head: you're stepping through the looking glass when you enter *SL*. Here things are the other way around: it's guys who have to make themselves look real sharp to get any attention. And forget the clothes you get for free—they aren't sharp enough.

INTRO
CHAPTER 1
CHAPTER 2
CHAPTER 3
CHAPTER 4
CHAPTER 5
CHAPTER 6
CHAPTER 7
CHAPTER 8
CHAPTER 9
CHAPTER 10
CHAPTER 11
CHAPTER 12
CHAPTER 13
APPENDICES

My favorite way to spend *SL* time? I like meeting and talking to new people. *Second Life* gave me a chance to use my French for the first time in quite a while—there are more and more residents from non–English-speaking countries. (Everyone will communicate in English of course, but you can quickly tell it's not their first language.)

DESMOND SHANG

My *Second Life* experience is quite astonishing, really. I make normal, antiquated, ordinary things commonly found in the 19th century, just for fun. Everything from lamp posts to Victorian homes.

For some reason, this sort of thing seems to be popular. I never expected it. Perhaps for many, the "anything goes" culture that pervades the online experience quickly becomes irksome.

So rather than taking money out of *Second Life* I bought an island, just for fun. Perhaps three or four people would enjoy living in a 19th-century seaside village to offset the cost a bit? I made a little tartan flag, opened the island Caledon, and the village filled up quickly. Suddenly there was a waiting list of about 50.

I didn't expect this kind of response. Nothing else to do but buy more land and make people happy, I suppose. The experience of it was rather like that of lighting a firecracker.

The community took off by itself quite without me, and as of this writing, hasn't slowed down. Within short order there were homes and shops, tea societies, formal parties, and this incredible sense of fun and growth. The sense of being a part of something both wonderful and larger than oneself seems to infect everyone.

I'm stunned by the community accomplishments. We have a trolley created by some talented residents that has become somewhat of a landmark, and the community raised thousands of real dollars for the American Cancer Society in the Relay for Life events. It's an honour to know them all.

The day-to-day is a bit like that of a handyman. I make sure Caledon is reasonably clean, fix a few things that need fixing, and answer questions. There are plenty of questions from the West Trade Imports Ltd antiques customers, as well. Now and then I add more land, which is always fun. It's all very low-key; I've yet to have even one nasty experience with anyone staying in Caledon.

Likely if I had done something else in the beginning, things would be very different now. This seems to be a perfect example of how a little decision has vast consequences down the line. I must confess, *Second Life* has been very much more rewarding than I ever thought it would be.

FRANCIS CHUNG

There's two things you need to know about me for this story to make sense.

Firstly, I love cars. I obsess about them. There's this route between San Francisco and Tahoe that takes you on some nice windy asphalt through the mountains—just a really great drive. I made that trip a few times in my Accord EX-R back in 2000, during my little stint in the bay during the whole Dot Com era. I have this recurring dream of taking that drive again in something with rear-wheel drive.

The second thing you need to know about me is that I'm a grad student, and the truth is, this isn't the glamorous and lucrative profession that they portray in movies and television. It's vaguely like taking a vow of poverty in the name of science. What this means is, tragically, that my means of getting around town consists of a pair of New Balance sneakers and public transit.

So this is where *Second Life* comes in—despite all its flaws and limitations, it does this one thing that you can't get anywhere else—it gives you this tool that lets you *make stuff*—a way to realize your dreams, albeit in a virtual space. One day I just decided, if I can't have a car in my first life, I'm going to have one in my second life. I'd live vicariously through *SL* until the day I can have a set of real wheels to call my own.

And if I'm going to have a car in my second life, I'll be damned if I can't have the coolest ride around. To me, there's absolutely nothing cooler than a '60s muscle car: V-8 in the front, drive at the back, dodgy handling, and way too much power. Guts and glory. That's what I was thinking when I started out on what eventually became the Dominus Shadow.

This being *Second Life*, it would just be inappropriate to just build a car and call it done. That would clearly be too mundane. Forgive the pun, but this pony's one trick would be to do *everything*. It had to do all the tricks that you might want, and then some; suicide doors, a gargantuan supercharger, hover-car mode, the list goes on. I think I have this personality type that's not really complete unless I'm obsessing about something. For now, though, I'm stuck on cars, and I guess that shows through just a little.

CHAPTER 9   TAO TAKASHI

I first heard about *Second Life* in fall 2005 in a report on the video blog Rocketboom. It sounded very interesting back then and I planned to join, but for some reason it took me four months to do so. But when I did it was immediately apparent to me that *Second Life* is my thing. Partly it's because of all the creativity you can see happening and you can take part in yourself, and partly it's because of the great community.

So I started immediately with doing all sorts of creative things like building my first house, designing my first T-shirt, programming my first script. After a while I heard about machinima and planned to check it out for myself. And as I have a video blog in real life I thought about doing the same in *Second Life*. And so *Tao Takashi on Air* was invented first as an experiment, but it's now an ongoing series. It covers various topics, like concerts from *Second Life* and real-life musicians, community events such as the *Second Life* Relay for Life or the *Second Life* birthday, and much more.

Doing machinima is great and challenging at once. On the one hand it's like most parts of *Second Life*: still a new field and you have great freedom in doing what you want. On the other hand you have to deal with certain limitations, such as not having a speech animation, or dealing with lag.

But while doing machinima is probably the area for which I am mostly known, it's not the only field I am working on. As I am a Python and Web developer in real life, I also try to combine these things with *Second Life*. One project coming out of this is the creation of *Second Life* TV, which reads RSS feeds from video blogs and displays those videos in-world. It's more of a research project, though, to experiment with different mechanisms of interaction, and thus might never be finished.

Also related is the creation of `http://planet.worldofsl.com/`, a *Second Life* blog aggregator which displays the most-recent blog posts from the *Second Life* blogosphere on one page. This gives the reader a quick overview of what's happening right now in the *Second Life* blogosphere and also gives new users a list of noteworthy blogs. Part of this is, of course, also my own blog at `http://taotakashi.wordpress.com`, in which I write about what I am doing and about what's going on in *Second Life* from my perspective.

BACCARA RHODES

Since making my first appearance in July of 2003 as Baccara Rhodes, I have been referred to as the "Social Doyenne" of *Second Life*. First and foremost, and setting the tone for my tenure in *Second Life*, I have tried to set a standard for taste, manners, and a life well-lived while building a personal community that I can be proud of. Although I always try to refer to this eloquent and elegant woman in the third person, she is an extension of my being and here I will refer to Baccara as I.

An early review from *The New York Times* in June of 2003 brought me to *Second Life*. From the beginning, it was clear that I would be here a very long time, so I laid a clear-cut path for the woman that I wished to be. In those early days, everyone learned together and shared each bit of knowledge— each day akin to an adventure, each tidbit of new information shared willingly among new friends.

Prior to *Second Life* becoming such a vital part of my everyday existence, I was an event planner in my "real life" as well as being in the flower business on a

wholesale level for many years. I had retired from those occupations; I had all kinds of visions for the road that lay ahead.

However, virtual life had other plans for me, and I found myself becoming the "event diva" within a short time. Shortly after I met Fey Brightwillow, one of *SL*'s earliest and best designers, we cofounded Spellbound Events. Early in *SL*, we put together the largest cohesive building, scripting, and animating team to date and staged the very first social- and community-service programs. On the Spellbound resume, you will find tributes to the imaginative stories of L. Frank Baum (author of *The Wonderful Wizard of Oz*) and J.M. Barrie (author of *Peter Pan*), as well as the largest weddings constructed in *Second Life*. Today I continue hosting large-scale weddings and social events at sim Stardust, as well as coordinating corporate and private projects.

Mash Mandala is my dear friend and *SL* partner. Together we operate the *SL* Depoz Ink and Stardust. First opened in April of 2005, Depoz became the first complete building center in our world, where residents could shop for everything needed to put together their own homes, and it expanded to a multisim location soon after. This has been a most successful collaboration as well as an extraordinary friendship across 2,500 miles. Together we operate several regions and make all decisions together in a "drama-free" partnership, enjoying good friends and good times for close to two years.

In *Second Life* virtually anyone can continually expand their horizons by having a battery of projects at one time. I participate in different arenas and today am preparing work with some exciting projects, such as languagelab.com and the new Eros Continent debuting toward the end of the year.

I have acted as project coordinator for some stages of the building of `http://languagelab.com` and will conduct user-interface classes for instructors who will begin learning to use *SL* in preparation for the teaching of English as a second language, as well as [teaching] foreign languages to English-speaking computer users. I am very excited to join longtime associate Stroker Serpentine at the Eros Super Continent Project by being the hostess and manager of a very special event sim for private group members to have special weddings and parties in the grand fashion for which I am well-known.

As one of the more "mature" [residents] of *SL*, I look at my world with a dewy-eyed wonder each morning. It is a world I have helped to create, and one of which I am very proud.

TARAS BALDERDASH

When I came to *Second Life* I didn't know I was on a spirit quest. I also didn't know I was a charity monk. But after a week of looking around at the miasma of casinos and clubs interspersed with homes, gardens, and wonders, I did know that *SL* was the next "big thing." OK, perhaps not *SL* itself, but the 3D metaverse of which *SL* is the best current implementation.

My avatar evolved quickly: first black clothing, then a beard, then something close to clerical robes using the built-in appearance editor. The result was a Russian monk avatar. But after another week the monk changed again, this time becoming the Taras of today: short, bald, tubby, 850-year-old Mongolian monk (sometimes shape-shifting into a shaman or dragon). In a world of 20-something hard-body avatars looking for a date, it was natural for me to want to stand out by being an ancient and celibate curiosity. I took up residence at the Elven Maiden Mausoleum, a place I still visit daily.

I began to evolve a new *SL*-only culture. This culture is the Avatarian Way, and the organization formed to pursue it is the Avatars of Change (AOC). I rewrote the ancient Chinese Yi Jing (I Ching) oracle, creating a version for *SL*. This "Oracle of *SL*" contains many instructions specific to our world, like "Fly out, teleport back" or "change your head." The texts are stored in an Oracle Orb, which hands them out in exchange for charitable donations.

It was in these early days that I met Kami Akula. She became a major AOC patroness, providing us land for our monastery. The AOC has group land now, but we will always be grateful to Kami.

Today the AOC has 70 members, more than 10K meters of land, and is sending contributions to Support for Healing in *SL* and Modest Needs (http://www.modestneeds.org) in real life. We have eight sacred spaces and more than 20 Oracle Orbs around *SL*. I have started to instruct members in the Avatarian Way,

CHAPTER 9

INTRO

PART I

PART II

PART III

APPENDICES

WHO ARE YOU?

given them the Avatarian Script to write in, and placed the first Orthodox Christian object in *SL*, St. Nicholas Antiochian Orthodox Church. We are preparing the first "well-field community" in *SL*, and adding two more Oracles of *SL*: the Yellow King's Garden Oracle and the ancient Chinese Forest of Changes Oracle.

More info at my blog: http://tarasbalderdash.blogspot.com/.

ANGEL FLUFFY

I do many different things in *Second Life*, using it for business, education, social interaction, exploration, and of course relaxation. To me, *SL* is a sort of shared dream free of annoying restrictions like the laws of physics. The dream is the sum of our choices and thus is empowering to participate in. I believe dreams tend toward goodness in the long term, because negativity is ultimately self-destructive, and when it ceases to be useful it becomes ugly. My dream is to understand the beautiful dreams around me...to make real the ones that only exist as ideas, and to improve upon the ones that already exist.

To make dreams into reality, I seek out other people who have good ideas, and I work with them to bring those ideas into (virtual) reality. I bring them into reality as a business, for fun, for a challenge, and simply for the joy of helping others. I improve upon existing dreams by first understanding them, then considering how they could better meet their purpose. I sometimes wonder what the purpose of the entire dream of *SL* is, and how I can improve that, too.

Each person creates their own purpose, both in *SL* and in real life. I think this is a large part of *SL*'s appeal—the ability to define your purpose free of real-life constraints. I firmly believe that no person is born with an intrinsic purpose—but that each person can make and then choose their own purpose in life. After all, if a purpose exists for you, yet it exists independently of you and not due to any of your choices, then how is it your purpose? Surely it would just be someone else's purpose which they have assigned to you? I believe that each person must one day accept the challenge of creating a purpose in life for themselves, and that some purposes are

better than others. Specifically, purposes which help other people and improve the world are better than purposes which don't. Each of us is challenged by life to choose to be on the side of the angels, to be for the glory, and then to find a way to make the good things from our dreams into reality.

That is why I am in *Second Life,* and what my lifestyle here is based on: making dreams into reality and making reality better.

IRIS OPHELIA

One of the biggest problems with the Internet since day one has been a lack of expression. Emoticons help, but there's always an uncrossable line where expressions, tones, and body language lie. *Second Life* has the means to break through it and, at the same time, remains just as far as any instant messaging service.

Most of us don't think about *SL* like a chat room. *Second Life* has become more than just a machine to support sellers and buyers. Subcultures and even castes from the real world, and also completely unique to this virtual world, have formed, building spaces and communities of their own within it. We have more than just businesses supported by these communities; we have magazines, newspapers, and mercenary-style blogs and websites, and even sets of unique celebrities. There is official government and policing, as well as militaristic and militia groups. There are preachers and criminals, weddings and divorces, dogs and cats. *Second Life* is a microcosm of reality. It's not the Internet, it's not a freeware game; sit down and think about it. It's something completely different. All this and, as it's still small in comparison, everyone is given much more power and much more potential to do good or bad than they are in the real world.

A lot of this goes without saying, so why would flighty little Iris waste her space on it? *Second Life* isn't just an IM program with bigger user pictures and emoticons. We have gestures, which move our whole avatar, play sounds, send messages, all depending on how they're set. The problem is that this whole world has been created, with so much to see and do and experience, and yet there's so little genuine emotion. The crying gesture is used as a joke 90% of the time. If you were really crying, how

9

INTRO

PART I

PART II

PART III

APPENDICES

WHO ARE YOU?

could you convey it in *Second Life*? The bigger problem that comes from this is that you can hurt someone and never even know it…or hurt someone and never feel the guilt you deserve.

How I earn my second living, how I craft my second look—those aren't the most important parts of how I live my second life. The most important aspect of how I interact in this virtual world is in emotions. There's a heart beating behind every avatar, including yours. We're not that far from the real world here, and we all have to make a choice to respect that—or ignore it. Here, there are fewer repercussions for a bad attitude. I choose to live my second life positively, helpfully, and passionately, and I hope you do too.

CHAPTER 9

CHERI HORTON

Cheri Horton might look like somewhat of a character—and perhaps an intimidating one, at that. I mean, she does have a pair of devil's horns, which, by the way, quickly became a permanent part of her appearance soon after she first began inhabiting the virtual world back in September 2005.

But the truth is, she is my genuine digital incarnation—a personal carbon copy who's made of pixels, yet exists as levelheadedly, organically, and sincerely in 3D simulated space as my physical-world self exists in meatspace. The traits that seep effortlessly through the permeable boundary from physical to virtual space include everything from philosophical principles to sexual predisposition. Only difference is, I am biologically male. But because I am transgender and identify partly as female in the physical world, it's really no big leap interacting in a 3D digital environment as the opposite sex. In fact, it's a pretty comfortable fit, just like the devil's horns.

The horns are highly symbolic. They represent individualism and independence, as well as defiance toward didactic and repressive values and restrictive, narrow-minded social mores.

And let's face it—they just look sexy as hell, not to mention the fact that they befit my interests, which I give voice to in *Second Life*, albeit only under controlled and consensual circumstances, just like offline. But I'll spare the juicy details of my physical-world deeds for perhaps another book, and instead stick to the grid, where I own a rather large castle that houses the Dashwood Dungeon, the place where I take on clients as a dominatrix.

True, I get paid to dominate my in-world customers, but money is far from the sole incentive. My *SL* gig as a dominatrix—and just interacting in *Second Life* in general— also provides a good vantage point to observe and write about simulated sex, gender, and adult avatar relationships, which I cover for my web site, `http://apogeevr.com`. Because in a virtual space like *Second Life*, as it turns out, one is oftentimes granted a more candid glimpse of true human nature.

But hey, don't let the horns and the penchant for BDSM give you the wrong impression. Cheri is no rogue, raging beast. And neither am I. Quite the contrary: outside the realm of these consensual activities, Cheri is composed, well-spoken, thoughtful, and polite, just like yours truly.

FORSETI SVAROG

I am Forseti Svarog, aka Giff Constable, VP of Business Development, The Electric Sheep Company. I discovered *Second Life* in late 2004 through a Linden Lab press release. I was hooked just by reading: User-generated world? Open IP rights? Virtual economy? Creating entrepreneurs out of creative talent? Oh, man! I created the avatar name Forseti Svarog on a whim, and realized too late that once you've built a reputation under one name, you can't really change. For a long time, Forseti was nonhuman because I did not like the way male human avatars looked, plus I enjoyed making avatars from scratch. At some point, my friend Launa [Fauna] gave me a skin to try, and Torrid [Midnight] made some hair I liked, and Forseti evolved into a human.

For a long time, *Second Life* was primarily a creative outlet for me. I am a painter, and prims and textures became an amazing new canvas. I have not actually picked up a brush since discovering *SL*. I also enjoyed the entrepreneurial spirit within *SL*. I

CHAPTER 9

INTRO

PART I

PART II

PART III

APPENDICES

WHO ARE YOU?

have been an entrepreneur several times in my career but at the time I was advising other technology entrepreneurs on how to sell or IPO their companies. *SL* became a fun hobby which kept my entrepreneurial flame flickering even in an amusingly non-serious way.

I have always been an art-history buff, but *SL* awoke a love of architecture and kicked off an incredibly fun learning curve. I started walking around New York City translating everything I saw into prims and textures. I decided I wanted to become a really good builder and realized the importance of great texturing. I devoured *Photoshop CS2 Bible: Professional Edition*. I examined how other builders I respected, like Barnesworth Anubis, Cory Edo, Aimee Weber, and Neil Protagonist, were solving problems.

In late 2005, I decided to start a company around *SL* and figured I would start on the creative side, build up a reputation, then shift into the business gears. Right around the same time, I met the Electric Sheep team and realized that it was silly to create my own when I could work with such smart, talented, and fun people.

My fascination with *SL* originated around ideas and concepts. I never expected the many relationships I have formed within the community over the years. The friends I have made from all walks of life—you know who you are—have turned out to be the most wonderful surprise of *Second Life*.

CHAPTER 10

MAKING MONEY

In recent years, virtual riches that translate into real-life wealth have become a very hot topic. There are more and more articles and stories about people earning a comfortable real-life income through their activities in virtual worlds. The vast majority of people who sign up for *Second Life* expect to make some money, and many freshly born residents hope to make a *lot* of money. After all, quite a few have succeeded, and their example continues to excite and motivate many thousands of would-be online millionaires.

So, can you get rich in *Second Life*? This chapter gives you a very detailed answer to that question. Briefly, the answer is yes you can—but only if you make the required effort. Getting rich in *Second Life* requires roughly as much effort, skill, and luck as getting rich in real life. Surprise, surprise! However, it *is* possible, and this chapter should increase your chances.

CONTENTS

MONEY: THE COLD, HARD FACTS

INTRO

PART I

PART II

PART III

APPENDICES

MONEY: THE COLD, HARD FACTS

There's one fact you have to keep in mind at all times: there are 250–320 Linden dollars to one good old US dollar. That means it costs hundreds of L$ to buy bubble gum in the real world—chew on that. The exchange rate fluctuates, but 90% of the time it has stayed within the limits quoted. It may surge or drop suddenly following an *SL* update that introduces a new money source/money sink such as a new stipend, or higher fees for sound and texture uploads. However, even then it is unlikely to break out of the 220–350 range in the foreseeable future.

The awful truth is that if you want to make meaningful money in *Second Life*—money that will actually make a difference in your real life—you must be prepared to put in quite a lot of time and effort. Simply getting an *SL* job isn't likely to make you a lot of dough; most likely, you'll have to be a little more skilled and/or inventive, and start a profitable virtual business of your own (Figure 10.1). *SL* job and business choices are discussed later in this chapter.

Figure 10.1: Owning a virtual business can give you plenty of real-life thrills.

ADDITIONAL INFO:
GETTING PAID

Many SL old-timers, when asked how they get L$, tend to shrug and state they simply buy 10 bucks' worth of Linden dollars from time to time. This is probably the best thing to do if you treat *Second Life* primarily as an opportunity to socialize and have adventures of all kinds and colors (see "Money Realities" sidebar).

SIDEBAR

RESIDENTS SPEAK:
MONEY REALITIES

"It is possible to make money in SL, but it's like living in a poor country where the exchange rate to the dollar is terrible. The most I can make in a day is about L$1,000, or approx. US$3. I'd rather do a day's work in real life and get paid £150. I think if you really put your heart into it, you probably could make about $100 a week from it, but it's going to take time, and a lot of hard work.

"You should view the game as a place for fun, or a profitable hobby. Don't think you're going to make your millions here, because that's very unlikely."

—stove Lu

"When you are first getting started, you are really better off just buying Lindens with a credit card or PayPal. Seriously. Work in SL pays less per hour of effort than any minimum-wage job in RL."

—Ceera Murakami

CHAPTER 10

TWO WAYS TO PROFIT

Fortunately, you can enrich yourself in more than one way in *Second Life*. You can make money in *Second Life*, and you can make more real-life money through or

CHAPTER 10

INTRO

PART I

PART II

PART III

APPENDICES

TWO WAYS TO PROFIT

thanks to *Second Life*. One often leads to the other. Making money in *SL* means you're earning money directly and solely through activity in the *SL* world: an *SL* job or running an *SL* business. Making money through *SL* means you apply knowledge and/or skills gained or perfected in the virtual world to real-life situations. In addition, you'll also encounter real-world companies making money on/in the virtual world, and *Second Life* business ventures making money in the real world.

Most *SL* members tend to think solely of making money *in Second Life*—after all, it's much more fun that way. However, *SL* magnates tend to make money on their *SL* activities both inside *Second Life* and in real life, and most professionals use their real-life skills in *SL*.

One *SL* resident who symbolizes success on the virtual path to riches is Anshe Chung, *Second Life*'s wealthiest denizen and owner of a virtual real-estate empire with an estimated worth of US$250,000 at the time of writing—that's right, a quarter million real American dollars (according to a May 2006 *Business Week* article). Anshe Chung's annual income is rumored to be in the low six figures. However, it is driven by both real estate sales/rentals and a money-exchange system that converts euros and US dollars into Linden dollars, and vice versa. The commissions charged on this real-world service mean that Anshe Chung makes money both inside and through *Second Life*.

Another notable symbol is the *SL* resident Kermitt Quirk. His Tringo game stands as an example of how *Second Life* can translate into real-life financial success. Having created Tringo as a game to be played inside *Second Life* only, Quirk went on to sell the game to a real-world game company, which developed it for the Nintendo Game Boy Advance—this on top of selling many copies inside the *SL* world at L$15,000 a pop.

> NOTE
>
> ADDITIONAL INFO:
> ## GAMING IN SL
>
> *Games of all sorts are a big feature of the SL landscape. You get a taste on Help Island—its take on Space Invaders is a real blast. Once you're on the mainland, you'll have plenty of gaming choices (Figure 10.2). For more on gaming, see Chapter 3.*

These two examples underscore what many new *SL* residents forget about: *Second Life*'s virtual world is part of the real world. You do not have to be another Kermitt Quirk to profit from that connection. For example, if your poor sales or salary-negotiation skills are preventing you from making more money in your real-life job,

SL can serve as your training arena. Or if you're having trouble breaking into an arts-related profession in real life—if your ambition is to be writer (an iffy choice, let me tell you), but real life isn't giving you a break because you have no experience, a job with one of the *SL* papers could be the first step to a literary career (see the "Help Wanted: Journalism" sidebar).

Figure 10.2: *Second Life is a gamer's heaven.*

SIDEBAR

RESIDENTS SPEAK:
HELP WANTED: JOURNALISM

Hello everyone,

I am the publisher for *SL Business* and we are currently looking for staff writers, columnists, and freelance writers. You can reach me in-world, of course, and also by email: highlyfocused@gmail.com.

Here is a list of opportunities that are available:

- **Staff writer:** The staff writer works closely with the editorial team in the coverage of the monthly editorial outline. You will be given subjects from the outline to research and draft content for submission to the editors. This is a salaried position and requires regular attendance in SL. Salary is discussed in-world.

- **Columnist:** The columnist covers one particular area and is usually a subject-matter expert. A columnist's submissions

CHAPTER 10

INTRO

PART I

PART II

PART III

APPENDICES

will appear in the monthly magazine and possibly in the weekly supplements. Columnists are paid per column at a rate of L$1,500/US$5.

 Freelance writer: The freelance writer picks up work that the editorial team may not be able to get to or lightens the load per se. Freelance writers that seek work from the magazine will receive subjects from the editorial team to research and draft for submission. Freelance writers are paid per article at a rate of L$1,500/US$5.

I'm looking forward to your response and if interested I'm looking forward to introducing you to the SL Business team. Thanks!

Hunter Glass
Publisher
SL Business Magazine

SL can also be very helpful in unearthing a hidden talent. If your everyday life doesn't give you the chance to develop your creativity, *Second Life* can be a very rewarding change of scenery. Chances are, sooner or later you'll be able to make a few hundred Linden dollars doing something you enjoy. Enjoyment is key to choosing the right money-making activity!

NOTE

ADDITIONAL INFO:
MAKING REAL-LIFE MONEY IN SECOND LIFE

The Electric Sheep Company is a good example of a real-world corporation that makes money from Second Life. Its services focus on providing advice and solutions to real-world companies interested in building real business in a virtual world.

MONEYMAKING VENTURES

Money really does grow on trees. *Second Life's* virtual world features "money trees." Money trees grow fruit that can be picked for money, and they can be hit for up to L$20 at a time; they're basically L$-distribution machines meant to help new *SL* residents. They can be loaded up with money through donations from the general public, as well as interested parties such as the owner of a store next to the tree. Money trees are meant to draw people to a certain spot

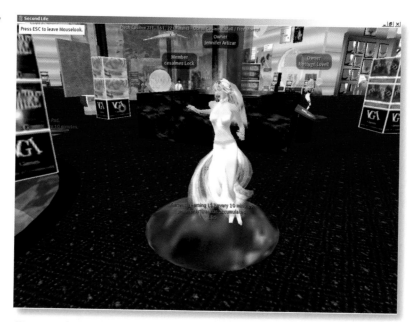

Figure 10.3: There really isn't such a thing as free money—not even in a virtual world.

(usually a commercial enterprise), and they succeed only too well: most often, they're tapped out. Unfortunately, this is partly due to *SL* resident abuse. If you've really set your heart on picking a fruit for L$10 or thereabouts, you may have to wait for quite a while.

NOTE

ADDITIONAL INFO:
FREE MONEY

"Free money" is a heavily advertised commodity in the virtual world. However, obtaining "free money" often requires as much or more effort than simply earning it (Figure 10.3).

You may also receive "free" money in the form of a stipend. There have been many changes to the stipend system. At one time, a stipend called "dwell" was paid

out to residents with the highest popularity ratings, with popularity being determined by the amount of traffic to a resident-owned destination (such as a store, or even a private home). At another, both Premium and Basic account holders received a weekly stipend. At the time of writing, only Premium account holders receive a stipend, and since Premium accounts cost money, the Linden dollars you receive aren't exactly free. Whatever new changes come to the stipend system, it seems more than likely that *some* sort of stipend will always be a feature.

It's highly unlikely all your *SL* needs will always be covered by your "free" money. Appetite grows while eating, and sooner or later you're bound to hanker for a top-shelf item whose price runs into the many thousands of Linden dollars. Patiently saving up stipend payments is a pain, and you might have to buy a few real-world dollars' worth of Linden dollars.

However, if you're not willing to stoop to that level, or if you actually *want* to make money in-world because it's fun, you have plenty of possibilities to choose from. At the time of writing, there aren't as many professions as in the real world—*Second Life* does not need the services of dentists or plumbers, for instance (however, there is at least one practicing psychologist). Don't worry—there are more than enough job types to choose from! The following sections cover *Second Life* employment and money-making opportunities, with comments on their earning power (at the time of writing).

ADDITIONAL INFO:
THE TAX MAN

Keep in mind that you may be required to report your virtual-world income to real-world tax authorities. The exact rules may differ depending on your place of residence in the real world; make sure you know what they are.

As you know by now, the money you make in *Second Life* is rarely worth much in real-world terms. However, it may be still worth your while because inside *Second Life*, the Linden dollar enjoys purchasing power that puts the US dollar to shame.

Generally speaking, things are cheap in *Second Life*. It is a world in which—right off the bat—you get stuff such as free houses and vehicles, to say nothing about all the clothes and various other items. On top of that, you can acquire tons of cool stuff for free, or at the symbolic price of L$1. And the "expensive" stuff simply isn't very expensive: at the time of writing, a state-of-the-art *SL* weapon firing "smart" projectiles costs less than L$3,000, or US$10. A few US dollars won't buy you much in real

life; but in *Second Life*, the same money buys you a whole lot of fun (Figure 10.4).

What's more, there is special magic in making money inside a virtual world. Earning the equivalent of a single real-life dollar feels more satisfying than making 50 dollars in real life. No matter how much effort you invest up front, money made in *Second Life* always feels free, and thus counts more. This special trait of virtual earnings is one of the most important

Figure 10.4: A lot of the time, Second Life *fun is either free or inexpensive.*

reasons why almost everyone is willing to invest an hour to make the equivalent of US$1, including many people who would recoil in horror upon being asked to work for US$20 per hour in real life. It's not hard to imagine numerous real-world companies holding intense meetings, even as you read this, to determine how to profit from that phenomenon....

The bottom line is this: making money in a virtual world is much more fun than in the real world. To keep it that way, don't focus on making money in itself, but on doing something you like that just happens to be profitable.

RESIDENTS SPEAK:
THE JOY OF MAKING MONEY

"If you enjoy doing something, the money eventually follows."

—Kate Proudhon

"One of the best ways to make money is to sell stuff, of course. Find what you are good at and what you have a passion for and build it.

> ← *With time and practice, residents will begin to show an interest and offer to buy whatever you have made. That's how I was eventually able to afford land, by designing and selling aircraft."*
>
> —Dustin Pomeray
>
> *"For most people, earning money is probably easier in the real world, so do enjoy* Second Life, *first and foremost. It is not a money-making tool; it is a game, a virtual community, a creative environment, and so much more."*
>
> —Elgyfu Wishbringer

In addition to the fun factor, the other big consideration in your choice of money-making activity is your money-making goal. Decide up front how much you need or want:

- Enough money to buy the *SL* items you want, and engage in activities you want. This sets your Linden-dollar needs in the low thousands per month. You can make enough to cover needs like that even by taking relatively low-paid, unskilled *SL* jobs.

- Enough money to cover the above, plus the real-life costs of a Premium membership, and possibly also low land-maintenance fees: To make that much money, you'll have to show some skill at an *SL* job, or run a modestly successful business of your own.

- Enough money to cover all *SL*-related costs, including low land-maintenance fees, plus put a meaningful amount of real-world currency in your pocket: Unless you're a genius scoring big with a brilliant business idea, a money goal like that means a commitment equivalent to a part-time job in real life. You have to be highly skilled, and/or run a successful, highly profitable business (Figure 10.5).

- Enough money to live on in the real world, nevermind *SL*-related costs: Face it—if that's your goal, you're looking at the time commitment of a regular full-time job. Not only that, but you have to be a razor-sharp businessperson willing to make a big up-front investment of time and money. Top *SL* animators can also make this income bracket.

In short, the only people likely to have the motivation to turn *Second Life* into a source of regular income are those who could easily make that much or more money in real life—but prefer to do it in *Second Life* because it's more exciting and fun. According to believable rumors, at the time of writing, the number of people living on income from *Second Life* is in the low three figures, and the number of people earning a meaningful real-life

Figure 10.5: *It isn't easy to make it big in* **Second Life**.

income in the low four figures. This isn't much in the scope of a quarter million active *SL* residents.

ADDITIONAL INFO:
LIFE IMITATES SECOND LIFE

You may find a real-world job in or through Second Life. *It does not have to be in network marketing or something similar, either. For example, a business or a social services organization may be looking for contractual employees for an online program that's being run in* Second Life*'s virtual world.*

Remember, the name of the game is fun. If making a financial killing in a virtual world turns you on, don't let anything stop you. Because if something can, it will—that's always how it goes with truly ambitious goals.

Now let's take a more detailed look at how you can earn money in *SL*.

INTRO
CHAPTER 1
CHAPTER 2
CHAPTER 3
CHAPTER 4
CHAPTER 5
CHAPTER 6
CHAPTER 7
CHAPTER 8
CHAPTER 9
CHAPTER 10
CHAPTER 11
CHAPTER 12
CHAPTER 13
APPENDICES

10

INTRO

PART I

PART II

PART III

APPENDICES

MONEYMAKING VENTURES

JOBS

The *Second Life* Knowledge Base contains a job guide at `http://secondlife.com/knowledgebase/article.php?id=077`. It is full of information but isn't comprehensive at the time of writing.

The Knowledge Base's job guide classifies jobs as skilled or unskilled according to whether they require real-life skills. However, special virtual-world skills do exist: you'll find many *Second Life* skills are mandatory for certain jobs. Note that *SL* skills often assume a different *form* than real-life skills do: for example, being a good dancer involves having good dance animations and has little to do with your dancing abilities in real life. A *Second Life* skill may simply be a script that gives its owner a certain ability.

NOTE

ADDITIONAL INFO:

SPEND MONEY TO MAKE MONEY

Many SL jobs require you to own certain items; others require an avatar with both outstanding looks and moves. Acquiring these could require a big investment. For example, to become a professional model, you'll need a great custom shape, skin, hair, and fairly expensive custom animations.

We'll now cover the most popular jobs in *Second Life*. Keep in mind that there are others, and that new job categories appear all the time. However, the professions listed here account for more than 90% of *SL* jobs.

CAMPING

"Camping" is *SL* slang for a job that does not require anything more than your presence. It often consists of sitting in a chair in exchange for L$10–20 per hour, with money being paid out every 5–15 minutes. These very, um, virtual jobs were highly popular when dwell stipends were paid out, and it made a lot of sense to pay people to stick around. In spite of the death of the dwell stipend, camping jobs still appear because there's a real-life rule that applies in *Second Life*: people draw people. *Second Life* is not a densely populated world. When you look at the world map while you're in the world, you'll see that green "people" icons tend to form

clusters. Therefore, it still makes sense for many business owners—especially retailers—to hire avatars to hang around for the equivalent of a few real-life cents per hour (Figure 10.6).

Figure 10.6: "Camping" acquires a new meaning in Second Life.

GREETER

A greeter job is an upscale camping job. In addition to simply being there, you're required to speak (type) a simple greeting from time to time, possibly perform a simple gesture such as a bow. As you would expect, you won't make a fortune even when your avatar looks really sharp. At the time of writing, the standard salary is L$50–100 per hour; you may also get tips. Naturally, this requires an avatar of above-average appearance, social skills, and charm. You may work as a temp—a couple of hours at a specific event—or you can work the *SL* version of full time, which tends to hover around 10 hours a week. Don't expect to earn more than a few thousand Linden dollars a month—10 or 12 real-life bucks. To make a couple of thousand more, you'll have to develop outstanding social skills and invest in your avatar's appearance.

However, being a greeter can be lots of fun if you simply like meeting lots of new people and watching action happen. It certainly gives you the opportunity to make new friends and can be the right choice if socializing is what you want most out of *Second Life*. The temp or one-off greeter jobs can be handy if you have a Basic membership. They'll let you pay rent on a little *SL* space of your own to store your prims. They also let you have a little pocket money for all those L$1 bargains that abound in the virtual world.

INTRO
CHAPTER 1
CHAPTER 2
CHAPTER 3
CHAPTER 4
CHAPTER 5
CHAPTER 6
CHAPTER 7
CHAPTER 8
CHAPTER 9
CHAPTER 10
CHAPTER 11
CHAPTER 12
CHAPTER 13
APPENDICES

ADDITIONAL INFO:
SOCIAL NETWORKING

Jobs that involve plenty of socializing and meeting new people, such as greeter or event host, can be very helpful if you're trying to get your newly formed business off the ground. You're likely to gain many customers from among SL residents you meet through your job. Just don't be too pushy! Some extra info in your profile and a custom calling card work just fine to draw attention to your other money-making activity.

SECURITY

Security jobs range from being a simple bouncer to an armed bodyguard; as you might expect, there are many more of the former than the latter. The simplest security jobs pay as little as L$50 per hour and usually do not require you to have any special equipment or to engage in any sort of combat. Bodyguard or special armed guard jobs are negotiable, but don't expect to get more than the high three figures. Very few security guards earn more than L$150 per hour.

Do *not* view a job in security as an open-ended opportunity to shoot people. As explained in Chapter 2, this makes you as much of a miscreant as any offenders you're dealing with. If shooting people is what you crave, go to a combat sim. That being said, the job does give you some virtual authority and can be great fun if you enjoy watching what people are up to in their second lives. These are basically the only reasons to take a security job; the pay is poor, and you don't get the same opportunities to socialize as a greeter does.

Most security-guard jobs require a steady time commitment of a few hours a week. There are not very many of them around, because a security guard is mostly for show; automated security systems do the job much better, and there are models available free of charge.

SHOP ATTENDANT/SALES REP

Most items you can buy in *Second Life* are sold directly by their owners—via ads in-world and in *SL* publications, through automated vendors, or in stores. Most stores

employ automated sales, but at the time of writing there's a new trend toward sales staffing. There are two kinds of jobs within that category. Being a shop attendant requires your physical presence in the shop and usually pays a low (two-figure) hourly wage, plus a small commission on sales made. Being a sales rep doesn't require scheduled presence inside a shop—it's roughly the *SL* equivalent of real-life traveling sales reps. At the time of writing,

Figure 10.7: Developing a social network is crucial to business success in Second Life.

neither job offers an opportunity for big income. However, this particular job sector is set to grow along with *Second Life*.

ADDITIONAL INFO:

JACK OF ALL TRADES

If you're a new SL citizen without a defined skill that would let you choose one of the SL professions without hesitation, consider trying out various jobs or working at two or more jobs in different professions at the same time. This makes it easier to find your true SL calling and also lets you develop a bigger social network—possibly the number-one prerequisite for success in money-making activities (Figure 10.7).

EVENT HOST/DJ

Event hosts organize and manage social events inside the virtual world: games, parties, fashion shows, etc. Of all the *SL* jobs discussed till now, this is the first that

INTRO
CHAPTER 1
CHAPTER 2
CHAPTER 3
CHAPTER 4
CHAPTER 5
CHAPTER 6
CHAPTER 7
CHAPTER 8
CHAPTER 9
CHAPTER 10
CHAPTER 11
CHAPTER 12
CHAPTER 13
APPENDICES

has true career potential. To begin with, event hosts make decent money, and there's a big market for their services: business owners stage many events to attract new customers. Although the hourly rate isn't great, tip income is higher than a greeter's. In addition, event hosts often receive a cut of event profits. However, be warned that the job's money-making potential greatly depends on your skills and experience. Obviously, a good Tringo host who makes the game more fun attracts more players, and an experienced, well-known event host boosts event attendance simply by being there. However, being there is the catch. Attaining an income of L$10,000 a month or better is likely to require a serious time commitment.

> **NOTE**
>
> **ADDITIONAL INFO:**
> ## HOSTING AS A STEPPING STONE
>
> *An event-hosting job is the ideal first step if you want to open an entertainment business of your own. Once you're an experienced event host, all you need is a copy of the game of your choice, and a space to hold game events. Game fans are likely to follow the host they like, so you'll have an audience right away. You may also rent both the game and the space, or possibly even negotiate a lease in exchange for a cut of the profits.*

In return, you get a great opportunity to socialize in the virtual world. Event hosting makes it easy for you to build a large social network, which can pay off big time—your virtual friends are likely to show up at events you host and give you good tips. *SL* event hosts who also run businesses of their own are likely to profit even more: some of the people they meet at events become their customers.

Figure 10.8: Get basic event-host training by attending the kind of events you'd like to host.

A successful event host must have strong social skills. A sense of humor, good writing skill, and the ability to type fast are essential. Attractive avatar appearance is another must—the more attractive, the better. Acquiring custom skin and clothing is a priority, and custom animations and gestures are very desirable too. Naturally, if you host specialized events such as games, you have to know how the games work (Figure 10.8).

A DJ is basically a highly specialized event host. You have to understand how audio streaming in MP3 format works—if you don't, consult the *SL* Knowledge Base at `http://secondlife.com/knowledgebase/article.php?id=083`. Naturally, you also have to have real-world DJ skills: you have to sense what your audience would like to hear next and react accordingly. Disc jockeys are both well-paid and in high demand. If you're good, you can expect to earn several thousand Linden dollars for a single session (two to four hours). This includes the hourly wage paid by the club/casino/establishment that hired you, plus tips from guests. Talented disc jockeys might well make the DJ job their *SL* career of choice: the high hourly earnings mean that working just a few hours a week can bring in a comfortable *SL* income (see the "Working as a Musician" sidebar).

NOTE

ADDITIONAL INFO:
WORKING AS A MUSICIAN

The Second Life Wiki's Guide to SL Jobs lists being a live musician as a viable job. It definitely is technically viable—basically, you're a DJ playing your own music, except that you need an instrument (an item attached to your avatar), plus a few custom animations. However, do not expect to make a living at this; at the time of writing, the chances of making it big as a musician in SL are roughly the same as in real life.

Event hosting and DJing are professions, not just jobs for unskilled workers. As you'll see, this also applies to many jobs listed as "unskilled" by the *SL* Guide to Jobs. Happily, it isn't hard to find entry-level positions that will let you gain experience (see the "Help Wanted: Various Fields" sidebar).

INTRO
CHAPTER 1
CHAPTER 2
CHAPTER 3
CHAPTER 4
CHAPTER 5
CHAPTER 6
CHAPTER 7
CHAPTER 8
CHAPTER 9
CHAPTER 10
CHAPTER 11
CHAPTER 12
CHAPTER 13
APPENDICES

CHAPTER 10

INTRO

PART I

PART II

PART III

APPENDICES

MONEYMAKING VENTURES

ADDITIONAL INFO:
HELP WANTED: VARIOUS FIELDS

JOB FAIR FOR ENTRY-LEVEL AND EXPERIENCED POSITIONS THIS SUNDAY

Expansion and growth! Two Island Sims of virtual entertainment need more Part Time staff. Job Fair is in the front courtyard of the Black Dragon Pub on VooDooLive Island. Managers will be on hand to interview and hire on the spot.

THESE JOBS DO NOT REQUIRE ANY PRIOR EXPERIENCE—TRAINING PROVIDED:

- *Dancer/Model—L$30 an hour to dance plus tips/FREE Designer clothes to participate in monthly designer showcase. Free Photoshopped portfolio and profile pictures.*

- *Event Host—Day and late-evening positions available—L$50 an hour plus tips*

- *Slingo/Bingo Host—After midnight SL time—L$50 a hour plus tips*

- *DJ (Drum N Bass, Hip Hop, Rave, Rock, Salsa, Top 40, '80s)— We give you the software and training you need to get started. 4 practice rooms available at all times. 4 radio streams available.*

SOME EXPERIENCE NEEDED FOR THESE POSITIONS:

- *Venue Manager & Assistant Manager—Six hours a week on-site. Knowledge of event posting and land tools a must.*

- *Magazine Associate Editor (Must have Photoshop)*

- *Writer for Magazine—L$500 per 400 word article*

- *Web Master—We have the domains and servers. We need simple websites developed and maintained to support our banner ad sales—flexibility and great income.*

← *If you can't make it to the Job Fair, please send an e-mail to* `voodooisland@gmail.com`.

DANCER/STRIPPER

The virtual world of *Second Life* features clubs and casinos galore (Figure 10.9). Practically all of them employ dancers to attract as many *SL* residents as possible. Most dancing jobs have set hours, but one-off gigs are a possibility and tend to pay more than regular jobs on a time-expended basis. The pay varies widely and depends on a dancer's skill and appearance. As you would expect, a successful dancer looks great (meaning

Figure 10.9: There's no shortage of clubs in Second Life.

an investment in avatar appearance) and moves great (meaning an investment in custom animations).

In addition to an hourly wage, dancers receive tips. Truly good dancers derive most of their income from tips, even allowing for the 20% cut that usually goes to the event holder/club or casino owner. Top dancers can make good money, with hourly earnings in the high three figures.

In *Second Life*, the line between dancers and strippers is thin: many *SL* residents do both. If that's what you'd like, you should invest in suitable animations. Strippers make even more money than dancers do, and it's an investment that quickly pays for itself.

INTRO
CHAPTER 1
CHAPTER 2
CHAPTER 3
CHAPTER 4
CHAPTER 5
CHAPTER 6
CHAPTER 7
CHAPTER 8
CHAPTER 9
CHAPTER 10
CHAPTER 11
CHAPTER 12
CHAPTER 13
APPENDICES

231

Given all the job flavors, it's not surprising that monthly earnings can vary widely. A beginner needs to try hard to make two or three thousand L$ per month, while a top dancer/good stripper will make that much in the course of a single working session (two to three hours). To stay at the top, you'll have to repeatedly invest in updating your avatar's appearance, and in new animations. It's the ideal job for anyone who yearns to be admired and likes to see practical proof of that admiration.

MODEL/PHOTOMODEL

This is another job that should appeal to anyone with an admiration deficit in real life. Modeling jobs are relatively scarce, however. If you want to embark on a modeling career, it might be wise to start out as a dancer and continue making money dancing while you invest in all the prerequisites to become a successful model. These involve great shape, skin, and animations (including special poses and catwalk animations). What's more, you'll need to work on your avatar's appearance constantly; modeling is a very competitive field. If you're interested in finding out more and possibly getting a lead on your first job, visit one of the modeling agencies that operate inside the virtual world (use the Search function).

There are two types of modeling jobs available: modeling in virtual flesh during fashion shows, and working as a photomodel. Pay varies wildly. Beginners make peanuts, but that's usually offset by free appearance enhancers (clothes, animations, attachments). Top models in either category are skilled professionals who may make thousands of L$ per hour and win prizes in competitions (see the "Help Wanted: Modeling" sidebar). Monthly earnings can reach five figures in Linden dollars.

SIDEBAR

RESIDENTS SPEAK:
HELP WANTED: MODELING

PHOTOMODELS WANTED

I am fixing to open up a studio of photos that I do. I want to post samples of work I do in the studio, so basically your picture would be put up on a wall with other pictures. I will pay you L$800 for your time. Should be like only 10 mins for me to find a pose for you and take the picture. You will get a free picture out of this.

If you are interested in doing this, send me a notecard in-game with your picture.

I'm only looking for about 6 people to do this, both males and females. I take all kind of avs. Look at my profile in game to find examples of my work. Thank you for your time.

—Sky Veloce

ALLURE TOP MODEL COMPETITION—ENTRIES DUE NLT SUNDAY AT MIDNIGHT

First Prize L$25K

Please join us in this exciting competition which will determine the Allure Top Model.

Allure Modeling Group is pleased to announce this competition to recognize the hard work and effort so many in SL put into professional modeling.

It is simple to enter—send three photos to Bruno Buckenburger. One should be a head shot. The other two are completely up to you.

On August 21, Allure will select the top 20 candidates.

Those 20 will have the opportunity to practice runway modeling, receive a free portfolio from Allure, and will be judged by some of the most recognized and admired industry professionals:

- *Bruno Buckenburger—President, BBVision & AllureNET Media*
- *Jenn McTeague—Allure Modeling Group Vice-President*
- *Janie Marlow—Clothing Designer, Mischief*
- *Alyssa Bijoux—Jewelry/Accessory Designer*
- *Sophie Stravinsky—Photographer, Sophiesticated Photography*

From this group of 20, five finalists will be selected to return and compete for the top prize and the honor of being named the Allure Top Model.

* * * * *PLEASE pick up a notecard with complete rules at the Allure Model Group office on the fifth floor of The Offices at Bareum Beach Towers: Bareum (150,99,67) or at Socle—The Allure Model Showcase Center: Bareum (211,9,45). Good luck!

INTRO
CHAPTER 1
CHAPTER 2
CHAPTER 3
CHAPTER 4
CHAPTER 5
CHAPTER 6
CHAPTER 7
CHAPTER 8
CHAPTER 9
CHAPTER 10
CHAPTER 11
CHAPTER 12
CHAPTER 13
APPENDICES

ESCORT

As discussed Chapters 2 and 3, virtual sex is a popular activity in *Second Life*. Predictably, there are plenty of *SL* people who make money from it—not only escorts, but also animators who create the necessary animations and gestures, and builders who sculpt sexual organs.

Making money on sexual favors is not easy in a virtual world where there's plenty of free sex on offer. A successful escort has to invest plenty of Linden dollars in avatar appearance, including the necessary sex-related attachments (your avatar comes *sans* sexual organs), and other special items (such as a Gensex bed). If you have the money, obtaining necessary gestures and animations isn't difficult (Figure 10.10).

Figure 10.10: Hmmm, wonder if I can get two moans for the price of one.

Escort "jobs" in clubs and other entertainment centers are advertised frequently and are much less shameful than in the real world. Pay consists mostly of "tips" paid by appreciative guests, usually minus a 20% cut for the event host/owner; sometimes there's a low hourly wage as well to discourage absenteeism. Top escorts work the way top call girls do, receiving clients in lushly appointed private surroundings. Earnings go as high as L$2,500 per half hour, but the average tends to be in the high three and low four figures per half hour. In either case, monthly earnings can be impressive, easily reaching five figures in Linden dollars.

ADDITIONAL INFO:
THE FOUNTAIN OF YOUTH

If you're so inclined, being a virtual escort has real career potential. The money's good and tends to get better with time; escorts don't age in Second Life. Many SL dancers and strippers make money on the side as escorts.

TEXTURER

A texturer uses an external application, such as Adobe Photoshop or Paint Shop Pro, to create original textures that are subsequently imported into and used in *Second Life*. Textures are what you apply to the surface of a prim to make it look a certain way (wood, metal, black, yellow, ridged, glossy, whatever). Texturing is a skill that is very much in demand, but there's also plenty of competition. Many builders are also texturers; however, if you're a texturer of outstanding skill, you can count on finding a well-paid job with a busy builder or clothing designer. You can also go into business for yourself—don't expect to earn megabucks on every original texture sale, though. Usually, custom textures are reasonably priced (under L$100), and you'll have to sell many to earn a meaningful amount of money. A good approach is to market a no-transfer eye-catching texture at an appealing price, and sell many copies. It's the sales volume that determines your profits.

Creating textures pays best if you're also a builder, and your original textures are part of your new products. If you're definitely not into building, do your best to form a mutually profitable partnership with a talented builder. Your earnings may vary wildly and are determined solely by your creativity and marketing skills. If you're a mute genius, you'll most likely give away most of your stuff for free. If you're a marketing genius as well as a talented texturer, you can expect monthly earnings in the five figures (Linden dollars).

ADDITIONAL INFO:
CREATIVE INSPIRATION

If you're interested in creating new textures, downloading the high-quality textures from http://secondlife.com/community/textures.php *is a good start. You'll be able to see what's possible and gain a yardstick to measure your own creative efforts.*

INTRO
CHAPTER 1
CHAPTER 2
CHAPTER 3
CHAPTER 4
CHAPTER 5
CHAPTER 6
CHAPTER 7
CHAPTER 8
CHAPTER 9
CHAPTER 10
CHAPTER 11
CHAPTER 12
CHAPTER 13
APPENDICES

235

CLOTHING DESIGNER

This is one of the most popular occupations in *Second Life* (Figure 10.11). Everyone tries their hand at it while editing their avatars' appearance, and very many *SL* residents take the next step and download the templates from http://secondlife.com/community/templates.php. The downloaded templates come with a tutorial that explains the basics of clothing design. However, if you're seriously thinking about making it a career, you

Figure 10.11: In Second Life, everyone has a go at clothing design at least once.

should attend some of the courses and tutorials offered inside the *SL* world. A few are listed in Chapter 2, including courses available free of charge. Look through *SL* Classifieds to find more.

A clothing designer is a skilled professional who has mastered the art of creating something in 2D and making it look good in a 3D environment. It is not easy to design clothing so that seams, pockets, buttons, etc. stay where they should when an avatar changes poses. Every clothing designer needs to have a few posing stands, which "freeze" avatars in selected poses. This makes it possible to get a better idea of how a clothing item will look when worn by a moving, dancing, gesticulating avatar. In addition, some clothing items may require scripting: a good example is a sequin dress that sparkles.

A *Second Life* career in clothing design is not for the faint of heart. If you decide to go for it, be prepared for very strong competition. *SL* residents aren't likely to spend money on items that are inferior to clothing that's offered for free or at the symbolic price of L$1, and plenty of designer items can be obtained in this way. Earnings vary wildly: top designers make great money, and achieving a monthly income in six figures

isn't impossible. However, most clothing designers make much less than that. Raking in enough to cover standard *SL* expenses plus business-related costs (store rental, texture uploads, advertising) is pretty tough going.

SCRIPTER

A scripter is someone who writes scripts in LSL—*Second Life*'s programming language. Many *SL* residents have real-life programming skills that they apply in *Second Life*, and there are many tutorials available inside the virtual world, as well as at http://rpgstats.com/wiki/index.php?title=Main_Page. Predictably, there are quite a few scripters in *Second Life*.

It's not easy to make money selling free-standing scripts, and most top-earning scripters are also builders. The best way to maximize scripting income is to write scripts for objects you created yourself, as long as you have the needed building skills. The scripters who don't do this tend to work in tandem with builders who lack scripting skills.

Given all these considerations, income derived from scripting can vary greatly. Top scripters who aren't builders but are part of a well-known team can earn a monthly income in the five figures; however, income depends on the partners' skills and marketing acumen. The hard truth is that adequate scripting skills plus good building skills are more likely to earn you good money than outstanding scripting skills on their own.

BUILDER/LANDSCAPER

The term "builder" covers a very wide variety of jobs, depending on the builder's specialization. A furniture maker is a builder; so is an architect; and so are jewelry makers, vehicle builders, and gunsmiths.

Every *SL* resident can have a shot at becoming a builder; it's easy to learn how to make basic, one-prim objects with *SL*'s prim-editing tools. However, thereafter the learning curve becomes much steeper. It takes experience to know up front what kind of prim is best for a task at hand. Chapter 7 is full of advice for everyone interested in creating objects inside *Second Life*.

A builder is someone who has conquered the steepening learning curve and reached the level of skill necessary to create attractive and useful items out of prims. A truly skilled builder can create attractive and useful items using the smallest number of prims possible. Prim density is always a concern because a simulator can handle a limited number of prims.

As mentioned earlier, many builders are also scripters, and quite a few are texturers. Skill requirements in each area can vary wildly. For example, a furniture maker has to be a good builder and texturer, but the scripting skill required is next to none (a simple "sit down" script may be copied from the chair in the Library). On the other hand, a gunsmith needs to be a good scripter to build weapons capable of dealing with increasingly sophisticated shields and security systems. Extra skills in other areas come in handy, too—for instance, an architect who builds prefab houses and includes streamed music and sound effects for opening/closing doors will enjoy an edge over a less-versatile competitor.

Most builders have their own businesses—sales outlets for what they build. Thus, the amount of money you can make as a builder in *Second Life* depends not only on your inventiveness and technical skills, but also on your marketing and sales acumen. Builders who are good in all of the mentioned areas can reach a monthly income in the six figures.

> NOTE
>
> ADDITIONAL INFO:
> ## THE IMPORTANCE OF BUILDERS
>
> *Becoming a builder is one of the most exciting career choices in* Second Life. *Talented builders are the creators of most of the virtual world's content; in that way, they're the creators of fun for everyone else, as well as for themselves.*

Landscapers are builders who are also accomplished at using *SL's* slightly tricky land-editing tools, and at creating plants (Figure 10.12). A realistic-looking plant involves not only delicate prim manipulation, but also scripting (so that it moves in the wind, and so on) and frequently the creation of a new custom texture or two.

Figure 10.12: Creating realistic-looking plants is a highly specialized skill in Second Life.

ANIMATOR

Animators are the most highly paid among single-skill professionals. Creating complex animations for *SL* avatars is a difficult job requiring the mastery of an external application: the *SL* Guide to Jobs has the details. There are relatively few animators inside the virtual world of *Second Life*. At the same time, there is a big and constantly growing demand for new animations. Good animators can earn monthly incomes in the six figures more easily than specialists in any other profession.

Many *SL* residents are inspired to try creating animations. If you're interested, a good place to start is the Animation Guide at `http://secondlife.com/knowledgebase/article.php?id=050`. Predictably, it's not an easy career choice if you don't have the real-life skills required. It is a highly specialized job: with few exceptions, the rule is that either you're an animator before you even enter *Second Life,* or you aren't. However, don't let this discourage you if you've set your heart on animating!

INTRO
CHAPTER 1
CHAPTER 2
CHAPTER 3
CHAPTER 4
CHAPTER 5
CHAPTER 6
CHAPTER 7
CHAPTER 8
CHAPTER 9
CHAPTER 10
CHAPTER 11
CHAPTER 12
CHAPTER 13
APPENDICES

REAL-ESTATE DEVELOPER AND SPECULATOR

In real life, real estate is regarded as a secure if long-term investment. In *Second Life*, real estate is a secure investment that pays off much more quickly. Real-estate speculation offers such attractive opportunities that almost everyone dabbles in it, and many *SL* people make it a permanent side occupation that delivers a steady stream of profits.

Becoming a big fish in the *SL* real-estate pool requires a substantial investment up front: the really big players order entire new islands from Linden Lab. Many real-estate barons are also skillful landscapers, while others order professional landscaping services from a specialist. Once land has been acquired, it is developed to increase its resale/rental value.

The most basic and common form of land development is flattening land throughout the parcel and applying a green grass texture. At the time of writing, the asking price for a First Land parcel like that hovers around L$3,000—a profit of nearly 600% (and that's after a drop in price of about L$2,000 over just a few weeks). However, professional real-estate developers go much further than that, often creating elaborate

Figure 10.13: Second Life *lets you rent your own little virtual paradise for just a few dollars a week.*

themed sims complete with custom-made, exotic vegetation; professionally scripted, sparkling waterfalls; and sandy beaches (Figure 10.13). Top developers also offer to customize land to client requests. Of course, all this carries a hefty price. Searching the Classifieds for land sales or clicking on the parcels offered for sale on the world map will quickly give you an idea of how things look, but here's just one example: at the time of writing, a nice, waterfront parcel of modest size (1,024 square meters) rents

for approximately L$1,500 a week, and sells for between L$35,000 and L$50,000 depending on location.

Real-estate developers come in many shapes and sizes. Some offer land complete with rental buildings. Others specialize in developing shopping malls and commercial centers, and renting out or selling space within to business owners. There are roughly as many varieties of real-estate opportunities as there are in real life—some may be missing, but there are *SL*-specific opportunities instead: You may not make any money on garages and parking lots, because an *SL* resident can fit a brigade of tanks or a fleet of spaceships into a single Inventory folder or storage prim. However, you can make good money on tiny 16-square-meter lots; renting out a lot like that for advertising purposes in a high-traffic area can bring in a very nice income.

The real-estate business market in *Second Life* is very exciting, with many new players making virtual fortunes—or going bust. Those that fail are usually land syndicates formed by groups of *SL* denizens for the purpose of creating a special community or micronation. Political infighting in a virtual reality is just as common as in the real world, though in *SL* any sad consequences are less painful.

CURRENCY TRADER/FINANCIAL SPECULATOR

Currency traders are businesspeople making real-world money by exchanging Linden dollars for US dollars or euros. Some trading agencies, including Linden Lab's LindeX, make a profit by charging a small commission on transactions; others, like Anshe Chung's currency exchange, make money on the spread between buy and sell rates. What's more, the Linden dollar's exchange rate fluctuates very sharply when compared against real-world currencies. These fluctuations represent good profit potential to financial speculators (see the "Currency Trading and Financial Speculation" sidebar). It does not seem proper to recommend such career choices in this guide: although the profit potential is very healthy, a misfortune can get you in real trouble, just as in the real world.

INTRO
CHAPTER 1
CHAPTER 2
CHAPTER 3
CHAPTER 4
CHAPTER 5
CHAPTER 6
CHAPTER 7
CHAPTER 8
CHAPTER 9
CHAPTER 10
CHAPTER 11
CHAPTER 12
CHAPTER 13
APPENDICES

If you want to make money on your money in a passive way, you can open an account with one of *Second Life*'s financial institutions. *SL* banks admit to being high-risk institutions, but they pay excellent interest rates. Banking operations are usually conducted via automated tellers that dispense notecards with instructions (see Figure 10.14).

Figure 10.14: *Second Life offers you the chance to bank via virtual ATMs.*

Always keep in mind that if you engage in any kind of financial speculation inside *Second Life*, you may lose your entire investment. Bank owners disclaim any responsibility for deposits and openly advise *SL* residents not to bet their life savings. What would you expect? They're virtual banks, after all.

NOTE

ADDITIONAL INFO:

WALL STREET IT AIN'T—YET

At the time of writing, Second Life does not have a stock exchange: the only institution claiming to be one is an operation for trading public shares of a single company (read: a real-estate speculator).

SIDEBAR

RESIDENTS SPEAK:

CURRENCY TRADING AND FINANCIAL SPECULATION

"If you're going to sell Lindens, use a limit sell, timed so you catch the market when it's going down. Your Lindens may take you a few days

to sell rather than being instant, but the effect is that you get about 6% more US dollars for your money. Getting a 6% bonus for 5 minutes work reading the LindeX is very worthwhile! Also, I would suggest avoiding using 3rd party exchange sites. The reason for this is simple— their prices will probably be higher than LL charges, because instead of just LL taking a cut, both LL and the site operator take a cut. There are two important business principles here: firstly, 'where possible, cut out the middleman,' and secondly, 'buy low, sell high.'

"If you're not going to sell your Lindens, yet, and you can afford to lose them entirely, stick them in Ginko or another high-risk/high-gain savings account. You might lose your money; there is always a chance of that. On the other hand, if you use it right, you can earn 3.3% interest per month on your balance, which almost offsets the 3.5% fee for selling L$. I'm not sure if this is a good way to make money on its own, but I think that if you get that 3.3% interest on all L$ before you sell them, and you time your selling of L$ to sell when the market is right, using a limit sell, your chances of making money are much better."

—Angel Fluffy

"I'm confused why people don't believe that banks like Ginko can pay their depositors such a robust interest rate. It's Second Life. Where else can someone make an investment of some time and 10 Lindens (to upload a texture), then sell 1,000 copies of their creation for 100 Lindens each, grossing L$100,000 from their small initial investment?

"As I explained in my article in The Democrat, banks in Second Life make money not only from high-interest loans (compared to real-world banks), but also from currency speculation, land deals, and lotteries. These are all, undoubtedly, risky 'investments,' but the fact is that some banks are able to return high interest rates to depositors. Ginko, for example, has been around for 2 years."

—Marla Truss

BECOMING A BUSINESS OWNER

Without question, the most rewarding way to make money in *Second Life* is by running your own business. It is rewarding in more ways than one, too. You'll make

INTRO
CHAPTER 1
CHAPTER 2
CHAPTER 3
CHAPTER 4
CHAPTER 5
CHAPTER 6
CHAPTER 7
CHAPTER 8
CHAPTER 9
CHAPTER 10
CHAPTER 11
CHAPTER 12
CHAPTER 13
APPENDICES

more money working for yourself than working for someone else, and by the very act of creating a business you'll be adding to the virtual world's content.

Starting a business is really easy. You do not need to go through any legalities; you don't even need a Premium account or any space of your own—you can advertise and promote your services through the Classifieds and in person. Remember that a well-developed social network is key!

If you do require space—for storage if nothing else—you can rent it. Special deals are often available as developers open up new malls and shopping centers (Figure 10.15).

Figure 10.15: Newly opened commercial centers often offer great rental deals to attract business.

NOTE

ADDITIONAL INFO:
FUN BEFORE PROFIT

Running a virtual business has a special magic all of its own; don't pressure yourself into thinking that you must make lots of money. Enjoy what you're doing, first and foremost.

SIDEBAR

RESIDENTS SPEAK:
RUNNING A BUSINESS IN SECOND LIFE

"The big income spinners are land [barons], although you won't make any friends doing that. Some DJs get paid quite well, but you have to

PART III · MONEYMAKING VENTURES

have the huge amount of time and resources to do it. Designing a line of clothes/furniture, etc. takes time but can pay dividends if you're willing to invest in it."

—Samia Perun

"A lot of people get the impression from their first land sale...that moving land in SL is pretty simple. It's not. To effectively make money as a land baron in SL you have to be able to invest quite a lot of money in tier. Depending on [values] and buyer trends, you can end up sitting on plots of land for indeterminate amounts of time.

"The best thing you can do in SL is develop content that people enjoy. Back in November of last year when I started out, I did club/sim management and made a little cash for a couple of months while I learned the system and applied my inherent talents to it...but in January of this year, I developed my very first product, which turned out to be quite a hit. I haven't paid my tier out of my own pocket ever since...and I'm at the US$125.00-a-month tier level now.

"Business development in SL can be pretty simple. Many people simply rent mall space and sell their products there. There are thousands of malls in the world, so there's never really an end to mall space availability, and it's relatively cheap. The downside to mall space rental is you have no control over directing traffic to your products.

"However, the best thing you can do if you want to make and sell products is to go Premium, and buy a nice plot of first land. This won't cost you any more than 10 dollars a month (easily payable even on a dancer's in-world salary).

—Suzanna Soyinka

INTRO
CHAPTER 1
CHAPTER 2
CHAPTER 3
CHAPTER 4
CHAPTER 5
CHAPTER 6
CHAPTER 7
CHAPTER 8
CHAPTER 9
CHAPTER 10
CHAPTER 11
CHAPTER 12
CHAPTER 13
APPENDICES

The plan that works best for most *SL* residents is to try out a few different occupations before choosing the one that's most enjoyable and profitable and turning it into a business. Also, most residents like the role-playing aspect of making a living in *Second Life*. Although they could easily fund a business effort from the everyday spare change in their pockets, they prefer to act as if *SL* earnings were their only possible source of income. A fledgling business owner often spends several hours a week working as an event host or a dancer to cover business startup expenses that would not buy a cup of coffee in the real world.

INTRO

PART I

PART II

PART III

APPENDICES

MONEYMAKING VENTURES

ADDITIONAL INFO:
PLAY THE FIELD

Do not limit yourself to any single occupation; try your hand at several to see what they're like. Many SL residents continue to earn income from multiple sources long after their primary moneymaker has taken off. Note also that most successful business owners tend to invest in real estate.

Starting a business is easy; what's not easy is making it a permanent and profitable concern. The final section of this chapter contains advice from a prominent *SL* businesswoman on how to achieve long-term success.

SECOND LIFE PROFESSIONALISM

Aimee Weber is the founder of Aimee Weber Studio Inc. (www.aimeeweber.com) and is one of *Second Life*'s most well-known and respected developers. Recognized for her considerable achievements in virtual fashion, education, marketing, machinima, and writing, Aimee is considered one of the foremost experts in virtual entrepreneurship. What follows is her advice.

Ladies and gentlemen, welcome to Intro to Advanced Business in *Second Life*; my name is Aimee Weber and I will be your professor today. To attend this class, you should already have an impressive mastery of at least one prerequisite skill in *SL*, such as scripting, building, texturing, terraforming, or project management. I know many of you are quite the hotshots in one or more of these areas, but today we will address the time-honored question of, "How can my skillz pay the billz?"

Going professional in *Second Life* may seem like the start of a dream job. You get to tinker with the bleeding edge of 3D Internet technology while at home, in your pajamas, and possibly drunk. But before you quit your day job, you're going to have to make some changes in your perspective on *SL* and how you present yourself to the virtual world.

Now I know from talking to many of you that these changes don't sit well with the fiercely libertarian nature of the *Second Life* demographic. You guys don't want to dance for the man, and that's fine. But try to stick with me here and maybe we can strike up enough compromise between being a freewheeling beatnik and a corporate tool to get the bills paid.

When a client is considering you for a project, they're taking a great risk in terms of money, time, and even reputation. It's therefore upon you to make them feel as comfortable and safe as possible choosing you for the job. Nothing accomplishes this like a proven history of achievement with a sea of happy customers in your wake. While your status as *SL*-Foo Grand Master Ninja will aid you greatly, you should focus on demonstrating a few other professional traits:

Finish your projects—This stream of consciousness we call a virtual world is littered with half-finished experiments and muses. While many are technically brilliant, they will likely give the impression that you're not a "follow-through" kinda person. Go ahead and take the extra steps to finish a project, document it, package it, and maybe even market it. This tells employers that you're willing and able to stick with them from start to finish on a project.

Meet your deadlines—You would be shocked at how much a deadline can change your perspective on work in *Second Life*. *SL* can be fun when you have all the time in the world to tinker and experiment, but now people are adjusting their schedules around your promised delivery date. You'll need to learn to prioritize and if necessary, learn to let go of low-priority features. I know some of you want things to be just perfect, but a project that arrives a month late is far from perfect. You can still take breaks to play *World of Warcraft*, watch *Doctor Who*, or look for Butterflies Gone Wild websites, but now you must budget that time!

Get experience, no matter what—You ask the Zen Master how you can get a job without experience, and how you can get experience without a job? The Zen Master says, "work for free." While Midnight City was (and still is) a nonprofit project for me, it has been invaluable in proving that I'm capable of managing a large-scale project. Charitable organizations like Relay for Life can also provide high-profile opportunities to spotlight your work and to get gleaming recommendations. Just remember, even though you're working for free, don't act as if you are working for free. The objective here is to get a reputable organization to vouch for your talent and professionalism, so make sure that's what they see!

Market yourself—Doing all the right things won't help you if nobody knows you're doing all the right things. Increase your visibility. Prospective employers are not looking for modesty; they need to know what you've done in the past and what you can do for them in the future.

Build a portfolio—Prospective clients are prepared to pay you money to do work for them, so don't start your relationship by making them work to learn about you. You should have a nicely organized portfolio that includes descriptions, photos, testimonials, and client contacts from your past projects. If your work has appeared in the press, be sure to include links.

INTRO
CHAPTER 1
CHAPTER 2
CHAPTER 3
CHAPTER 4
CHAPTER 5
CHAPTER 6
CHAPTER 7
CHAPTER 8
CHAPTER 9
CHAPTER 10
CHAPTER 11
CHAPTER 12
CHAPTER 13
APPENDICES

Get a website—I won't say that this is essential, but it's a tremendous help in creating the perception that you are a stable entity in the industry. Having the website could also increase your Google visibility associated with *Second Life* and may land you the occasional contract deal right off the street. If you can't afford a website, consider entering yourself and your accomplishments on the SL History Wiki (`http://history.secondserver.net/index.php/Main_Page`).

Network—I know many residents are self-proclaimed recluses and the idea of networking feels unnatural, insincere, or downright painful to them. The truth is, the more people you can stay in contact with on a regular basis, the more opportunities will likely come your way. This is a fact of life. If attending the occasional virtual mixer feels like torture, consider hiring somebody a bit more boisterous who can act as your agent while you continue your monastic pursuits.

Operate as a business—Now this part I hate with a capital 8. But if I can do it, you can do it...and by that I mean if I *have* to do it, you damn well had better do it! Seriously though, real-world organizations have a standard process by which they get things done. You will always be in a stronger position if you can integrate yourself into their process rather than being a confusing exception in their corporate flow control. That means yummy paperwork:

> **Write proposals**—These can vary widely depending on the task at hand, but most will include a statement describing your client's problem, your solution to the problem, a breakdown of cost, your needs/requirements, and some amount of self-promotion describing why you are the best person for the job.

> **Submit invoices**—Don't be caught off guard when a client requests an invoice! Microsoft Word and Excel provide templates for invoices, so take the time to familiarize yourself with them.

> **Make presentations**—You may be asked to give a telephone or live presentation, and that means public speaking! Once again, if you're shy, consider teaming up with somebody who can do a good job wheeling and dealing in front of a crowd.

THE SECOND LIFE DEVELOPER DIRECTORY

When real-world corporations approach Linden Lab about projects, they are normally directed to the *Second Life* Developer Directory (`http://secondlife.com/developers/directory.php`). This directory lists *Second Life* residents with a proven track record of professional success in *SL*.

But how does one get on this list? Linden Lab's senior vice president, Robin Harper, had this to say:

"I think the best way to get on the list is to send in your name and skill set, and a great portfolio—pics, happy clients, etc. It also really helps to be able to show that you are able to work on a 'professional' level. That is, you are ready to manage things like deadlines, invoicing, milestones, and progress reports."

When asked to elaborate on professionalism, Robin went on to say, "You might find that you need to do RL presentations, so public-speaking skills and salesmanship are also critical. I think setting expectations is part of being professional. People need to know what they're getting into, and you need to be realistic about what you can promise. In the long run that makes everyone a lot happier!"

SO...YOU SURE YOU WANNA DO THIS?

Nobody knows what will become of this budding platform or if grooming a career in *Second Life* is a fruitful endeavor. If the phrase "get rich quick" finds its way into your thoughts about *Second Life*, I recommend you run away very fast. *Second Life* professionals work very long, hard hours and many have been doing this for years with only moderate payoffs. I'm not trying to discourage anybody. Instead, new residents looking for instant gratification in the world of *Second Life* business should try to maintain more-reasonable goals.

However, if you have talent, patience, passion, and just a touch of obsessive compulsive disorder, there may be some great opportunities waiting for you in *Second Life*. I leave you with this quote from Robin:

"Second Life is getting a lot of visibility lately, as you know. If someone is serious about building a developer business, this is a great time to get involved."

Class dismissed!

CHAPTER 11
REAL RESIDENTS

Second Life lets you craft your persona to be anything or anyone you want. This chapter offers a look at some of possibilities through profiles of real residents who have achieved a measure of notoriety.

In-world notoriety is influenced by many factors and is achieved in any number of ways. Some residents create unique, recognizable avatars whose engagement with the community makes it a world worth living in. Some foster civic-minded and educational activities. Others may have a measurable impact on the real world's perception of *Second Life*, and in doing so, change the shape and direction of its evolution. Others exercise their creativity in building and scripting, and still others create successful companies and well-run regions.

This chapter profiles a handful of interesting residents in a world almost 1 million strong; there are, of course, many, many more.

> **NOTE**
>
> **ADDITIONAL INFO:**
> **AVOIDING REPETITION**
>
> *Some residents are so influential and well-known that they were mentioned in many of the resident-provided sidebars. To avoid redundancy, we removed duplicate entries.*

CONTENTS

THE ARTIST: DANCOYOTE ANTONELLI

Over the years, more than a few residents have experimented with *Second Life* as an artistic medium, through sculptures and interactive installations: AngryBeth Shortbread, Arahan Claveau, Nylon Pinkey, Stella Costello, and The Port collective spring immediately to mind. In mid to late 2006, there's seemingly been a mini Renaissance of artists entering the field, many of them established professionals from other media. Among them is Dancoyote Antonelli, a real-life artist who created *SL*'s Museum of Hyperformalism. Dancoyote's artwork pushes the boundaries of *Second Life*, exploring both interactive artwork and live performance, most especially with a widely praised performance that combines flying dance animations, music, and particle effects (think Cirque du Soleil but more psychedelic). Many believe Antonelli has created a breakthrough that establishes *Second Life* as a new form for artists; in any case, his works are sure to inspire even more aesthetic milestones in the metaverse.

THE METAVERSE BIG THREE: BASKERVILLE, SIBLEY HATHOR, AND REUBEN TAPIOCA

BASKERVILLE

SIBLEY HATHOR

REUBEN TAPIOCA

It began with an island, the first that Linden Lab had put on the open market for resident auction. After the subsequent bidding war had ended, Fizik, the owner of a UK branding agency called Rivers Run Red, had opened up shop on the isle he now called Avalon. That was early 2004, and it was the first corridor of real-world business and marketing into *SL*. Though Fizik met with stiff early resistance from residents who feared this would lead to an explosion of corporate influence and

PART III   APPENDICES   REAL RESIDENTS

pervasive real-world advertising, the world has (so far) proven resilient to the arrival of large companies—most of whom have set up shop on islands that residents can opt to visit or ignore. Some of the first appeared on Fizik's Avalon, including 20th Century Fox with a virtual-world screening of footage from *X-Men III*. In late 2005 and early 2006, two large competitors to Fizik emerged: The Electric Sheep Company of Sibley Hathor began creating *SL*-based experiences for companies like Major League Baseball and Lego, and Millions of Us, the company founded by former Linden Lab staffer Reuben Tapioca, started building *Second Life* projects for clients like Warner Records and Toyota. Taken together, these residents and their companies represent the "big three" in terms of bringing real-world money and power into *Second Life*.

THE BUSINESSWOMAN: ANSHE CHUNG

No list of the rich and famous is complete without mentioning Ms. Chung, owner of Dreamland, an entire continent, and thousands of dollars worth of oceanfront property across the world. In *SL*-related media, US$150,000 is the dollar figure you'll read most—it's the amount Linden Lab estimates Anshe makes per year from her in-world real-estate business, with her *SL*/RL partner Guni Greenstein through their company, Anshe Chung Studios. Ms. Chung has arguably become *Second Life*'s most prominent avatar in the outside world, appearing on a May 2006 cover of *Business Week* beside the appropriate title, "Virtual World, Real Money." The story launched the explosion of interest in outside corporations and organizations in this quirky online world, and as such, the face of Anshe launched millions of real-world dollars into *Second Life*.

THE ENGINEER: FRANCIS CHUNG

Ms. Chung made a gun and a hug and changed the world. Created back in mid 2004, the Seburo handgun was and still is among the most fully formed weapons in *SL*, with muzzle flashes and spent casings that trail wisps of gunsmoke when they exit the chamber. The hug was just as complex, enabling avatars to embrace each other. (A simple enough task, you'd think, until you consider that each avatar has to be perfectly positioned even before two custom animations can be launched.) For such a social world, inventing a hug was profoundly powerful, eventually unleashing an entire industry of custom animations that brought residents together, from kisses to the

most acrobatic sex imaginable. Continuing her inventiveness into 2006, Francis's Dominus Shadow, a finely detailed muscle car, became the must-have vehicle of *Second Life*. Most impressive of all, in a summer-'06 fundraiser for the American Cancer Society, it auctioned for the L$ equivalent of nearly US$2,000. With such skills, it's no surprise that Millions of Us (see "The Metaverse Big Three" earlier in this chapter) hired Francis to create the *SL* version of the Toyota Scion.

THE EDUCATOR: BRACE CORAL

When new residents come to the world, confused and disoriented, it's often Brace who helps. She is the founder of New Citizens Incorporated (formed in November 2004), a group for veteran residents who want to assist newbies. It began on a tiny plot of land that gradually expanded into a kind of college of *Second Life*, offering round-the-clock classes in everything from using the interface to building. Tens of thousands of residents who would have otherwise quit in frustration owe a great debt to Brace and her 350+ volunteers.

THE FURRY KING: ARITO COTTON

Furries—fans of anthropomorphic cartoon animals like you'd see in an early Disney cartoon—are easily the most recognized subculture in *Second Life*. Arito joined the

world in the summer of 2003 (he was among the very first furries to do so), and soon after that, fashioned an attachable suit with paws, a tail, and other mammalian trappings, creating what's believed to be the very first furry avatar in *Second Life*. From there Arito brought in furry friends Liam Roark, Michi Lumin, and Eltee Statosky, who went on to found Luskwood, *SL's* first furry community, in late 2003. (Still an active and dynamic community, Luskwood has nearly 500 members.) The foxlike Arito is also the main creator of Taco, a cell-shaded island that's a tribute to furry humor and cartoons, and one of the most distinct locations in *Second Life*.

THE FILMMAKER: ROBBIE DINGO

Dingo is a relative newcomer to *SL*, but his first two *Second Life*-based machinimas catapulted him into a position among the very best artists working in the medium—initially with "A Better Life," the moving story of a man confined to a wheelchair who finds himself transported into *SL*, then with "Stage," which depicts the circle of life and the passing of generations with the use of impressive visual effects. Also noteworthy is his step-by-step video depiction of creating the guitar for Suzanne Vega's appearance in *Second Life*. With these movies and more, Robbie Dingo has demonstrated just how far *SL* machinima has come—and how much more ground it can break. Check out some of his creations on this book's companion CD.

FROM LINDEN LAB:
SECOND LIFE MOVIEMAKING MAESTROS

"Skydive" *by Cage McCoy and Reitsuki Kojima*

Second Life experience from beginning to end.

"Second Life Trailer" by Javier Puff

This machinima has a real cinematic feel, uses a nice mix of motion graphics and titling, and is nicely edited together.

"Better Life" by Robbie Dingo

Moving video, possibly the best movie made in Second Life!

"Primitives in the Wild" by BuhBuhCuh Fairchild

One of the first real movies made in Second Life, it is a wonderful spoof documentary on Second Life objects.

"Second Take" by Total Boffin

One of the finest montages of Second Life places, activities, and people.

"Tour of the Solar System" by Aimee Weber

This movie reveals some of the real potential of Second Life machinima in the field of education.

"Game Over" by Pierce Portocarrero

An interesting, quirky piece from one of Second Life's machinima pioneers.

—Eric Linden

THE CELEBRITY GUEST STAR: CORY DOCTOROW

The Boing Boing blogger and novelist (shown here with a character from his latest work) doesn't visit *Second Life* often, but when he does, his impact is deep and ongoing. In late 2003 and in 2005 (during my days as an embedded reporter for Linden Lab) I invited Cory to discuss his latest novels. These visits (and his mention

of them on Boing Boing) helped spur other luminaries to make a *Second Life* appearance, including Lawrence Lessig, Joi Ito, Thomas Barnett (author of *The Pentagon's New Map*), technology writer Julian Dibbell, and Mark Warner (former governor of Virginia). So Cory's few visits have helped spread *Second Life*'s influence far and wide, from futurists and the technorati to educators, authors, and politicians. Though writers like Vernor Vinge and Neal Stephenson came before him with their speculative novels about the metaverse, Doctorow is the first author to affect the direction, growth, and culture of an actual online world. As an avatar, no less.

THE HOSTESS: JENNA FAIRPLAY

Within months of joining *SL* in late 2004, Jenna launched The Edge, a nightclub-*cum*-casino-*cum*-sex club, and since then it's consistently been one of the most popular spots in the world, the hangout of choice for thousands every week, especially newbies. This could be because of the fairly strange secret behind Ms. Fairplay's success: she runs The Edge, she once told me, based on Maslow's hierarchy of needs, in which the newbie's urge to feel safe and accepted in a strange MMO comes first, and sex, fun, and friends come second. Her continued success suggests she's not wrong.

THE PUBLISHER: KATT KONGO

Although there have been numerous attempts to create an in-world newspaper, it was Katt Kongo who succeeded where so many had failed. (Unsurprisingly, she had nearly

INTRO
CHAPTER 1
CHAPTER 2
CHAPTER 3
CHAPTER 4
CHAPTER 5
CHAPTER 6
CHAPTER 7
CHAPTER 8
CHAPTER 9
CHAPTER 10
CHAPTER 11
CHAPTER 12
CHAPTER 13
APPENDICES

a decade of professional experience as a real-world journalist to draw from.) Launched in fall of 2005, within a year her biweekly *Metaverse Messenger* was reportedly attracting a monthly circulation of nearly 50,000, evolving into the grid's leading voice for information, advertising, and community. The sidebar "Residents on Movers and Shakers: Katt Kongo's Take" contains Katt's ideas about important *SL* residents.

SIDEBAR

RESIDENTS SPEAK:
SL MOVERS AND SHAKERS: KATO KONGO'S TAKE

Taco Rubio—*Usually the king of irrelevance, when he does have something relevant to say, residents and Linden Lab employees alike listen to him.*

Boliver Oddfellow—*CEO of Infinite Vision Media, Bo has coordinated events such as a 12-hour live music fest in Dublin and the Infinite Mind series, including Suzanne Vega's SL debut.*

Spin Martin—*He developed Slackstreet Entertainment, with SL's first record label (Multiverse Records) and the Hipcast Expo Center. In his first life, he's known as Eric Rice, a renowned blogger and public speaker (*http://ericrice.com*).*

Sitearm Madonna—*The consultant for many large-scale projects, such as Dublin, Sitearm has her finger on the pulse of SL. Her networking skills mean that she has a huge list of SL and first-life contacts.*

Zafu Diamond—*As founder of the Support for Healing website (*http://supportforhealing.com/*) and island sim (resources for those with mental illnesses), Diamond has helped many SL residents. With plans for expansion, he and his team will be able to help an unlimited amount of people cope with depression, anxiety, addictions, disabilities, and more.*

Tateru Nino—*As the Mentor group in SL grew larger, it clearly needed a leader. Nino stepped up to fill that role, coordinating development*

> of the newbie learning centers (Help Island), and teaching hundreds of newbies in the process.

Alexander Bard—*Bard founded the Second Citizen forums, one of the most widely read SL forums. He has provided a place for residents to speak their minds without fear of being banned from Second Life.*

THE HEART: JADE LILY

Long before many outside the community saw the potential of *SL* as a tool for social change and nonprofit fundraising, Jade Lily did. (Also among the first to leverage *Second Life* for charitable causes were Bhodi Silverman and ReallyRick Metropolitan—see Chapter 12.) In 2004, the petite brunette took pains to create a donation system for residents to sponsor Jade's real-life running team for the American Cancer Society's annual Relay for Life. She was unable to get the venerable nonprofit's support for the effort that year, but she did so in 2005, working with an ACS staffer who eventually joined *Second Life* as RC Mars. The inaugural *SL* version of the Relay raised over US$5,000. In 2006, with Jade overseeing dozens of volunteers, *Second Life*'s Relay for Life became a race track traversing several dozen acres, created to resemble a microcosm of the real world. That combined with numerous parties, auctions, and Jade's tireless efforts led the 2006 Relay to raise over US$40,000 in the war against cancer. Now, of course, the value of *SL* as a tool for making the real world a better place is unquestioned, and a number of respected nonprofits, including Techsoup.org, Creative Commons, and the Omidyar Network, have created a space in the world. Credit for this belongs just as much to Jade Lily as it does to Linden Lab. And it is Jade who deserves the greatest credit for proving to the *SL* community that it was, indeed, a genuine community, able to come together for a common purpose and do great things.

THE SOUL: TORLEY LINDEN

In *Second Life*, a "Linden" last name denotes a staffer with Linden Lab. In this rare case, however, we are speaking of a person who made the world fall in love with her a year before joining the company's payroll, when she was "Torley Torgeson." Reading her exhaustively enthused blog entries (http://torley.com) will give you a sense for why she knows and is adored by everyone. Her real-life Asperger's condition seems to be a key to her charisma: offline it's difficult for her to perceive or communicate emotions; in-world, where most communication is through chat and IM text, she's mesmerizing with empathy and charm. This power has not diminished even after she became a Linden employee; instead, it has been enhanced twice over. Though just a Community Team member, in the world Torley arguably has more social impact than even Cory Ondrejka, the head of development, or Philip Rosedale, the CEO himself. While Linden Lab management has the ability to pull the world's plug, it's Torley who holds the power to move the world.

THE HISTORIAN: EGGY LIPPMAN

A seasoned and talented builder in his own right, Eggy is among the earliest *SL* residents, having joined the world in April 2003, and he's a gregarious socializer of the first order. But perhaps his main claim to fame is becoming the world's archivist—he is one of the main creators of the *Second Life* History Wiki (http://history.secondserver.net/), a document of *SL*'s development from early Alpha period to now, and beyond. As of fall 2006, the Wiki boasts over 1,000 entries, noting cultural milestones and technological leaps throughout the years. With so many changes happening so rapidly, it's the *SL* History Wiki that veteran residents (and sometimes Lindens!) turn to.

THE VISIONARY: GWYNETH LLEWELYN

Read Gwyneth's *SL* blog long enough (conveniently located at `http://gwynethllewelyn.net`), and you'll begin to believe that Ms. Llewelyn knows more about where Linden Lab should take *Second Life* in the near future than anyone in the actual company does. And more crucially, she can explain her reasoning. She makes long, thoughtful posts on the technology and culture of *Second Life*; she's a longtime participant in *SL*'s several intellectual chat circles, and a cofounder of the self-governed Neufreistadt democratic community/experiment. See the sidebar "Residents on Movers and Shakers: Gwyneth Llewelyn's Take" for ideas straight from the horse's mouth.

SIDEBAR

RESIDENTS SPEAK:
SL MOVERS AND SHAKERS: GWYNETH LLEWELYN'S TAKE

FASHION

Chip Midnight—*Mostly because he has provided the whole community with so many templates, guides, tutorials, and helpful hints.*

BUILDING

Bill Stirling—*I would like to encourage people that brought real architecture into* Second Life. *In that case, Bill Stirling would be my first choice, with* **Jauani Wu** *a close second, and* **Moon Adamant** *probably next...[they show] that SL is becoming a mature platform for real-life architects, and this is what is going to encourage people to become professionals.*

ANIMATIONS

It's a hard choice between **Craig Altman** *with his Duo Dances,* **Beau Perkins** *with his hilarious animations (and an overwhelmingly good customer support & encouragement policy), or* **Owen Khan** *with his*

INTRO
CHAPTER 1
CHAPTER 2
CHAPTER 3
CHAPTER 4
CHAPTER 5
CHAPTER 6
CHAPTER 7
CHAPTER 8
CHAPTER 9
CHAPTER 10
CHAPTER 11
CHAPTER 12
CHAPTER 13
APPENDICES

legendary dances. However, the prize will go to **Web Page**—*since he's the guy doing practically all animations for machinima, and these will set the standards for the future.*

THE MUSICIAN: FROGG MARLOWE

When he came to *SL* in mid 2005, he was a recently homeless, down-on-his-luck musician sleeping on a friend's couch. That friend happened to be *SL* live musician Jaycatt Nico, and it was through Nico that Frogg launched his own career as a performer in *Second Life*. Offering a unique selection of alt-folk originals accompanied by solid guitar and harmonica work, the aptly named Frogg (his avatar is a 6-foot amphibian) established a vast following, eventually leading (in late summer of 2006) to prominent mention in a *Rolling Stone* article on *SL*'s burgeoning music scene. By then, Suzanne Vega, Duran Duran, and other big-scene musicians were appearing as themselves in *Second Life*, but in large part it was Frogg who proved the potential of avatar as pop star.

SIDEBAR
ADDITIONAL INFO:
SL MOVERS AND SHAKERS: FROGG MARLOWE'S TAKE

EVENT HOSTING

It's such a close tie between **Tom Bukowski** *(founder of Digital Cultures group) and* **Selaras Partridge** *(founder of The Ethical Group) that I'll have them both. These are the guys that appeal to the SL crowd that loves intelligent chatting. :)*

MIXED-MEDIA EVENT HOSTING

SNOOPYbrown Zamboni—*SNOOPYbrown is the reference on "mixed-media" events. He was the first to bring some real people and real*

conferences inside Second Life. *His real-life job at the Accelerating Change Foundation and his participation in the Future Salon series make him a reference for everyone who is determined to bring the focus of the limelight from RL inside SL. At those times when people still discussed if SL was a "country," SNOOPYbrown treated it precisely like that, "opening shop" for his Future Salons in SL, as if it were one of several US cities where the Futurists meet.*

RL-in-SL Business

Hiro Pendragon—*Hiro Pendragon has all the skills and requirements to be a successful community focus in* Second Life: *technical prowess, a strong and moving charisma, an excellent way to make people be at ease, writing skill, and the ability to create in a very short time a truly huge network of contacts, with tendrils of information flowing to a central point. He stands for his good reputation—his word is all you require to establish a relationship. Thus, it is no small wonder that his own company thrives.*

Others

And on a personal note, **Eloise Pasteur** *and* **Sudane Erato***. Both will be probably footnotes in SL's history; but both have influenced me a lot.*

THE IMPRESARIO: SPIN MARTIN

Before he became an avatar, Spin Martin was renowned around the Internet as Eric Rice, well-known blogger and DJ who was also among the first podcasters and videobloggers. Inspired by Lawrence Lessig's *Second Life* appearance in early 2006, Spin stormed the grid and took his talents with him, founding Slackstreet, an island devoted to music and podcast recording. He then bought up Multiverse Records with the aim of launching an *SL*-based label. Numerous podcasters have since joined *Second Life*, including former

INTRO
CHAPTER 1
CHAPTER 2
CHAPTER 3
CHAPTER 4
CHAPTER 5
CHAPTER 6
CHAPTER 7
CHAPTER 8
CHAPTER 9
CHAPTER 10
CHAPTER 11
CHAPTER 12
CHAPTER 13
APPENDICES

MTV VJ Adam Curry, but Spin deserves much credit for taking audio-based *Second Life* content to the next level after live streamed music.

THE WEB 2.0 MASTER: CRISTIANO MIDNIGHT

Sometime in 2004, Linden Lab added a feature to *Second Life*'s screenshot-creation tools, enabling residents to send an image to someone's e-mail address. The original idea was to create one-to-one viral marketing, but it was Cristiano who turned it into *Second Life*'s first Web 2.0 mash-up. His Snapzilla website (`http://www.slpics.com/`) is the Flickr of the metaverse, a growing compendium of more than 100,000 screenshots that residents share, rate, and comment upon. In doing this, he's created a site that's become, in effect, the public face of *Second Life* on the Web. And with the closing of the official *Second Life* forums in September 2006, Cristiano will no doubt expand his web-based empire even further.

THE LIGHTNING ROD: PROKOFY NEVA

Every society needs its dissidents, and every free society attracts those who would aspire to that role. To many, Mr. Neva earned that title with his notion of the Feted Inner Core (FIC)—in Neva's mind, at least, a shadowy, informal conspiracy between *Second Life*'s top content creators and Linden Lab, who secretly plot to create a techno-utopia where the average user is marginalized. He's an activist dismissed as an irrelevant extremist by the mainstream, but whose thought still manages to define the terms of the debate. ("Smash the FIC" is the "No blood for oil" of *SL*.) Some will point to Mr. Neva's dire 2005 prediction that *Second Life* would never surpass 40,000 registered users as evidence that his time as a dissident has passed, but there's no denying that the FIC concept has nonetheless infected the world, as seen in parodies, slogans, and everyday speech. Also worth mentioning here is Ulrika Zugzwang, firebrand founder of

PART III

REAL RESIDENTS

APPENDICES

PART II

PART I

INTRO

264

the Neualtenburg Projekt, originally an experiment in socialist democracy on an island simulator of the same name—and after a bitter dispute, now known as Neufreistadt, another exercise in democratic self-governance founded by Gwyneth Lllewylyn (see listing), among others.

THE MENTOR: TATERU NINO

Usually dressed in blue crushed velvet like a hip Mary Poppins, Tateru is the Mother of Mentors, offering a warm and encouraging hand to the hundreds of volunteer support mentors who see her as their informal leader—and to the thousands of new residents who've gained their footing and found a place in *Second Life*, thanks to her help. (Many of these people have created a Cult of Tateru group and built a shrine in her honor.)

RESIDENTS SPEAK:
SL MOVERS AND SHAKERS: HANK HOODOO, SATCHMO PROTOTYPE, AND FORSETI SVAROG'S TAKE

Adam Zaius—*Adam's skills are diverse. He is a talented builder and scripter, develops* Second Life *commerce portal SecondServer.net (*http://secondserver.net/*), and has founded development company Gigas and the Azure Islands real estate empire.*

The libsecondlife Team—*Linden Lab has always prided itself on putting power in the hands of its users. The libsecondlife project (*http://www.libsecondlife.org*), an open-source group effort spearheaded by bushing Spatula, Eddy Striker, Baba Yamamoto, and Adam Zaius, takes this one step further and reverse engineers the* Second Life *protocol, allowing developers to interact with* Second Life *in ways well beyond what Linden Lab intended to be possible.*

Lumiere Noir—*Lumiere is the creator of The Ivory Tower Library of Primitives, the definitive resource for new users learning their way around* Second Life*'s powerful and idiosyncratic modeling tools. No one*

11

INTRO

PART I

PART II

PART III

APPENDICES

REAL RESIDENTS

has yet improved on the Ivory Tower, so Lumiere's work is influential on generation after generation of Second Life builders.

Pierce Portocarrero—*Pierce has pioneered and mastered machinima—video made from captured screen footage—in Second Life, and in the process been instrumental in creating the best way to show and explain the virtual world to outsiders.*

Starax Statosky—*Starax embodied the reclusive genius in Second Life; unlike many of these names he was never a very public figure, but the Magic Wand he created is a legendary item, a perfect demonstration of the chaos and creativity possible in Second Life.*

Tao Takashi—*Tao has been involved in many things around SL, but we in particular appreciate his efforts in creating World of SL, a Second Life blog aggregator. The SL blogosphere continues to expand, and it has become incredibly hard to keep track of it all. Tao's website makes this important job easier.*

Travis Lambert—*Travis runs the Shelter, a social gathering spot that does a great job welcoming new SL residents in a safe and friendly environment. The Shelter, run entirely as a nonprofit, is one of the longest-running and most valuable SL institutions.*

Walker Spaight—*In his virtual-world identity, Walker Spaight edits the tabloid Second Life Herald, which he took over after founder Urizenus Sklaar retired. He is also a voice on Johnny Ming's SecondCast podcast. In his real-life identity as freelance journalist Mark Wallace, Walker covers Second Life for prestigious real-life publications and blogs about virtual worlds at the popular* http://3pointd.com/.

CHAPTER 11

THE SCRIPTER: CATHERINE OMEGA

The alpha and the omega—Catherine came to the world when the world barely existed, way back in the prehistoric, pre-Beta period of January 2003. She began to master the Linden Script Language and went on to cofound and edit the LSL Scripting

Wiki (http://secondlife.com/badgeo/), the ultimate, indispensable resource for the thousands who came after her, seeking to program in the code that makes *Second Life* come alive with user-created interactivity.

I began my gig as Linden Lab's official "embedded journalist" in April, 2003 (back then I was known as "Hamlet Linden"), and one of the first residents I met was a slender brunette with a utility belt who lived in a mansion by the sea. Catherine Omega told me she built the place and was now constructing a tram system so people could reach it from the nearby mountain, and that was impressive enough. But she wasn't finished. Almost casually, she mentioned that she built this place while she was homeless in real life. She used a desktop computer made with parts she acquired through various means, including from a dumpster outside a computer store. She used a coffee can to get a wireless Internet signal in the rough-and-tumble apartment building she was squatting in at the time. "Cat's da smartz!", her friend Lyra Muse told me, and so she was (and is).

It was right then and there that I decided *Second Life* would be the story of my career. If this young and tiny world with a population in the hundreds already had such extraordinary people among them, I knew even more wonderful stories were sure to come as it grew.

THE CONVENTIONEERS: FLIPPERPA AND JENNYFUR PEREGRINE

When the real-life husband-and-wife team first approached Linden Lab with the idea of throwing a real-life convention for residents, it must have seemed impossible to pull off. And for that matter, after role-playing an alternate persona online, who would want to show off their real-life face in public? But the first *Second Life* Community Convention (SLCC), held in the fall of 2005 in Manhattan, was a success; it attracted residents from around the world. The second SLCC (in 2006) was even more grand, with nearly 500 residents in attendance, some coming from as far away as Australia and France, and numerous major

media outlets swarming to cover it. What began as a fan convention had become a trade expo, too, with numerous real-life companies and organizations hovering around it, looking to invest millions of dollars. And so the goth-inflected couple found itself in charge of a convention that was part Burning Man, part high-tech business expo, all *Second Life*. The couple talks about important *SL* residents in the sidebar "Residents on Movers and Shakers: FlipperPA and Jennyfur Peregrine's Take."

RESIDENTS SPEAK:
SL MOVERS AND SHAKERS: FLIPPERPA AND JENNYFUR PEREGRINE'S TAKE

Bub Linden: *Bub didn't just bring an amazing eye towards graphic design sorely needed for Linden Lab's Web presence; he also brought a fun-loving spirit and instantly became one of the most popular Lindens. His ability to engage residents' enthusiasm in photo shoots and energize the populace to put SL's best foot forward in marketing campaigns is amazing. More than anyone, Bub humanizes Linden Lab to a lot of the residents.*

Darko Cellardoor: *Second Life's best known stoner, with a heart of gold and a penchant for fine literature.*

Jai Nomad: *Jai has been involved in many of the themed areas on the mainland, including the villages of Taber, Boardman, Brown, and Indigo. The GNUbie Store in Indigo was the original freebie market within Second Life, allowing new residents the opportunity to learn by example from some of Second Life's most prolific content creators.*

Munchflower Zaius: *One of Second Life's most popular content creators, whose original motto was, "Slutwear sells!" She's quite an expert at music trivia, and part of the estranged intellectual crowd.*

Obscuro Valkyrie: *Obscuro started the original Second Life vampire role-play group, Vampire Empire. It is one of the most active communities in Second Life and has been since it was founded in 2003. Very few themed communities make it that long!*

Siggy Romulus: *Second Life's original wiseass and trouble maker is also quite a well-known content creator. Siggy is a proud Australian who also hosts his own weekly radio show.*

Stroker Serpentine: *"My name is Stroker, and I am a pervert."* *Stroker's quote from the beginning of the 2006 Second Life Community Convention said it all; he has parlayed that perversion into being the top seller on SLBoutique.com, and a huge X-rated sales empire.*

Ulrika Zugzwang: *A lightning rod to be sure, Ulrika is a highly intelligent liberal who founded Neualtenburg. A self-described social democrat, she was a driving force behind many of the concepts of how government should be handled in SL: always a touchy topic! She also is an expert level animator and scripter.*

Washu Zebrastripe: *One of the biggest markets in Second Life is hair attachments. Washu has always maintained a low profile, but was the original prim-hair designer. Washu's Wigz inspired a renaissance in hair design, with full stores and simulators now dedicated to the art of prim-hair sculpting. She's also got a great sense of humor and is always fun to be around.*

THE FASHIONISTA: NEPHILAINE PROTAGONIST

(PIXEL DOLLS)
CORSET SUIT.
L$100
M/NC/T
INCLUDES
SHIRT, PANTS

Like Aimee Weber, Nephilaine's proven the power to create not just a viable business in avatar fashion, but a unique persona that's just as important to her success. Her avatar is a delicate belle flavored with goth and industrial stylings, and her Pixel Dolls boutique was one of the first clothing emporiums to dominate *SL*. She's often too busy designing to socialize, and her social network seems to be based largely on her loyal customer base and—just as key—on the numerous now-successful fashion designers she taught and encouraged on the way up. She often teams with her real-life husband Neil Protagonist, a professional effects designer and artist in the game industry. Together, creating her Pixel Dolls stores or contributing the fashions to Neil's anime-themed Nakama city, they are an unbeatable force of creativity.

CHAPTER

11

INTRO

PART I

PART II

PART III

APPENDICES

REAL RESIDENTS

THE GAME GOD: KERMITT QUIRK

A combination of Tetris and Bingo with a gambling hook, Tringo, created in late 2004, has consumed the community of *SL*; it's played 24/7 in casinos, nightclubs, and game rooms. Its success was based not just on its ease of play and its gambling aspect, but on a clever franchise system Kermitt created that gave buyers an incentive to host Tringo games of their own. Kermitt sold hundreds of copies, and his success leaped to whole new levels when the rights for the game were sold for a Game Boy Advance port. This was possible, of course, because Linden Lab allows residents to retain the intellectual property rights over their creations. Nearly a year later, however, Kermitt Quirk remains the only major success story for this policy—and as such, remains among the top role model for realizing the *Second Life* dream.

THE GRID QUEEN: BACCARA RHODES

Often seen sashaying through the world in a Versace evening gown, Baccara's avatar is a woman of a certain age, and by sheer force of personality she transformed herself into the grande dame of *SL*. Her language is elegant and often high-flown, and she tolerates no vulgar speech. She once decided on a whim to move into the combat-enabled war zone, and scolded the gamers there for their rude behavior; outraged, they launched a series of terrorist attacks culminating in the kidnapping of a monkey in an art gallery rigged with proximity mines. (But they never threatened Baccara directly, because, one of them sheepishly admitted, she had too many powerful friends for them to risk that.)

Since then, Baccara has used her real-life experience as a wedding and bar mitzvah planner to organize numerous elaborate weddings and projects that involve dozens of creators, including a 32-acre tribute to *The Wizard of Oz* in 2004 and a 48-acre tribute to the world of Peter Pan in 2005. It's projects like this that helped make her the central connector of diverse and often insular groups of builders and scripters with the socializers and casual gamers they rarely interact with otherwise. Now a successful businesswoman, Baccara is the co-owner of Home Depoz (as the name suggests, a retail outlet for houseware and furniture) and Stardust (a prime location for parties and weddings which she, of course, plans).

THE COMMUNITY BUILDER: THE SOJOURNER

A one-woman demonstration of the power of *Second Life* as a social tool, Ms. Sojourner has been a tireless volunteer and organizer in *SL* for nearly two years as a founder of Shockproof, a support group for stroke survivors, and as an event planner and organizer on the Dreams sim, home to endless building contests and holiday fairs to benefit a good cause.

THE BRAND: AIMEE WEBER

Full-disclosure: Ms. Weber occasionally contributes to my New World Notes blog, but she's earned her place on this list numerous times, first as a fashion designer who became successful based not only on her massive sales and distinct style, but for the brand identity she created around it—an outrageously brash, flirty, distinctly tipsy punk-rock ballerina

with blue butterfly wings. To frame this personality (and a prime consumer location), she built the island of Midnight City, a virtual New York with textures and lighting to rival the best from *Grand Theft Auto*. Not satisfied with doing just that, Aimee also became an innovator in immersive educational experiences, working, for example, with the San Francisco Exploratorium to create a 3D model demonstrating how eclipses work, and for the National Oceanic and Atmospheric Administration to simulate a tsunami's effect on the shoreline. In the commercial realm, Aimee created two of the first *SL* experiences for major-real world corporations—an in-world "listening booth" done up to look like a hip New York loft for Warner Brothers singer Regina Spektor, and a virtual retail site for American Apparel. In the sidebar "Residents on Movers and Shakers: Aimee Weber's Take" Aimee discusses residents who interest her.

SIDEBAR

RESIDENTS SPEAK:
SL MOVERS AND SHAKERS: AIMEE WEBER'S TAKE

Ama Omega—*Dark Life creator and expert programmer.*

Bel Muse—*Nexus Prime founder and Second Look website creator, her early work set the stage for SL works to come.*

BuhBuhCuh Fairchild—*BBC is the leader in Second Life's machinima movement. His efforts have propelled movies in SL from a useless curiosity into a budding industry.*

Cienna Rand—*Technical guru and the mother of IRC's #SecondLife channel. Via IRC Cienna is the leader of a whole tech underground in SL.*

Johnny Ming—*Johnny Ming started and runs SecondCast, the most successful podcast in Second Life.*

Kris Ritter—*Kris Ritter was an early builder who created one of the first enormous projects, Heaven and Hell, I saw. It was an inspiration for me in my formative years of SL.*

Mistress Midnight—*Fashion designer and founder of Midnight City.*

Nylon Pinkney—*Introduced a hand-drawn "cartoon" alternative to the generally accepted photo-quality texture work that dominated SL.*

qDot Bunnyhug—*Uh... *blush* you know...sexy stuff.*

Rathe Underthorn—*Technical expert known for pervasive advertising billboards.*

Trinity Serpentine—*The voice of* Second Life, *Trin and her cohost Nala Galatea are the most successful streaming DJs in* Second Life.

Xylor Baysklef—*Created a variety of SL wonders including XYObject, which is scripted to automatically create large objects, and XYText, which fills an enormous need for text displays in SL.*

CHAPTER 12

A CULTURAL TIMELINE

"I'm not building a game," Philip Linden once said, "I'm building a new country." And in many ways, the history of *Second Life* thus far resembles the first centuries of America itself; *Second Life* grew from sparsely inhabited arcadia and a few natives to a place of colonists and pioneers, then on to a diverse and richly tapestried place with a population larger than Boston and still growing. This chapter is devoted to that history, and to some of the personal and cultural milestones that happened along the way.

CONTENTS

FIRST ERA—2001 THROUGH EARLY 2003: PRE-HISTORIC, PRE-BETA

First created as a platform to test virtual reality and touch-interface technology, *LindenWorld* came into existence in 2001. In the beginning, avatars were known as Primitars, awkward robots composed of prims, which roamed the earth on stubby legs, occasionally terraforming it with ground-shaking grenades. They shared the world with snakelike creatures called Ators and rock-eating birds.

Redubbed *Second Life*, the world opened to non-Lindens in March 2002, welcoming small tribes of Alpha and closed Beta citizens by limited invitation. Land was shared in common, and tiny, close-knit tribes of tinkerers and utopians took root. (See the "Early-History Memories" sidebar.)

SECOND ERA—SUMMER 2003: NATIVES VERSUS COLONISTS

Public Beta of *Second Life* began in April 2003, and while most settlers intermingled with the original residents, cultural rifts appeared. Back then, the continent was tiny and three sims were known as The Outlands, where combat was allowed, even encouraged. The Outlands often became a battleground to act out these conflicts.

SIDEBAR

RESIDENTS SPEAK:
EARLY-HISTORY MEMORIES

"I had been searching for the Metaverse since I read Snow Crash... *I found* Second Life *mentioned in a GameSpy.com forum that was discussing the inadequacies of MMORPGs shown at 2002's E3. When I checked the link, I immediately knew I had found my Metaverse. That was in August 2002, and after a few excited e-mails to Linden Lab, I was allowed into* LindenWorld *in early September.* LindenWorld *was the pre-Second Life world, basically SL without water.*

"I heard that about 50 users had logged [in] before I arrived, but there were only about five regulars that I would see each week. If six people

were in-world at the same time it was a *PAR-TAY! A couple months later we moved from LindenWorld to Second Life, and there were peaks of 20 people on at the same time. They mostly hung out in the same area—around the 'newbie corral.'*

"In the early months the culture was definitely create-centric. At least I was. I love creating, and socializing is secondary for me. My most memorable event was one weekend (while the Lindens were away), BuhBuhCuh and I decided to build a bunch of Neo-Tokyo structures overshadowing the little downtown city the Lindens had built."

—bUTTONpUSHER Jones

"I've been living my second life for well over two years. Much as how Forrest Gump frequently found himself at the crossroads of historic events, it quickly became apparent to me, Torley Linden (née Torgeson), how many pioneering adventures I'd become caught up in. And not just as an observer, but a participant—something which continues for many resis (my shorthand for "residents") to this day and beyond.

"My eyes close and memories spill forth: one of my earliest and fondest dates to late 2004, when a seemingly innocuous sim, Meins, came into the acquisition of Kex Godel. She was one of my earliest mentors, often found floating on a cloud in the classic Ahern-Morris Welcome Area. Amongst friends, we jestingly buzzed about how 'KEX IS A LAND BARON!' As sandboxes of the fertile imagination are entirely appropriate in Second Life, numerous experiments were birthed in Kexland.

"Our own Thomas Edison, Francis Chung—of "guns and hugs" fame, whose profile in New World Notes in fact led me into Second Life in the first place—constructed what I'd dub the "Frananthema Macrobuild." A towering mass, many stories high, decorated with sinister Giger-esque etchings, some parts resembling an epic flying swordsman flick's fight setting.

"The significance of this quickly becomes apparent when you think of, say, Donald Trump's skyscrapers—empires, dynasties! What eventually happened was Meins changed hands to the Gigas Group.

"And then what?

INTRO

PART I

PART II

PART III

APPENDICES

SECOND ERA

"The Macrobuild was eventually taken down—de-rezzed—and what cropped up was a cyberpunky residential neighborhood. I could almost feel Gigas cofounder Adam Zaius grinning from ear to ear as he took me for a tour and showed me his spinning artworks. It was sad to see the tower go, but 'twasn't indicative of any empire falling, but rather, one rising.

"In hindsight, if you've connected the dots, you'll notice that these are the roots of what would become the Azure Islands, an expanding resident-run continent which has proved influential to other would-be empire builders. Second Life's island estates are booming and there's no end in sight. Plus, it's just gorgeous to sit on its beaches; not too many moons ago, I hung out with old friends in a tiki hut atmosphere.

"More threads tie into our tapestry:

"Adam Zaius and Oz Spade of Gigas wound up creating the official Linden in-world offices. They're not used as much as I'd like to see, but their style of decadent elegance in tandem with practicality is very much apparent—and oft-copied to this day.

"Francis Chung would go on to create even greater things, collaborating on the Wet Ikon ROAM project with Rathe Underthorn, a jetpack device that automatically flew you from any point A to any point B on the main continent. While ROAM disbanded earlier this year, I believe its conception encouraged the Lindens to implement direct, point-to-point teleportation. A YUGE (as Trump would say) societal change! At last, resis were no longer bound to fly to a destination from Telehubs, those beautiful-but-damned timewasters.

"Kex Godel's early SL Preferences FAQ ended up inspiring me to write some of my own and proofread other resis' documentation, which eventually led to my getting hired at Linden Lab. So I stay very close to my roots to this day, recognizing you cannot possibly have a destination without a point of origin. Kex also got to go to SL Views, a Linden-sponsored roundtable where leading residents could share their ideas and concerns with the company in person. I'm proud of her and grateful I met her, and many others who've helped me in my travels.

"And me, Torley Linden? As an avatar forever voyaging with my watermelon fetish, I'm still finding my way stumbling across fun times,

many of them now recognized as monumentally important, some of them not, but...it's all about the experience.

"If the journey's the reward, then Second Life has paid for itself many times over. Best US$10 I ever spent."

—Torley Linden

"I have been a resident of Second Life since July of 2003. It was a time when there was barely a landscape at all; bits of buildings dotting the world here and there and many days less than 50 people ever logged on at one time.

"There is no way to talk about my most cherished memories of Second Life without talking about the events. Somewhere during my early days, I began to stage events to publicize my early builds. It became apparent that my friends and indeed our residents at large were much more interested in the fun than the build, and so before long, I was back in the party business. (I had been an event planner for most of my professional life, but now retired. Sometimes we try to escape our past, but it often grabs us again.)

"After a score of early soirees, (fashion shows, store openings, and of course weddings) fashion designer Fey Brightwillow and I founded Spellbound Events, the first cohesive building, scripting, and animating team in Second Life. After deciding that storybook lore was our real love, we looked around for an idea that we thought would interest the entire community, male and female of all ages.

"So in Summer 2004, we gathered the Spellbound members together and staged Oz on one of the few private sims existing in SL at the time, Evie Fairchild's Island of Cayman. SL was barely a year past the beta stage, and yet Oz drew hundreds of visitors from our still-tiny world. Many came back repeatedly to put on the munchkin avatars provided, and dance the night away with their favorite characters, follow the yellow brick road, and watch the witch melt.

"Months passed, and the members of Spellbound quickly got restless to repeat the fun in an improved way. Therefore, I came to visit Linden Lab to ask for help to stage yet another community event, one of a size that

12

INTRO

PART I

PART II

PART III

APPENDICES

SECOND ERA

Second Life *had never seen: a trip through early 20th-century London and a tribute to Peter Pan. The Lindens tried a pilot donation of three sims for a three-month period. We would have six weeks to construct our vision, and six weeks for the world at large to visit it.*

"And visit it they did. They came in droves, by the thousands, logging an unprecedented number of visitor hours. People came repeatedly to role-play in Edwardian costume, [or as] raggedy boys, pirates, or Indian children. They chatted on the streets of London, foiled would-be bank robbers, flew out the Darlings' window across the water past the Jolly Roger in search of the Lost Boys, and had swordfights with Captain Hook himself.

"It was a window to the soul of what Second Life *was and could really be as a community. Everything was provided free of charge. People came, played, and enjoyed in the spirit of good fellowship. It was a most special time. Even the* New York Times *covered the event in a story about* Second Life, *capturing its spirit forevermore.*

"As I reflect on the early days, I remember how I marveled at the creativity of people. Every day some new way of making magic was happening. Today I see building groups formed whose sole purpose is constructing large projects but more of a commercial nature, which is just as wonderful. And no matter what the purpose, the idea of camaraderie to a single goal is an incredible benefit to Second Life. *The work is more exacting and the standards are tougher but I still believe that our motives are the same.* Second Life *as a world wishes to be the best it can be.*

"As our world has grown, events like Neverland are more difficult to arrange. Impossible no; nothing ever is. Each time I meet a wide-eyed new avatar I hear in them the amazement that is Second Life. *They can immediately understand all that is possible. At any age, you are returned to an age of innocence. Your creativity is restored. In any life, it hardly gets any better than that."*

—Baccara Rhodes

WAR OF THE JESSIE WALL

During public Beta, players of *World War II Online (WWIIOL)*, a massively multiplayer online Allies vs. Axis military strategy game, discovered *Second Life* and arrived by the

hundreds, using the building tools to meet and plan tactics for *WWIIOL*. They formed a group called WWIIOLers and unsurprisingly, they also built weapons and fortresses. This sudden influx of combat-minded residents was a culture shock to many. Before their arrival, many peaceful residents had put down roots and built homes in The Outlands, and they were upset by the arrival of armed avatars who opened fire on them in their own homes.

Open battle broke out between the WWIIOLers and indigenous resisters, and much of it centered around the Jessie Wall, an imposing barrier that separated the civilized districts of *Second Life* from the war zone (Figure 12.1). The wall also became a billboard for pro- and antiwar sentiment over the war in Iraq, which was raging in the real world, and that spurred the antagonism even further. (Most of the WWIIOLers supported the war; many of the residents nearby did not.) Robot turrets, teleporting bullets, and other weapons were built and deployed in what was, in

Figure 12.1: The WWIIOLers defend their territory in Jessie.

retrospect, a conflict to define the nature of *Second Life*: pacifist utopia, or gun-happy libertarian free-for-all. The battle was quelled eventually, and clashes like it are largely made moot by the continued growth of the world, with more than enough space for both pacifists and war gamers to be in *SL* without them even meeting each other, if they so choose.

SECOND ERA—SUMMER 2003: REVOLUTION!

As society forms, so does social upheaval. The most pronounced example in *SL* was the reaction to Linden Lab's "tax policy." Residents were being taxed (L$ were deducted from their accounts automatically) for objects they instantiated in-world. To the Lindens, this seemed like a simple way to prevent residents from overheating the servers with too many objects. But the Lindens got way more than they expected.

INTRO
CHAPTER 1
CHAPTER 2
CHAPTER 3
CHAPTER 4
CHAPTER 5
CHAPTER 6
CHAPTER 7
CHAPTER 8
CHAPTER 9
CHAPTER 10
CHAPTER 11
CHAPTER 12
CHAPTER 13
APPENDICES

THE TEA CRATE REBELLION OF JULY '03

Objecting most strongly to Linden's tax policy was Americana, a group devoted to creating tributes to US landmarks. Feeling punished for their public-works project, Americana unleashed a protest suitable to their name, dropping giant tea crates across the world and setting their American landmarks on fire. A cat named Fleabite Beach sent out a Thoreau-style proclamation against "Mad King Linden," and led the revolutionaries into the streets with muskets and signs emblazoned with the words "Born Free: Taxed to Death!" (Figure 12.2) Much of the citizenry was drawn into the insurrection, either as rebels or redcoat "Linden loyalists."

Figure 12.2: Fleabite Beach and other tax revolters pose in 2006 for a reunion portrait.

But from conflict comes community, because it was one of the first times residents saw themselves together in a grid-wide struggle. And though the Lindens may not admit it, the protests helped encourage them to end the tax system.

THIRD ERA—WINTER 2003: A NEW NATION IS BORN

During this period, Linden Lab made three policy decisions that were considered radical at the time:

1. To end monthly subscriptions (the standard revenue model for almost all MMOs) and instead, begin charging monthly "land use" fees for virtual land

2. To announce a laissez-faire policy on buying and selling the official in-world currency on the open market for real money

3. To recognize residents' legally enforceable intellectual-property rights over the objects and scripts they created within the world

NOVEMBER 14, 2003: IP INDEPENDENCE DAY!

Advised by *Free Culture* author and Stanford law professor Lawrence Lessig (Figure 12.3)— basically making him the Thomas Jefferson of *Second Life*—Linden Lab established a new policy, dedicated to the proposition that residents should retain intellectual-property rights over works they create in-world. The impact was not felt immediately, but that coupled with the ability to trade L$ for US$ spurred the growth of a substantial mercantile class (artisans, entertainers, shopkeepers, weaponsmiths, etc.).

Figure 12.3. Lawrence Lessig

RESIDENTS SPEAK:
THE HISTORY OF LUSKWOOD

"The beginnings of 'Furry in SL' certainly were not planned. The right people, at the right time, doing the right things, led to a sort of perfect environment for Luskwood to have its genesis.

"September 2003: Michi Lumin and Eltee Statosky had recently 'migrated' from a furry-oriented text-based virtual world, and 3D seemed like the next natural progression. Michi had brought Liam along with her from anime-based mush/mud environments.

"While SL was promising, it seemed to confine you, at first glance, to a human avatar. Around this time, Eltee was running around with fox ears and a tail stuck to the normal human avatar, which was the closest thing SL had to furries. This was around the time when Arito Cotton was

CHAPTER 12

INTRO

PART I

PART II

PART III

APPENDICES

THIRD ERA

 experimenting with attachments to make an avatar which would be worn over the human avatar.

"Needless to say, Arito's first attempt went over well (even though he doesn't like to show that avatar to this day—it was certainly embryonic compared to what we have now). But word spread fast, and it wasn't long before Arito had made four or five custom prim avatars for other people.

"Michi, Eltee, and Liam met up with Arito, and saw some of his avatars. Gathering at Eltee's small plot in Lusk, Michi worked with Arito to create the dragon avatar that she still wears to this day, and Liam, who was essentially the second furry-avatar maker in SL, began making his own with the group.

"Nightly, the group would get together and just build and talk. On one of these nights, Liam made a wooden owl lamp and joked that the group should call themselves Luskwood. Working in Lusk and Olive (Arito's first plot—which Luskwood still owns), the four refined their personal avatars over a few weeks, added scripts, and took them on as their main personas.

"Back then, events were pretty much global—the world was small, and "Show and Tell" events happened pretty much daily, announced personally by the Lindens. After the Lusk crew showed up at some of these events with their new creations, public interest began to mount. People began to come to Lusk to see the new developments that the Luskwood group was creating, and interest in these anthropomorphic prim avatars spread.

"Over the next few weeks, the group ended up with well over 30 requests for custom furry avatars. Thirty furries in SL was considered quite a number then, and the Luskwood custom waiting list began to grow from one month to several months; each avatar took about a week to complete. Eventually, Arito figured that Luskwood could sell a "basic" avatar, which would only have to be built once, and would be sold as modifiable so that the end user could easily change hair color or add customization to his or her own liking.

"The vendor—the first avatar vendor in SL, built in the same wooden style as Liam's owl lamp—inherited the name Luskwood Creatures. Arito

← figured that Luskwood would sell at most 100 of these avatars, declaring that if they sold more, he would 'eat a plywood prim. In real life.'

figured that Luskwood would sell at most 100 of these avatars, declaring that if they sold more, he would 'eat a plywood prim. In real life.'

"To date, Luskwood has sold 23,000 avatars, and Arito has yet to eat a single block of wood."

—Michi Lumin

FOURTH ERA—LATE 2003 THROUGH EARLY 2004: EXPANDING THE FRONTIER

The great land rush began in December 2003, when Linden ended the tax system, eliminated monthly subscriptions, and adopted virtual-land usage fees as a revenue model. In the beginning, Linden held "land grabs" for new territory, similar to claim-staking events in the American frontier. *SL* residents by the dozens would hover around real estate controlled by "Governor Linden" and wait for the Lindens to release it to the open market at the top of the hour. Eventually the Lindens civilized this process with an auction system, in which plots of land and entire continents are put on the open market, both for Linden dollars and US dollars. The first island was put on the block on January 7th, 2004—and the rights to own it were sold for over US$1,200 to Fizik Baskerville (see Chapter 11 for more on Fizik). The day after news hit that Fizik owned a real-world commercial branding agency and was planning on using *SL* as a marketing platform, protestors were there to greet him, waving "Boycott the Island" signs.

From the moment the land-ownership policy began, real estate was rapidly claimed, bought, and sold, even as the company added new continents and private islands to keep up with demand. The "land barons" began to emerge, using their business acumen to acquire large swaths of territory, then charging a "rental" fee to other residents.

THE IMMIGRANT EXPERIENCE

Throughout the first three years, waves of Net-based cultures arrived: the technorati who read about *SL* on sites like Slashdot and Boing Boing, hard-core gamers who

12

INTRO

PART I

PART II

PART III

APPENDICES

FIFTH ERA

were looking for an online building-block set to play around with, the furries (of course!), anime fans, and more. Impelled by policy changes or led en masse by pioneers, many were expatriates from other online worlds, seeking a place where they could make their own rules. After *Second Life* accounts were made free in mid 2006—previously there was a monthly subscriber fee, and later a US$10 sign-up charge for basic accounts—many apparent "immigrants" were in fact simply existing account holders who were starting secondary accounts.

CHAPTER 12 | FIFTH ERA—MID 2004 THROUGH MID 2005: INDUSTRIAL REVOLUTION

Significant integration of Web-based technology into *SL* began in June 2004 with the ability to stream audio onto land, and to incorporate custom animations with avatars. Later in the year came the ability to stream QuickTime video and the ability to export .xml data, and soon afterward, the means to create heads-up displays that let residents customize the interface with new functionality. Each of these innovations fostered whole industries: live music performance and DJs, machinima, in-world advertising, e-commerce websites, and more. On a cultural level, this is roughly when influential residents like SNOOPYbrown Zamboni (aka Jerry Paffendorf, currently Futurist in Residence with The Electric Sheep Company) began to speak of *Second Life* as a kind of 3D Web, a new medium that merged an online world with interfaces previously associated with the World Wide Web.

SIDEBAR | FROM LINDEN LAB: BREAKING THROUGH

"While Second Life *has always received plenty of publicity and news coverage, I think the breakthrough happened in June 2004, with a Reuters wire story featured in* USA Today *and on* MSNBC *describing how residents owned virtual land. This culminated with Philip speaking live on CNN. A lot of us Lindens ran over to the bar across the street, watched his segment, then had a little celebratory drink before going back to work. That was the first time we understood that* Second Life *was going to make a difference."*

—Catherine Linden

RESIDENTS SPEAK:
MILESTONES IN THE LINDEN SCRIPTING LANGUAGE

"The history of Scripting in Second Life can be divided into two categories—first, the points at which functions are placed into the eager hands of residents, and second, the points at which residents apply those functions in combination with existing ones to create working items, usually in an entirely unpredictable manner. For instance, objects which create other objects moving at high speed have been possible since at least January 2003; it has also been possible to have objects which give people money. Was the development of guns firing bullets which actually enrich the victim rather than harm them initially envisaged? I imagine not.

"Still, there have been certain points in the evolution of the Linden Scripting Language (Mark Two—Mark One was a very different beast, not to be mentioned in polite company) which one could call 'landmarks.' Perhaps the first is the development in release 0.6 (April 2003) of a function allowing the reading of notecards by scripts, which allows for considerable storage and retrieval of information.

"In 1.1 (October 2003) we find the introduction of llParticleSystem, the function allowing the generation of swirling patterns, firestorms, smoke clouds, rain, and immense torrents of teddy bears. Perhaps more significantly in terms of effects on the economy, in release 1.4 (June 2004) we see functions allowing for encryption and also for communication with Second Life via the protocol known as XML-RPC, which would make large-scale commercial enterprises such as SLExchange far more practical.

"Returning to more cosmetic (and thus more central to the nature of Second Life) functions, in release 1.6 (March 2005) we see enhanced abilities to detect what an avatar is doing—allowing for the invention of the highly popular Animation Overrides. In 1.7 (October 2005) we have functions allowing the movement of attachments via llSetPos et al, which greatly enhanced the field of avatar creation—now tails could wag, wings flap, clockwork keys rotate.

"In 1.8 (December 2005) functions allowing the banning of people from land parcels by script were introduced, allowing security devices to take

CHAPTER 12

INTRO

PART I

PART II

PART III

APPENDICES

FIFTH ERA

advantage of the protection functions of the world itself. And recently in 1.10 (May 2006) we have llHTTPRequest expanding on the previous method of communication with Aethernet entities, allowing a script to further exploit the powers of machines far separated from the grid.

"Still, the ingenuity of residents when it comes to finding new uses for things continues to produce new results from old material. Only in May 2006 was it discovered that llSetPrimitiveParams could be used to move an object and any passenger an indefinite distance in a mere fraction of a second. The true effect of scripting on the world is defined less by the tools provided and the original intentions behind them, and more by the relentless efforts of residents to use every means at their disposal to affect the grid as they see fit."

—Ordinal Malaprop

MEETING THE LOVEMAKERS

While many people are prone to giggle at the idea of residents using *SL*'s animation technology for making their avatars have close encounters of the most intimate kind, often it's just a kind of entertaining icebreaker that leads to genuine friendship. Two residents I interviewed engaged in a bout of passion like this as a kind of fun role-playing, as if their avatars were stars of an adult movie—then later on, struck up a conversation and

Figure 12.4: Phil and Snow demonstrate an animation that helped grow their business—and their real-life relationship.

became close (but not romantic) friends. They became so close, in fact, that when one of them was left homeless by the Katrina disaster, the other reached out, and without ever having met him, she purchased a bus ticket for him to her home and let him crash on her couch for several weeks.

On another occasion, I interviewed Phil Murdock and Snow Hare of PM Adult, an animation and toy emporium they co-owned, and learned that their business partnership had made them a couple in real life. Their first kiss was an animation they were creating for their customers, and they tested it out on themselves. (Figure 12.4) It was, Phil told me, "awesome and special. Just as special as the first in real life."

SIXTH ERA—SUMMER 2005 THROUGH PRESENT: BOOM TIME

As of this writing, the world is experiencing a boom period. Kermitt Quirk's Tringo not only became an *SL* phenomenon during the sixth era; it became a Game Boy Advance title in April 2006 and started undergoing development as a television show.

Also during this time, Linden Lab launched the LindeX, an internal L$-for-US$ commodities market, effectively transforming virtual currency into a micropayment system. Constant stories in the media (the BBC, ABC, and the cover story for *BusinessWeek* in May 2006) described wonders and wealth beyond measure, spurring another wave of immigrants, many of them entrepreneurs—and carpetbaggers.

All this attention helped fuel the rise of metaverse development companies such as Rivers Run Red, Bedazzle, The Electric Sheep Company, Millions of Us, and more, offering production services for real-world clients paying real cash. In tentative steps, studios like these brought the first real corporations into *Second Life*: Adidas, Reebok, Warner Bros., Major League Baseball, Starwood Hotels, Toyota, and other legacy institutions. The entrance of *Second Life* into the "Web 2.0" pantheon along with user-created content portals like MySpace and YouTube was well under way.

ADVENTURES IN MIXED REALITY

Second Life was designed to keep reality and the online world as separate as possible, but the real world always finds a way of sneaking through, from major personalities in arts, culture, and politics to very real businesses on the Fortune 500 list.

REAL-WORLD FIGURES

As I remember it, bringing real names into *Second Life* was first suggested by Web developer Jim Linden, in the days when I was still Linden Lab's "embedded reporter." I had just had my first "Hamlet Linden Book Club" with Cory Doctorow, though at the time his avatar was called CoryDoctorow Electric—his surname taken from the default list. "Why not just make his name Cory Doctorow?", Jim asked casually. "We can do that on the

Mark Warner

Figure 12.5: Governor Warner, the avatar

server." And so the next time Cory entered the world to talk about his latest novel, he was called Cory Doctorow. His fellow novelist Ellen *The Bug* Ullman and game designer Harvey *Deus Ex* Smith had similar experiences. Then came technology guru and venture capitalist Joi Ito and (in a series of summer-'06 appearances sponsored by public radio's *The Infinite Mind*), famed singer and "mother of the MP3" Suzanne Vega. MIT technology designer John Maeda, Internet visionary Howard *Smart Mobs* Rheingold, politician Mark Warner (Figure 12.5; see the sidebar "Governor Warner's Second Life") and legendary novelist Kurt Vonnegut (Figure 12.6) also got in on the action. (As it happens, the idea to give residents a limited choice of surnames to choose from was presaged in Vonnegut's novel *Slapstick*, in which everyone in America is given a new name to create immediate affiliations between individuals who might not otherwise have anything in common. This created, in effect, instant families.) As we go to press in late 2006, these notable figures will soon be joined by all the members of '80s supergroup Duran Duran, who'll appear as themselves on an island experience created by Fizik Baskerville (see Chapter 11) and his Rivers Run Red.

In the near future, Linden Lab is expected to allow residents to designate avatar surnames of their choice, and many will surely come to the world with their real names. Perhaps many will choose their real surname while maintaining their avatar's first name. This is what I did when I left the company to write my own book on *Second*

Life, in early 2006. By then, Hamlet Linden had already become more recognizable than my real-life name: Google listed it about half as much as my real name, but Googling my actual name turned up New World Notes and Hamlet Linden as the first two hits. And what began three years ago as a split-second choice to make "Hamlet" my first name in *SL* resulted in a name I'm now stuck with. Were I to start fresh with an entirely new avatar title, I would also need to start a whole new walk on the karmic cycle of Internet being.

Figure 12.6: The avatar of Kurt Vonnegut

As *Second Life* becomes even more important to the Internet, so will the names of *SL* avatars—choose wisely.

ADDITIONAL INFO:
GOVERNOR WARNER'S SECOND LIFE

In August 2006 the former governor of Virginia took on avatar form, flew onto a stage, and met with a group of residents to discuss war in Iraq, terrorism, abortion, and his political action committee (which now has a branch in SL). It was a culmination of numerous visits to SL by real-world figures on the international political scene, including Lawrence Lessig (January '06), who pleaded a case before the Supreme Court; and Thomas P.M. Barnett (October '05), who worked for Donald Rumsfeld in the Pentagon and briefed Senator John Kerry during and after his bid for President in 2004. Anything now seems possible in Second Life.

REAL-WORLD COMPANIES

American Apparel, Warner Brothers, Major League Baseball, Toyota, Adidas, and Starwood Hotels are just a few of the real-world companies that have a permanent/ongoing presence in *SL*. Primarily brought into the grid by the Metaverse Big Three (see Chapter 11) studios, these companies are engaging with residents through "branded experiences" that are meant to be promotion for them and fun for the community. Buy American Apparel clothes and Adidas shoes for your avatar, purchase a low-priced replica of a Toyota Scion to tool around in, watch a re-creation of a baseball game between the Yankees and the Red Sox, visit a prototype hotel design from Starwood (owners of the Westin, Sheraton, and W chains), then listen to the music of Regina Spektor, available in New York–style loft sites sponsored by Warner Brothers Records. By the time you read this, of course, these companies and their experiences will no doubt be joined by countless others, providing residents with a chance (if they're interested) to merge real-world consumerism with their second lives.

SIDEBAR

RESIDENTS SPEAK:
FASHION MILESTONES

"Fashion in Second Life *moves at Internet speed—and so does the underlying technology that gives* Second Life *such a dynamic and expressive way to customize an avatar.*

"The first major innovation was the emergence of 'photorealistic' skins. The default system skins are not very realistic-looking, either in terms of musculature or skin tones. Innovative content developers decided they could 'hack' the Second Life *default by—at first—creating files to replace the stock files which came with the* Second Life *viewer. Later, the idea of using a 'full-body tattoo' to store the skin texture made it easier, simpler, and safer for residents to find and buy a skin which not only looked incredible but permitted a diverse range of makeup, shading, and body-hair options, all things the default skins were not especially well suited to do in a believable way.*

"The next major fashion innovation was the use of prims for hair and shoes. Using a collection of linked and specially textured prims as hair caused a fashion revolution, because many were dissatisfied with the options available in the default avatar-adjustment sliders. Prim hair changed all of that, and quickly. Soon after, people began to experiment ➡

with prim shoes which permitted developers to make realistic looking three-dimensional footwear—everything from athletic sneakers to boots any real-life dominatrix would be proud to stash in her closet.

"The final and most recent fashion revolution was the introduction of the flexible prim shapes in the 1.10 software release. Flexible prims allow three prim shapes (cylinders, prisms, and cubes) to react to the movement from in-world physics. From the day of 1.10's release, flexiprims took the fashion world completely by storm—from swaying minis to superhero capes and elegant wedding trains, the world of *Second Life* fashion just hasn't been the same since flexiprims arrived on the scene.

"Although *Second Life* definitely has its own fashion ebb and flow, the popular styles in-world often come from real-world inspiration. As just one example, this year's fashion trends have seen a revival of popular '80s couture such as leg warmers, plaid patterns, dresses and shorts with tights, and frilly embellished shirts.

"In general, most garments and shoes in *Second Life* tend more toward sassy (the uncharitable might even make that 'trashy') than classy, but in a virtual world where you can set the size of your avatar's butt using a slider and show off killer abs because of a developer's skill in Photoshop, why not dare to bare? That's the attitude of most residents and there is no shortage of revealing wild styles to tempt and tantalize."

—Celebrity Trollop

BUILDING COMMUNITY: BURNING LIFE

A tribute to the famed Burning Man festival held every year during Labor Day weekend, the Linden Lab–sponsored Burning Life is *SL* at its most free-form. What begins as an untouched flat island becomes, in the space of days, a kind of shared hallucination: the sculpture of a giant hand with a giant magnifying glass, frying the world; a human-sized, rideable Pac-Man tribute; a 3D re-creation of Edvard Munch's "The Scream" that lets *you* become the screamer on the boardwalk. The

INTRO
PART I
PART II
PART III
APPENDICES
BUILDING COMMUNITY:
MAKING A DIFFERENCE

first Burning Life was in 2003, and it's grown twice as large each year, culminating in the ritual burning of the giant wooden man (Figure 12.7) then disappearing as quickly as it came.

Figure 12.7: Artemis Fate, Krysss Galatea, Torrid Midnight, Gonta Maltz, and Maxx Mackenzie re-create Burning Life

BUILDING COMMUNITY: MAKING A DIFFERENCE

Thanks to the work of Jade Lily and Aimee Weber (see Chapter 11), along with their army of volunteers, *SL*'s Relay for Life raised nearly $40,000 for the American Cancer Society through a combination of telethon pledging and auctions. This topped an effort spearheaded by ReallyRick Metropolitan in the wake of the Katrina Hurricane disaster (and thus with little advance notice) to rally residents and launch dozens if not hundreds of impromptu events, parties, raffles, and other fund-raisers (Figure 12.8),

Figure 12.8: A Katrina donation site

a collective effort that eventually raised over $10,000 in donations, most of it going to the Red Cross.

The first known *SL* fundraiser began in April of 2004, launched by a casino magnate named Jason Foo. Before his second life, Jason was an active-duty Marine who saw fierce action in Iraq, the Philippines, and Afghanistan (where a mine killed his best friend and shattered one of Jason's kneecaps). Forced into retirement by this injury but unable to work, he turned to *Second Life* to supplement his VA benefits. As he became successful in-world, Jason reached out to fellow vets, creating donation boxes in his casinos to benefit a veterans-support group called New Directions; the group raised hundreds of US dollars.

In June 2004 a group fundraiser was coordinated by Bhodi Silverman and volunteers to benefit the online rights group the Electronic Frontier Foundation. Working with Gaming Open Market, a L$-to-US$ currency-exchange site popular at the time, Bhodi and her team held events and auctions that raised the L$ equivalent of US$1,768—extraordinary for an era in which the world was just several thousand active residents.

Both these efforts occurred very soon after Linden Lab enabled residents to buy and sell L$ for real currency. It's good to remember that among the very first uses of this ability was to make a beneficial impact on real people beyond the bounds of *SL*.

LINDEN-SPONSORED EVENTS

Once key attractions in life on the grid, official events put on by Linden Lab now compete with the dozens of other activities going on every hour. Besides Burning Life (see "Building Community" in this chapter), the company hosts at least two regular events. Check the Lindens' group blog (`http://blog.secondlife.com`) to find out more.

Town Halls. Usually held on a monthly basis, these are occasions to meet top Linden staff including Philip, Cory, and Community Development VP Robin Harper, to discuss issues affecting *SL*, and get word of system upgrades and planned changes. While these meetings often attract a capacity crowd, the Lindens take pains to make sure residents can participate, giving out "repeaters" (devices that transmit the Town Hall chat anywhere in the grid) or pointing residents to the Internet server where they can listen in.

The *Second Life* Game Developer Contest. Held annually, this is where resident game developers showcase their projects, be they first-person shooters, real-time strategy, or a variety of other genres. Previous contests have been judged by veteran

professionals like Harvey "*Deus Ex*" Smith and Doug "*Thief: The Dark Project*" Church. Most recently the games were judged by popular choice, based on the most pay-to-play action.

Linden Land. In late 2003, the company opened up an amusement park, inviting residents to build and maintain rides and contests. With roller coasters and arcade games, it was the most ambitious building and scripting *SL* had seen. Sinatra Cartier's jarring Spook House ride still stands.

New Moves for a New World. In July 2004, to inaugurate the recently added custom animation tools of version 1.4, Linden Lab sponsored a contest that challenged residents to create videos demonstrating their coolest moves. The semifinalists were presented at a hipster nightclub in San Francisco. Appropriately, Ulrika Zugzang's re-creation of Michael Jackson's classic "Thriller" video (featuring zombie choreography) took the grand prize.

Campus *Second Life* Launch. Reaching out to the academic world, VP of Community Development Robin Harper launched a new initiative for colleges and universities interested in using the grid as a pedagogical tool. Early adopters included Aaron Delwiche, an assistant professor at Trinity University, and University of Texas at Austin's Anne Beamish, who used it to teach principles of social design for her architecture students. Many educators and institutions followed, including Harvard's Berkman Center and USC's Annenberg Center on Public Diplomacy, both of which conducted lectures and events from their own *SL* islands.

Opening of the Teen Grid. Responding to countless requests from frustrated adolescents and their parents, Linden Lab opened up a separate realm of *Second Life* in August 2005, reserved for residents between ages 13 and 17. Growing slowly, Teen *Second Life* now has 45,000 residents, and it often acts as a training ground for teens preparing to enter "the mature grid." (Australian Liaison Nicole Linden even introduced a welcoming party for teen residents who turn 18 and are thus eligible for this graduation.)

100,000-Resident Party. After years of steady growth, *Second Life* went from several hundred residents during the Beta period, to several thousand throughout to tens of thousand, finally culminating to 100,000 at the very end of 2005 (an ideal holiday gift). The occasion was marked by Linden-sponsored celebrations throughout the grid—and a party at Linden Lab headquarters in San Francisco.

"Bells and Spurs" at South by Southwest. The brainchild of writer/director Eric Linden, the six-minute machinima made entirely in *Second Life* made its public debut at the famed SXSW interactive/film/music festival in March 2006. Featuring

a cast of dozens and lip-sync animation (so avatars are actually depicted speaking dialog), the cowboy poem of ornery gunslingers in a deadly showdown was a showcase for *Second Life* as a filmmakers' tool.

SIDEBAR

ADDITIONAL INFO:
THE SECOND LIFE COMMUNITY CONVENTION

The brainchild of FlipperPA and Jennyfur Peregrine (see the previous chapter) the first SLCC was in 2005 in New York and attracted 100-plus attendees. (While not an official Linden Lab event, the company and others help with sponsorship, and the Lindens appear there in force.) On a dare, Philip gave the first keynote dressed up to resemble his SL avatar, Rolling Stones T-shirt and sequined codpiece included. That was when the world had a scant 60,000 registered users, and those times are long gone; for SLCC 2006, held in August, the world was fast approaching 500,000 residents, and nearly 500 of them attended the convention. By then, SLCC was no longer just an occasion for parties and exchanging SL tips, but also a business convention, with companies that do business in Second Life *making announcements about deals they'd struck with major corporations.*

The official SLCC site is http://slconvention.com/. *Keep an eye on it for news on dates and places for the next convention. And if you do go, remember that when meeting each other in person, SL residents—even Lindens—generally call each other by their avatar names. That's whether they look like a version of their alter egos or come without the fur, devil horns, alien skin, robot gear, and other enhancements you've come to identify them by in-world. What's amazing is how natural this feels, and how familiar you can quickly get with hundreds of people you've known only through 3D graphics.*

CHAPTER 13

THE FUTURE AND IMPACT OF SECOND LIFE

If you've made it this far, you're well prepared
for your second life. You know by now what a
virtual world is, who you can expect to meet
in one, how to get around *Second Life*, how to
create an identity for yourself, how to make
friends, earn money, explore your new world,
and add to the user-generated content that
brings it alive. If you've applied the lessons of
this book, you should be able to settle in for a
good long stay.

What might that extended stay look like? In
Chapter 13 we'll explore the answer to this
question by discussing the impact of *Second Life*
along with what the future might hold for it.

CONTENTS

HOW LONG WILL THIS LAST?

Most massively multiplayer online games see their players stick around for a little less than a year, on average. But as we've seen, *Second Life* is not really a game. It has no fixed goals to accomplish, no scores by which to measure your progress through the world. Success is judged in the same way people judge success in real life: according to how much money, love, fame, family, fulfillment, and so on you amass; it's completely up to you to say whether your second life is a success, and how you came to that decision. And it's completely up to you as to when the experience begins and ends. Most MMO players leave their games because they've experienced all the content that the developers were able to produce. Even if new content is coming down the pike in the form of expansion packs, it's often such a small variation on what they've seen before that many players aren't willing to put in the time. They'd rather move on. For all intents and purposes, they've seen it all.

In *Second Life*, it's nearly impossible to have seen it all. As long as new residents continue to stream into the world, *Second Life* will always have a practically limitless supply of new content to experience, new places to go, new people to meet, and new things to do. New residents mean new content-creators, new sites and sounds, new in-world tools and Web-to-world mashups, new clothes, new communities, and just new *stuff*—the kind of thing that makes *Second Life* so fascinating in the first place.

But will the residents continue to come? It looks that way to many people. *Second Life*'s growth curve has been unusual among virtual worlds. For most MMOs—that is, games like *World of Warcraft* or *Ultima Online*—the population tends to spike soon after the game is released, and gradually fall back to some equilibrium point over time (or die off altogether, if the developers are unlucky). *Second Life*, on the other hand, never saw the early spike but has seen slow and steady growth ever since it appeared. It's the kind of growth curve that's characteristic of the way many important new technologies are adopted, according to Jerry Paffendorf, futurist in residence with the Electric Sheep Company, a development house doing work in *Second Life*. "The story of *Second Life* has been the story of this little virtual world that only had a thousand users," Paffendorf says. "Then it was the story of this little virtual world that only had 10,000 users. Then it only had 50,000 users. Then only 100,000. Now it only has 700,000 users, and soon it'll only have a million, and so on."

The implications of this kind of growth continuing could well be world-changing. Though it took *Second Life* nearly three years to reach 100,000 registered users, late 2006 saw the addition of around 100,000 new users every month! That's mighty

impressive growth, but what's most notable is not the number of users, but just how those people have begun to use their world.

Second Life is often held up as the perfect place to get your fantasy on—and yes, there's no other place like it for becoming something you aren't, or even for working out just what it is you want to be. In a sense, it's the epitome of the "walled garden," a place where reality dare not intrude and whatever fiction you want to create in the world is just as valid as anything your neighbor is constructing. Nowhere else can you be a bipedal fox decked out in sci-fi commando gear at the helm of your own spaceship with as much specificity and detail as in *Second Life*. Elves, witches, vampires, robots, yachtsmen, dominatrices, race car drivers, fashionistas, steampunks—the list goes on and on. If you can imagine it in *Second Life*, chances are you can become it. It's the perfect world for letting your flights of fancy run free.

But as the months pass and more and more users stream into the world, an interesting thing is happening: rather than think of *Second Life* as a place apart, a place sealed off from the real world, more and more users are coming to see the virtual world as merely an extension of what they do elsewhere on the Internet, and even an extension of what they do offline.

If that's the case, then the continued growth of *Second Life* could mark an important phenomenon with regard not just to the virtual world but to the World Wide Web in general, and by extension to the real world around us. You may have the skills to live your second life by this point, but it's also worth thinking about what having a second life means in the context of your first one.

CHAPTER 13
THE NEXT GENERATION OF THE INTERNET?

Here's a simple example: Shopping, of course, is one of the most popular activities in *Second Life*. But did you know that you could search and shop for books and other items on Amazon.com from within the virtual world? The results are displayed in 3D, and when you find something you just can't resist, the *Second Life* client lets you launch the Amazon page in an external web browser to make your purchase.

What's remarkable about the Amazon site in *Second Life* is that it wasn't designed by Linden Lab but by a handful of Amazon developers who joined *Second Life* and are living out their fantasies as...Amazon developers. To them, *Second Life* is just another place to do what they spend most of the day doing anyway, and to be who they already are.

INTRO
CHAPTER 1
CHAPTER 2
CHAPTER 3
CHAPTER 4
CHAPTER 5
CHAPTER 6
CHAPTER 7
CHAPTER 8
CHAPTER 9
CHAPTER 10
CHAPTER 11
CHAPTER 12
CHAPTER 13
APPENDICES

In fact, *Second Life* is becoming that to more and more people. As the population expands, residents are increasingly using *Second Life* as simply another way to connect to each other. They also use it to access information on the Internet or the World Wide Web, albeit in a far richer and more colorful way than via traditional Web browsers. At

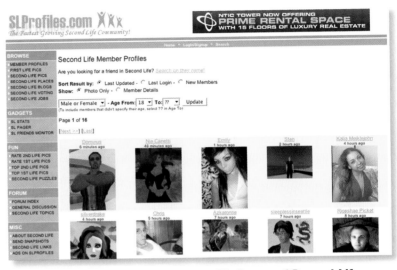

Figure 13.1: SLProfiles.com, the MySpace of Second Life

the same time, as *Second Life* has become a more open technological platform, residents have begun to create ways to use the Web to enhance their second lives. A website called SLProfiles.com, for instance, created by *Second Life* resident Yo Brewster, acts as a kind of MySpace for *SL* residents (Figure 13.1). Residents can create pages devoted to their first- and second-life profiles (pages that are just as colorful—or as colorfully ugly—as MySpace pages), maintain friends lists and lists of favorite places in *SL*, publish a blog through the site, even communicate via the Web with users who are logged into *Second Life*. Within three months of the site's launch, almost 1,000 users had signed up.

As *Second Life* users reach out to the online world of the Web, both the Web and the offline world are reaching back into *Second Life*. Though *Second Life* may be known as a fantasy world, it's increasingly being used as a marketing platform for real products from among the real world's best-known companies. In 2006, the real-world brands that made an entrance into *Second Life* included the following:

- Starwood Hotels, which used *Second Life* to prototype and show off its new Aloft chain of hotels (Figure 13.2);

- Toyota Motor Corp., which released a driveable model of its Scion xB in the virtual world;

- Adidas, which now sells virtual versions of its a3 Microride shoes—complete with "bounce" functionality;

Hipster clothing retailer American Apparel, which opened an outlet in *Second Life* that sells virtual versions of its colorful clothing and offers discounts on purchases of the real thing.

Figure 13.2: The virtual Aloft hotel

The entertainment industry has also found ways to take advantage of *Second Life*:

Singer-songwriter Regina Spektor released her last album in *Second Life* more than a week before it was available in stores;

20th Century Fox screened portions of *X-Men: The Last Stand* in *Second Life* simultaneously with its premiere at the Cannes film festival;

The Infinite Mind, a public radio show hosted by John Hockenberry, now does regular broadcasts from within *Second Life*;

Hit '80s new-wave music group Duran Duran is building a four-sim "futuristic utopia" where the band will play gigs, interact with fans, and showcase new acts.

At the same time that advertising and entertainment ventures are discovering *Second Life*, everyone from doctors to educators to the U.S. government is finding ways to use it:

A doctor's re-creation of the hallucinatory experiences of schizophrenics seeks to raise awareness of the disease among the healthy; *Second Life* is also home to at least one psychologist who practices there;

- Harvard Law School offers a course in "persuasive, empathic argument in the Internet space" that is taught partially within *Second Life*;

- The city of Hanover, NH, was re-created in *Second Life* by Dartmouth College for use in improving response measures in case of crisis;

- Both the State Department and the CIA are said to have established a presence in *Second Life*.

Discounts on T-shirts at your local American Apparel? A preview of a new album from a major label? A course at Harvard? And you thought this was supposed to be a fantasy world!

In fact, while *Second Life* continues to see just as much role-play, community-building, and fantasy-realization as ever, more and more of the projects that are being launched in the virtual world are designed more to be useful than anything else. The companies that have come into *Second Life* over the last year are using it not as some wild way to give people new identities, but simply as they'd use a website: to get the word out, hear feedback, and conduct business. These kinds of uses for *Second Life* have only just begun, but the sense among those who are pursuing them is that they've been more successes than failures. And they're the kind of successes that have built on each other. Because the Web is inherently supports user-created content and collaboration, *Second Life* is a kind of virtual world 2.0, a place where, like Web 2.0, the things that flourish are mashups, wikis, social software, and concepts organized around communities and customized content.

Not all of these things are good replacements for what we do today on the World Wide Web, of course. Reading a newspaper is far easier on a website than it is in a 3D online world. But imagine being able to click through a story and get launched into a 3D re-creation of the location where the story took place, where you could walk around and discuss the events with other readers who happened to be there at the same time. Instead of replacing the Web, *Second Life* holds vast potential to enhance it. Although the Web may never transform itself completely into something akin to *Second Life*, it's quite likely that 3D spaces will become an integral part of the online experience in the very near future, for a very large number of people.

So if you've made it this far through the book and you're wondering how useful your newfound skills at navigating the virtual world will be, the answer is probably that they'll be as useful as you want to make them. How long will your tenure in *Second Life* be? As long as you're connected to the Web, most likely. It's not just a virtual world you've entered. Welcome to the next generation of the Internet.

AN EXTRAORDINARILY RADICAL IDEA

To some people, of course, using *Second Life* as an extension of the World Wide Web is the most outlandish use of all. According to the skeptics, three-dimensional online worlds are hard to get around (or else why would you need a guidebook?), they don't add much more functionality to the Web than a graphical chat room, and their text-based predecessors were just as powerful but never took off like the true believers expect worlds like *Second Life* to do. Don't drink the Kool-Aid, they say, it'll just leave a bad taste in your mouth.

It's true that the virtual worlds and 3D Web technologies that have come before have languished and fallen largely into disuse. The 1980s and early 1990s saw the rise of text-based MUDs (multi-user dungeons) and their variants (MUSHes, MUCKs, TinyMUDs and more), some of which featured almost as much user-created content as *Second Life*. But despite the fact that some people preferred the mental graphics system used in text-based worlds (commonly known as "the imagination"), MUDs and their cousins were never able to garner a wide audience. Though some of the earliest text-based worlds are still inhabited today, they exist largely as novelty backwaters, not as places that attract innovative new developments in online business and experiments in connectivity.

The words "3D Web" also bring to mind, for some people, a failed attempt to bring 3D environments to the World Wide Web itself in the mid 1990s. VRML, the Virtual Reality Modeling Language, can be used to describe 3D objects and environments for use in web pages and other applications. First defined in 1994, VRML enjoyed a few years of popularity, but then fell largely into disuse. Though some CAD and 3D modeling programs still support the format, it's hard to find people who still rely on it as a robust mode of communication. VRML has been superceded by X3D, which is being promoted as a standard format for 3D computer graphics. But although the X3D community is growing, it has yet to make a widespread impact on how people browse and use the Web.

So when the subject of 3D virtual worlds comes up, many people are understandably skeptical. Any disruptive new technology often engenders the same kind of skepticism, says Mitch Kapor. Besides being chairman of the board at Linden Lab, Kapor is also the creator of the Lotus 1-2-3 spreadsheet application and chairman of the Mozilla Foundation. When he began his career in computing, the idea that there would one day be a desktop computer on every desktop was an outlandish proposition.

INTRO
CHAPTER 1
CHAPTER 2
CHAPTER 3
CHAPTER 4
CHAPTER 5
CHAPTER 6
CHAPTER 7
CHAPTER 8
CHAPTER 9
CHAPTER 10
CHAPTER 11
CHAPTER 12
CHAPTER 13
APPENDICES

CHAPTER 13

INTRO

PART I

PART II

PART III

APPENDICES

AN EXTRAORDINARILY
RADICAL IDEA

"It is very difficult to remember a time, even if you were alive then, when people did not have huge amounts of computing power at their fingertips," Kapor says. "But I can assure you that that was an extraordinarily radical idea." The same thing now goes for virtual worlds, Kapor says. "It's still a very radical idea that these are somehow going to be important and mainstream, and it's still only a very small fraction of the world's population that understands and appreciates that. We are very early; we are the early, early adopters."

SIDEBAR

FROM LINDEN LAB:
THE FUTURE OF SECOND LIFE

When Linden Lab chairman of the board Mitch Kapor addressed the Second Life Community Convention in the summer of 2006, he gave a convincing account of Second Life as a disruptive technology, one that would shake up the way most of the world goes about their daily business. But he also sounded a note of warning: to keep moving forward, the early adopters will have to remain open-minded and share their world with as broad a range of residents as possible.

"I think you are in a blessed position. You are the pioneers and the founders of this new world, and you have unbelievably great opportunities to put your stamp, to leave a legacy, to create things which will endure and have value. The opportunity to participate in the creation of a new world is really a rare one, and so I hope you cherish it. And you'll face challenges. In every disruptive technology I've seen, there has always been a dynamic in which the early adopters begin to be pushed aside as the whatever it is begins to become mainstream. There will be tensions as the frontier is civilized, on all sides, of people who like it the way it is, and people who want it to be what it might become.

"But the most important thing I want to say and leave you with is that with the privilege of creating a new world or new worlds, I believe, comes responsibility. And really the responsibility is to make that new world a better place. There is no one vision or value of what that better place will be, it will be slightly different or maybe very different to different people. But in a new world free of a lot of the constraints we're used to, which empowers individuals, my hope is that Second Life will continue to be a world that is more inclusive than the terrestrial world and will enable groups of people that are marginalized in the real world to be first-class citizens and residents.

> "It's still very early. I'm hoping that inclusiveness and Second Life *being a level playing field for everyone remains and increases as a core value. And finally I would just say to each of you, I hope you would think carefully about what a better world means to you, and as you go about Second Life you do things, build things, and interact in ways that further your own vision of that better world."*
>
> —Mitch Kapor

Even *Second Life* creator Philip Rosedale allows for the possibility that *SL* may not be the future of connectivity. But one doubts he really believes that. In any case, *Second Life* remains the only metaverse that matters at the moment: the most open, most inclusive, most technologically robust, and most rapidly growing virtual world around. And indications are that it will continue to be that for a long time to come. (See the sidebar "How We Got Here; Where We're Going.")

SIDEBAR

ADDITIONAL INFO:
HOW WE GOT HERE; WHERE WE'RE GOING

To some, the very idea of a 3D graphical world that exists only on the Internet is a foreign concept. For most people above a certain age, a new technology like Second Life *can be difficult to integrate into their lives. But by the same token, those who've grown up with similar technologies will have a far easier time incorporating new developments. Computer games are the technology that's probably done most to pave the way for SL's adoption.*

The first multiuser graphical worlds appeared in 1996, with the advent of an online game called Meridian 59. *Since then, massively multiplayer online games like* Ultima Online, EverQuest, Lineage, *and* World of Warcraft, *to name only a few, have made 3D online worlds commonplace for a new generation of gamers. And though many gamers are unsure what to make of a world where there aren't any orcs to slay, they've mastered getting around the world itself—the biggest obstacle to adoption.*

And just as MMOs are preparing people for an age of 3D online worlds, various other Internet-based applications and technologies are doing

INTRO

CHAPTER 1

CHAPTER 2

CHAPTER 3

CHAPTER 4

CHAPTER 5

CHAPTER 6

CHAPTER 7

CHAPTER 8

CHAPTER 9

CHAPTER 10

CHAPTER 11

CHAPTER 12

CHAPTER 13

APPENDICES

13

INTRO

PART I

PART II

PART III

APPENDICES

AN EXTRAORDINARILY
RADICAL IDEA

much the same thing. Though MySpace is not a virtual world, it is very much a Web-based social space in many of the same ways as Second Life: it is filled with user-created content, and with people forming new communities and trying on new personas. And with a staggering 100 million members, it will soon be funneling people into 3D worlds that go one step beyond the flat web pages of MySpace. Such a move is already happening: Korean social site CyWorld, a crudely 3D version of MySpace, launched a U.S. version in 2006, and 3D chat network IMVU recently added additional content-creation capabilities for its users. Applications like Google Maps and Google Earth have added powerful custom content capabilities in recent months and are becoming much more functional single-user virtual worlds.

For people who've grown up in the embrace of such technologies, the migration to a place like Second Life—which offers most everything these other worlds do, and more—will be second nature. If Second Life can continue to scale its capacity and continue to smooth the user experience with new features and releases, it should be around for a very long time to come.

As I write this, more than 700,000 people have checked out *Second Life* at least once. By the time you read these words, that number will have grown to more than a million if growth continues at the levels from the second half of 2006. Probably half of those people will be regular visitors to the world, dipping in at least once in any given 60-day period. Something like 100,000 different people will log on in

Figure 13.3: Listen to the new Regina Spektor album or just hang out with friends.

a given day, and at the busiest times there will be around 25,000 different avatars occupying the world.

Already, the effects of having so many different people in the space are being felt. Besides the projects, builds, and initiatives listed toward the beginning of this chapter, a number of trends at work in *Second Life* could have broader ramifications in terms of shaping people's offline lives. But perhaps the most important of these is the way *Second Life* helps connect people. The listening station where Regina Spektor's album plays in *Second Life* is not just a place to hear good music; it's also a place to hang out with friends, meet new people, and expand the boundaries of your virtual life (Figure 13.3). In such an online environment, interactions that were formerly limited or went only in one direction—consuming media online, for instance—now take on much richer form. (See the sidebar "Take Me Out to the Ball Game.")

SIDEBAR

RESIDENTS SPEAK:
TAKE ME OUT TO THE BALL GAME

When the Electric Sheep Company set out to re-create Major League Baseball's Home Run Derby in Second Life, *their task was to do more than simply show off the league's heaviest hitters. By re-creating a real-world baseball stadium in* Second Life *and populating the field with bobble-headed sluggers, they not only brought the real game into the virtual world, but they provided a social focus around which people could gather and, most importantly, add their own entertainment to the experience of watching the game. Blogger Eric Rice was there, and he notes how much more a part of the experience he felt in* Second Life *than in any other online context:*

"Tonight, a bunch of friends and I went to a baseball stadium, bought some hats and jerseys, some of us got some bling jewelry (Go RED SOX). Naturally, we had big foam fingers, hot dogs, beers. We talked smack, we cheered, we chatted it up. We watched the sun go down, we watched the boats in the drink, and we cheered for fireworks. And we watched home run after home run after home run.

"Now, if you stop reading here, there's nothing out of the ordinary going on. I participated in what millions participate in all the time. The only difference: my friends were scattered across the USA and the world. And I was a Boston-clad avatar.

INTRO
CHAPTER 1
CHAPTER 2
CHAPTER 3
CHAPTER 4
CHAPTER 5
CHAPTER 6
CHAPTER 7
CHAPTER 8
CHAPTER 9
CHAPTER 10
CHAPTER 11
CHAPTER 12
CHAPTER 13
APPENDICES

"Do androids dream of home run kings? They do if those kings are the Electric Sheep Company, the metaverse design consultancy that knocked it out of the park by bringing Major League Baseball into Second Life.

"They built a stadium. They sold tickets. They created schwag—real schwag, not the frivolous nonsense we really don't care about—schwag of importance. And while we sat around with our foamie hands and hot dogs, we all watched the stream of the Derby piped into Second Life via ESPN HD (and commercial-free, I might add), we all did everything I mentioned above.

"Here's a secret: You can't really do this in real life. Well, not without plane tickets, season tickets, and a helluva lot of work. Sure, we can sit in IRC or other chat rooms and assume we are watching the same thing. But there's nothing quite like the shared experience of doing it together.

"Homeboy Makaio and others rezzed some kayaks way out in the water, and I followed suit. We got some boats out in the drink. It was close as we could come to brawlin' with oars for long drives out of the park. We took photos and shared 'em. The massive towers, the views of the oceans—all the stuff people love doing at PacBell/SBC/AT&T park here in the Bay Area. You just love being at the park. Because, things like that are baseball.

"MLB hit a home run, because they didn't do the stereotypical thing we expect big companies to do—they didn't talk at us, they played with us. They entertained us. They were there having fun too."

—Eric Rice

FROM TOYS TO TOOLS

As we pointed out in Chapter 10, several thousand people derive a significant boost to their incomes from their activities within *Second Life*. Most of these people are retailers—vendors of clothing, avatars, animations, scripted weapons and vehicles,

even genitalia—who make the content they've created available to other users at a small price.

It's instructive to contemplate just what's being bought and sold here. Are these really skirts, haircuts, dances, guns, cars, and private parts? Well, yes and no. It goes without saying that these things don't have quite the same function as their real-life counterparts. A prim skirt will cover your *Second Life* self just fine, but you've still got to keep your first-life self dressed in the kind of clothing that would be acceptable in the physical world. In a sense, the outfit you

Figure 13.4: *Some of the micro-entertainments on sale in Second Life*

buy your avatar is a small piece of media, like a video clip or MP3 music file, a "micro-entertainment" purchased for a few cents as one of a stream of such purchases that add up to a rich online experience (Figure 13.4).

That makes the person who created that piece of content a kind of game developer on a micro scale. In fact, there's no real term for what this kind of "micro-developer" actually is. It's almost like being a momentary movie producer, except that what you're creating isn't a narrative but a component of a story, one that the audience member (who's also a kind of movie director) can mash up with all the other components of the scene, which have been created by all the other micro-producers.

Perhaps most important when talking about *Second Life*'s impact on the Web and on the rest of the world is the fact that all of these micro-producers are getting a lot of micro-payments for their work. Some of them earn enough to support themselves without having a job in real life, but that's not really the point. The point is that there's a new kind of work going on here; a new kind of labor market is developing. By dint of the fact that anyone can produce and distribute practically anything in *Second Life*, a market has developed for purchasing content in chunks much smaller than a $50 video game.

INTRO
CHAPTER 1
CHAPTER 2
CHAPTER 3
CHAPTER 4
CHAPTER 5
CHAPTER 6
CHAPTER 7
CHAPTER 8
CHAPTER 9
CHAPTER 10
CHAPTER 11
CHAPTER 12
CHAPTER 13
APPENDICES

CHAPTER 13

INTRO

PART I

PART II

PART III

APPENDICES

And because the costs of production are so low, the market is open to a far broader range of participants. Yes, you too can become a developer in *Second Life*; that's the whole point. And if you live in a place like China or India, where average incomes are low in comparison to the rest of the world, your *Second Life* income may be a significant boost. (Note that the necessary broadband penetration is hardly universal, and some places have yet to accept payment systems like PayPal and other systems that help turn your Lindens into cold, hard cash, but those things are on their way.) It's interesting to think about: perhaps a place like *Second Life* could help level the playing field on a global basis. Its impact is exceedingly small at the moment, but if it grows the way Linden Lab thinks it will, it would help raise a significant number of fortunes.

Second Life, of course, isn't the first place this new kind of market has developed. What the phenomenon resembles is just what's happening on the Web, as the medium morphs into the collection of technologies and principles known as Web 2.0, in which more and more people are mashing up more and more sites and applications, creating a broader and broader development community, and charging on a piecemeal basis rather than for whole chunks of consolidated content at once. Just look at the market for music: with the rise of file-sharing sites and services like the iTunes Music Store, albums sales have dropped sharply in recent years, while sales of $0.99 downloads are way up.

The micro-content that is traded in *Second Life* resembles the Web in another way as well. It's entertaining to dress your avatar up in virtual clothing and sit it in a virtual castle, mansion, office, or even a broken-down virtual shack, but it serves a more important purpose at the same time. The virtual accoutrements you adorn and surround yourself with are the things that help define your presence in the virtual world—much like the design of a MySpace page, a website, or a blog helps define your presence on the Web. That virtual outfit you've been admiring is more than just a decoration: it's a message, a way to transmit information to the people around you about just who you are in this context. And the people around you in *Second Life* may be friends, they may be strangers, they may be business contacts, or they may be Nick Rhodes from Duran Duran, who's quite a fan of the virtual world. As you go about your virtual life, ask yourself: do I want to invite these people to a castle, a mansion, an office, or a shack? For many people, at some point these things stop being toys, and instead become the tools of their online interactions, the fabric of a life online that serves many of the same functions as the offline portion of their lives.

ADDITIONAL INFO:
DURAN DURAN MOVES INTO SECOND LIFE

When Duran Duran keyboardist and songwriter Nick Rhodes was first introduced to Second Life in mid 2006, he was instantly captivated by what he saw. "I just thought, this is what I've been waiting for," he recalls. "It's everything that I'd hoped for, and that people had been predicting for the Internet from virtually its inception—if you'll pardon the pun."

Soon, with the help of Rivers Run Red, a virtual-world branding and services company, the '80s new-wave music group was planning a "futuristic utopia" for Second Life, a four-sim wonderland where the band would play concerts, interact with fans, showcase new acts, and simply provide a place for residents to hang out and be entertained.

To Rhodes, Second Life has as much potential to revolutionize the music and entertainment industry as MTV did when it first came on the scene. Duran Duran, of course, has been at the forefront of entertainment technology throughout the band's nearly 30-year history. They've been on the leading edge of video and digital entertainment, so it only makes sense that they become the first major act to take up residence in Second Life.

For Rhodes, entering Second Life is a natural evolution for the band. "I love beautiful songs about the reality of our lives, but I also like sci-fi fantasy," he said. "I think Second Life is the beginning of it. There are inevitably going to be many, many, many other virtual sites that spring up that are equally as good and eventually will become the next level of it. But right now, this is the most exciting place for us to be."

So to prepare for the future of *Second Life*, the best advice we could give would be to assume that it's here to stay. Most likely, *Second Life* will come to resemble nothing so much as a 3D extension of the World Wide Web. Wild fantasies will be able to be realized there, even as more and more real-world functions will move into the world. It may be that we will one day do much of our business in virtual worlds like *Second Life*. Already it's not hard to imagine holding a full-time job there, attending a class there, developing a product there, doing your shopping there, and even falling in love there. As the population and possibilities grow, all these things will only come more easily.

And as we look a bit further out, places like *Second Life* could also become integral to how we interact with the real world. As virtual worlds like Google Earth begin to more accurately mirror the real world, 3D online spaces may become simply part of how we get the news and information we need every day. Imagine logging onto *Second Life* to visit a replica of your local hipster neighborhood. You can check out the bands that are playing, listen to some music, shop for clothes or music files, bump into your friends who are doing the same thing, and perhaps even encounter some interesting piece of art or a flyer for a party that takes you to some other part of the virtual world entirely—or that leads you to discover something new about the offline world. This comingling of the real and virtual worlds could become one of the most powerful uses for a platform like *Second Life* (as futurist Jerry Paffendorf explains in the sidebar "The Mario Brothers Would Be Blown Away").

In any case, the virtual world is not to be taken lightly. That might seem to be in sharp contrast with the idea that you can do anything, be anything, fly anywhere, and discover whole new forms of play in *Second Life*. That's all very true, but it's also true that the world holds far more potential than simple recreation does. It is a place of recreation and re-creation both; a way to explore new places and a way to harness the power of community in relation to the places we've already been. It's a world of imagination and play, but it's also a world of utility and hard work. It's your world; make of it what you will.

SIDEBAR

ADDITIONAL INFO:
THE MARIO BROTHERS WOULD BE BLOWN AWAY

"Second Life and related metaverse technologies like multiverse promise the gradual addition of a social 3D layer on top of the Web," according to Jerry Paffendorf. Far from being a walled garden, *Second Life* is positioned to become an integral tool of browsing the Web, connecting via the Internet, and even of interacting with the real world around us. And *Second Life* is only the beginning.

"At a basic level we're experimenting with turning life and the planet into a Web-connected video game where we create and file-share experiences, some tracking-back to reality, some not," Paffendorf says. *"Mirror-world technologies like Google Earth will further shrink the world and lead to surprising global insights by giving us the big-picture view that David Gelernter called 'topsight.' In the late '50s we marveled at the first photograph of the entire planet seen from space. Now we're building out the globe in 3D and lighting it up with*

location-specific information. People will use this interface to the planet to help manage and publish their lives, explore distant places, identify and support problem areas, re-create local landscapes in the real world, make informed political decisions, and better understand the movement of people, ideas, and money—as well as don giant fire-breathing monster avatars and slog through virtual cities. Christopher Columbus, Adam Smith, Thomas Jefferson, Godzilla, and the Mario Brothers would be equally blown away."

INTRO

CHAPTER 1

CHAPTER 2

CHAPTER 3

CHAPTER 4

CHAPTER 5

CHAPTER 6

CHAPTER 7

CHAPTER 8

CHAPTER 9

CHAPTER 10

CHAPTER 11

CHAPTER 12

CHAPTER 13

APPENDICES

APPENDICES

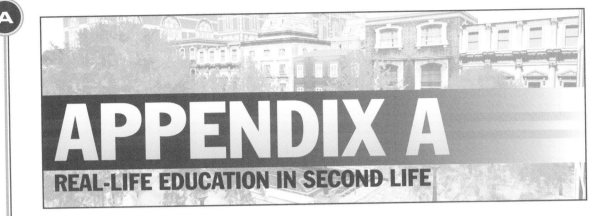

APPENDIX A

REAL-LIFE EDUCATION IN SECOND LIFE

My name in *Second Life* is Pathfinder Linden, and my primary focus at Linden Lab is how to use *Second Life* as a platform for real-life education. Please feel free to contact me in-world and visit my personal website at `http://zero.hastypastry.net/pathfinder/`. I hope you find this appendix useful, and I hope to meet you soon in Second Life!

Figure 1: Building interactive molecular models—dopamine

The goal of all educators is to teach students essential skills that will help them become productive and successful members of society. Leveraging new technologies for education, particularly ones that students already use as part of their daily lives, is a key way to make learning both effective and engaging!

We live in a world that is becoming more networked every day, and the Internet has grown into an essential medium for communication, socialization, and creative expression. Virtual worlds like *Second Life* represent the future of human interaction in a globally networked world, and students who have grown up with the Internet naturally swim in these waters. These "digital natives" eagerly embrace tools such as instant messaging, social networking spaces, and massively multiplayer online games. And as the students of today grow into the leaders of tomorrow, they will bring these technologies into the workplace, making their use an essential part of the future of work and business.

Second Life is a broad platform for many different kinds of activities [Figure 1], and real-life education in *Second Life* is a growing area of interest for many educators. Educators are currently using *Second Life* with students to explore distance learning, simulation, new media studies, and cooperative work.

As an educator, how do you get started? This appendix gives you some tips on how to get integrated into the educator community in *Second Life*, specific examples of what educators are currently doing, and ideas on how to be successful in your exploration.

APPENDIX
A
INTRO
PART I
PART II
PART III
APPENDICES
APPENDIX A

COLLEAGUES AND COLLABORATORS

Educators are most successful when they find colleagues and collaborators in real life to help them work through new teaching ideas and projects. Educators using *Second Life* face the same challenge, so the first thing to do is get connected with the growing community of real-life educators actively exploring *Second Life*. Share your ideas and project plans, listen to the experience of people who may be working along similar lines, and you'll be off to a great start!

The first place to go is the Educators Mailing List, which you can subscribe to at `https://lists.secondlife.com/cgi-bin/mailman/listinfo/educators`. This very active list is a great place to interact with other real-life educators exploring how to effectively use *Second Life* for academic purposes. Your next stop should be the Education Wiki (`http://www.simteach.com/wiki/index.php?title=Second_Life_Education_Wiki`), which serves as a clearinghouse for education-related information and links to useful resources. By leveraging the work of educators who have already used *Second Life* and engaging in discussions with other educators, you'll hit the ground running. Once your projects in *Second Life* are underway, be sure to share your own insights and knowledge on both the wiki and the mailing list. This will help grow the collective knowledge base for everyone!

There is also general page with more details on Education in Second Life located at `http://secondlife.com/education`. And for a frequently updated list of interesting third-party websites and press articles, be sure to check out `http://del.icio.us/secondlife/education`.

Ready to dive into *Second Life* now? The first thing you should do when you log in is join the Real Life Education group. This group is open for anyone to join, and it's a great way to stay in touch with educators while you're in-world. Click the Find button and search under Groups for "Real Life Education," click the Join button, and you'll be all set! Educators are encouraged to send instant messages to the group to coordinate in-world meetings and announce education-related events.

Congratulations! You're now connected with other educators around the world using *Second Life* for real-life education. Don't be afraid to ask questions, share your ideas and plans, attend some in-world meetings with other educators and students, and enjoy your newfound community of like-minded colleagues (Figure 2)!

Figure 2: Grad students meeting in-world to discuss research ethics

A
APPENDIX
INTRO
PART I
PART II
PART III
APPENDICES
APPENDIX A

GETTING LAND IN SECOND LIFE

To have a place of permanence where you and your students can build and work requires owning land. One way educators accomplish this is to find colleagues who already own land in *Second Life* and share some of their available space. There are also other options for educators who wish to try out *Second Life* or own a large space of their own.

First of all, there is a *Campus:Second Life* offer where Linden Lab provides educators with an acre of land for free for the duration of a specific class. This is a one-time trial opportunity for educators wishing to explore *Second Life* for the first time, and you won't have to pay anything to temporarily use the land. Linden Lab requires a syllabus for the planned class, as well as a general summary at the end of the class on how *Second Life* worked out for you as a platform. Full details on how you can sign up for *Campus:Second Life* can be found at `http://secondlife.com/csl`.

If you wish to own a permanent plot of land, Linden Lab has special educational pricing for private islands. A private island will allow you to completely control access to your learning environment (e.g., optionally restrict access to just students and faculty) and gives you 16 acres of land to use however you like. This is an ideal setup if you want to create a true Intranet in *Second Life* and have a persistent virtual classroom. For verified real-world academic institutions and 501(c)(3) non-profit organizations using islands to support their organization's official work, the current fee for a 16-acre private island is a one-time US$980 setup charge and US$150 per month for maintenance. For more details, please email `education@lindenlab.com`.

If you wish to buy a small plot of land on the mainland in *Second Life*, that's also possible. Linden Lab doesn't offer educational discounts for this type of land, and the land-management tools are not as comprehensive as the ones for private islands. For more information on how to purchase land on the mainland and the associated fees, please see `http://secondlife.com/community/land.php`.

Once you've got land and are ready to start the actual development of your in-world space, you can either do all the building and scripting work yourself or work with one of the many resident-run development companies in *Second Life*. A comprehensive collection of developers is listed at `http://secondlife.com/developers/directory.php`; and be sure to ask other folks on the Educators Mailing List for recommendations. Linden Lab provides the building tools and land, while the development and creative work is entirely up to you!

EXAMPLES OF EDUCATION PLACES IN SECOND LIFE

There are hundreds of real-life educators using *Second Life* for academic purposes, dozens of different universities working on projects, and thousands of acres of virtual land across the world where they're doing it! Here are some tips on how to find these places and some examples of current educational projects.

While you're in-world, be sure to visit the Campus region (Figure 3). This area is the main hub for classes participating in the *Campus:Second Life* program, and it's a great place to meet students and educators currently working on projects. There are also classes and projects being held on plots of land on the mainland across *Second Life* as well as on private islands. When you visit the Campus region, look for a kiosk sign that reads "Looking for Real Life Education Places in Second Life?" Click on it and you'll get a notecard with landmarks to more places. Be sure to

Figure 3: Two kiosks you should visit on the Campus region

also click on the kiosk nearby that reads "SLED PICAYUNE." That will give you the latest copy of an excellent weekly publication written by educators all about current education projects in *Second Life*.

Harvard's Berkman Center owns a private island called Berkman, where they've re-created Harvard's Austin Hall to use for in-world conferences and meetings (Figure 4). This space is a great example of how to re-create parts of a real-world campus in *Second Life*, and they've also successfully used it for "mixed reality" conference events. Harvard Law School professors Charlie and Rebecca Nesson are also using Berkman island with an upcoming course, giving students a new medium for exploration and collaborative work.

Figure 4: Harvard's Berkman Center and Austin Hall

The New Media Consortium (Figure 5) has created an experimental space called NMC Campus where they are exploring learning and collaboration in *Second Life*. This group is very active, and you can read more about their latest work on their NMC Campus Observe" blog at http://www.nmc.org/sl.

Figure 5: The New Media Consortium campus

A group of librarians with the Alliance Library System in Illinois has created Info Island, where they're exploring innovative exhibits of information, holding live in-world meetings with real-life authors, and providing space for other educators and non-profit organizations. They recently set up an immersive exhibit with information from the Library of Congress on the Declaration of

INTRO
CHAPTER 1
CHAPTER 2
CHAPTER 3
CHAPTER 4
CHAPTER 5
CHAPTER 6
CHAPTER 7
CHAPTER 8
CHAPTER 9
CHAPTER 10
CHAPTER 11
CHAPTER 12
CHAPTER 13
APPENDICES

Independence (Figure 6), including dioramas, streamed audio, and even period furniture! Read more about their current work at `http://infoisland.org/`.

Figure 6: The Declaration of Independence exhibit at Info Island

Figure 7: The International Spaceflight Museum

The International Spaceflight Museum (Figure 7) is a great example of using *Second Life* to create something that would be almost impossible to build in real life. This private island includes built-to-scale rockets, interactive models of the solar system, detailed information about satellite designs, and planetary observation decks. Learn more here: `http://slcreativity.org/wiki/index.php?title=International_Space_Flight_Museum`.

Second Life resident The Sojourner is a stroke survivor and has created a space called Dreams (Figure 8) that offers self-help support groups and education for other stroke survivors. Dreams is a supportive and creative environment where people dealing with stroke recovery can keep their minds sharp by engaging in collaborative community events and round-table discussions. Many stroke survivors deal with physical mobility limitations and paralysis in real life, issues they are free from while exploring the world of *Second Life*.

Figure 8: Dreams

Second Life resident Aura Lily has a passion for ancient Egypt and has been using *Second Life* to re-create the artifacts and architecture of ancient Egypt using maps drawn by Napoleon's engineers. She's currently working on an accurate re-creation of temples and buildings from the real-life island of Philae. Aura's work (Figure 9) is a great example of how *Second Life* can be used as an immersive way to explore ancient architecture and culture.

As you can see, there is a wide range of educational activities in *Second Life*, and these are just a few examples. For more, please see the list of Top 20 Educational Locations in *Second Life* at `http://www.simteach.com/wiki/index.php?title=Top_20_Educational_Locations_in_Second_Life`).

Figure 9: Ancient Egypt and immersive archaeology

SUCCESSFUL STRATEGIES

As the saying goes, "Pioneers are the people who catch arrows in their backs." Being a pioneering educator in *Second Life* is definitely a challenge, and academia in general sometimes discourages educators from exploring new teaching methodologies that appear a bit "out there." Here are seven tips to help you be as successful as possible in using *Second Life* for real-life education.

1) Spend as much time as possible exploring *Second Life*.

This sounds obvious, but it's most critical. To fully understand the potential of *Second Life* as a platform, you'll need to dedicate some time getting to learn how *Second Life* works, how people interact, and what the overall community is like. Reading this book is a great start! Keep it next to your computer while you explore in-world. Talk to every resident you meet and don't be afraid to ask questions.

2) Talk to other educators who are currently using *Second Life* for real-life education purposes.

Get plugged into the existing educator community as soon as possible. They will help you better frame your ideas, as well as give you new ones!

3) Come up with clear and measurable goals for your academic use of *Second Life*.

Every course curriculum has clear goals, and your work in *Second Life* should have clear goals as well. Keep them in focus, and do your best to measure your accomplishments. This will be good ammunition for you when trying to convince other faculty that your projects in *Second Life* have merit.

INTRO
CHAPTER 1
CHAPTER 2
CHAPTER 3
CHAPTER 4
CHAPTER 5
CHAPTER 6
CHAPTER 7
CHAPTER 8
CHAPTER 9
CHAPTER 10
CHAPTER 11
CHAPTER 12
CHAPTER 13
APPENDICES

4) Publish or perish!

Write a paper about your experiences in *Second Life*. Get it published in a peer-reviewed journal. Keep a public blog about your work, and encourage other colleagues to visit it. Get your students to blog about their work in *Second Life*. Contribute to the Education Wiki. As a pioneer, what you learn in using *Second Life* for real-life education is a priceless resource for others who will follow. Share the knowledge!

5) Remember that *Second Life* is a platform for a wide range of activities.

While you explore *Second Life*, you'll meet an incredible range of residents all using *Second Life* in different ways and for different purposes. In many ways *Second Life* is like the Web, representing the broadest possible range of interests and people you can imagine. Embrace this diversity! If you wish to have a very private area where you can completely control your environment, remember the private-island option.

6) Work at unlearning.

Second Life is a new medium that is unlike anything else you've experienced. As human beings, when we are faced with a completely new medium for creativity and interaction, we instinctively compare it to preexisting mediums and then apply our old ways of thinking to re-create old models.

When the motion-picture camera was invented, it was initially stuck on a fixed pole and used to film plays on a single stage. Only after many years did directors think "Maybe I can film with multiple cameras and cut between them. Or maybe I can move the camera around while filming!" That insight was the birth of film montage. In a similar example, when educators first explored the Web, they simply scanned books and put them online. Both of these are examples of how we typically embrace new mediums.

Unlearn your old ways of thinking. Don't re-create preexisting models of education. If you want to teach biology, why build a virtual classroom with desks and a blackboard in *Second Life* when you could build a whole interactive human cell?

7) Learn from your students.

Your students have most likely grown up with the Internet. They have always lived in a world where computers, instant messaging, email, and multiplayer games exist and are used daily. If they've never experienced *Second Life* before, they'll probably take to it like a fish to water and use it in ways you could never imagine. Learn as much as you can from them and their experiences, as the future of virtual worlds like *Second Life* and all new technologies truly belongs to the digital natives!

—John Lester (aka Pathfinder Linden)

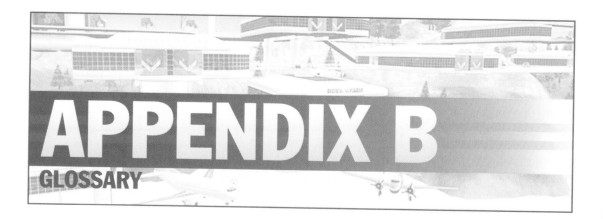

APPENDIX B
GLOSSARY

This appendix contains definitions of popular *SL* terms and abbreviations. Note that selecting *Second Life* Help from the pull-down Help menu opens a panel that contains a link to an in-world glossary of *SL* terms.

ad space: A tiny land parcel (most frequently, 16 square meters) used for advertising purposes: signs, billboards, etc. Can also be used as storage space (see "storage").

AFK: Away from keyboard. AFK means a resident may appear to be online, but there's no one at the keyboard typing. This tells people you are online, but not responding. Typing "AFK" in chat causes your avatar to display "[AWAY]" after its name. After 30 minutes of inactivity, you will be logged off automatically.

allocation: 1) The total amount of land a resident/account can own or otherwise hold. Premium subscribers receive an allocation for 512m² at no additional Land Use Cost; 2) The total amount of land a group can own. A group cannot own land unless it has an allocation equal or greater than the land size. Group allocation is donated by group members, who pay for the amount they donate (in addition to any land they themselves own), regardless of whether the group is currently using the allocation.

alpha channel: The transparency channel in image files such as textures.

animation: Avatar animation, or a sequence of avatar moves scripted in an external application (most commonly, Poser) and imported into *Second Life.*

AO: Animation override; generally a scripted object that plays specific animations in response to your character's actions. These animations take over (or override) default animations (walking, etc.).

AR: Short for Abuse Report, accessed from the Help pull-down menu and sent in when being griefed by someone (see "to grief; griefer").

attachment: A virtual object that can be attached to an avatar (for example, a hat, a gun, or a ring).

INTRO
CHAPTER 1
CHAPTER 2
CHAPTER 3
CHAPTER 4
CHAPTER 5
CHAPTER 6
CHAPTER 7
CHAPTER 8
CHAPTER 9
CHAPTER 10
CHAPTER 11
CHAPTER 12
CHAPTER 13
APPENDICES

av, avi, avie: Short for "avatar."

ban: 1) The act of explicitly forbidding entry. Landowners have ban tools to prevent specified residents from entering their land; 2) To add someone to your ban list and thus eject them from your land; 3) The permanent removal of someone from *Second Life*. This can be done only by Linden Lab. Thankfully, most people who break the rules learn to behave well before this happens. Not to be confused with a suspension, which is a time-out of sorts.

build: 1) To make something out of primitives; 2) An object composed of one or more primitives; 3) An engineering term for a specific version of the *Second Life* (or other) software.

bump: 1) The act of pushing another resident, either by running into them, hitting them with a physical object, or using a scripted object to apply a force to them; 2) A projectile designed to push residents. These projectiles are usually named "bump." Improperly scripted bump objects occasionally litter no-script areas, as their scripts are disabled (thus preventing them from deleting themselves); 3) Adding a comment to a forum post to place it at the top of the topic's list. Forum topics are sorted with most-recent postings at the top. Bumping an old post can get it back to where people will notice it—often done when the post has fallen off the first page.

camping job: A virtual job that involves staying in one place—sitting in a chair, dancing on a dance pad—in exchange for a few Linden dollars paid out every 10 or 15 minutes.

charter member: An *SL* resident who has lived in-world almost since it began.

Classifieds: Advertisement listings in the *SL* Search window.

covenant: A set of rules and regulations governing a particular estate (see "estate").

damage: Describes any region marked "Not Safe," where *Second Life*'s rules of damage and death are in effect. Any scripted object can be set to damage avatars (usually by firing damage-enabled projectiles). An avatar that takes lethal damage is instantly teleported to its home location. The overwhelming majority of *Second Life* is not damage-enabled.

dance ball, dance pad: Objects scripted to animate avatars, making them dance.

debug menu: A menu that is hidden by default but includes some useful advanced commands. It can be toggled on and off by hitting Ctrl-Alt-Shift-D.

deep-think: Related to sim performance. A deep-think happens when a physical interaction within a sim is taking a very long time to compute. A deep-think can be caused by a large number of colliding physical objects, when a physical object is stuck in an awkward position, or when advanced shapes are interacting in some weird

way. Symptoms of a deep-think are slow avatar movement, your avatar continuing to move after it should have stopped, or logging-off issues. You may still be able to chat normally while moving and other physical movement are impaired.

estate: An administrative unit of private or group-owned virtual land (usually a region or a collection of regions) with special tools for large-scale real-estate management.

First Land: The specially priced, 512-square-meter land parcel offered to *SL* account holders who can purchase land. You may purchase First Land only once.

first life: Real life or "RL."

flexiprim: A flexible prim used as a building block in *SL* (see "prim").

furry: An anthropomorphic animal avatar, usually bipedal. Furries comprise one of *SL*'s prominent resident groups.

gesture: A mix of avatar animation, sound, and sometimes special effects activated by a typed command or keyboard shortcut.

Gorean: A member of the Gor community based on the real-world novels of John Norman, in which master/slave relationships are the norm.

grid: Slang for the *SL* virtual world and its server network, as in "the grid is down" or "the grid is up again."

to grief; griefer: To bother or harass another *SL* resident through offensive actions; an *SL* resident who bothers other residents. Griefing violates *Second Life* community standards.

Help Island, HI: The place most new residents reach having passed through OI (Orientation Island). Mentors often help out new residents here.

home: The in-world location your avatar considers the center of its *Second Life* existence. You can teleport directly home at any time by opening the World menu and choosing Teleport Home. You can change your login location so you always start *Second Life* at home. If you wander (or march) into a damage-enabled area and are killed, your avatar will teleport home immediately (none the worse for the experience).

IM: Instant message

Inventory: The collection of clothing, objects, textures, etc. that your avatar possesses in-world. Your Inventory travels with you and you can use any of it at any time.

in-world: Anything that takes place within the virtual environment of *Second Life*. Also, the state of being logged into *Second Life*.

INTRO
CHAPTER 1
CHAPTER 2
CHAPTER 3
CHAPTER 4
CHAPTER 5
CHAPTER 6
CHAPTER 7
CHAPTER 8
CHAPTER 9
CHAPTER 10
CHAPTER 11
CHAPTER 12
CHAPTER 13
APPENDICES

island: A simulator/region that is detached from the main continent and accessible only by directly teleporting to it (i.e., "Cayman is an island sim."). Sometimes also used in the more general definition of the word, to refer to a small land mass surrounded by water.

L$: A Linden dollar (L$ or "Lindens") is the in-world currency. Most transactions in-world take place in L$.

LL: Linden Lab, the creators of *Second Life*.

lag: 1) The delay inherent to a connection between two computers on the Internet, especially an unusually long delay between a client and a server; 2) A delay or interruption in a network or Internet connection caused by slow response times and/ or lost or missing data. 3) Slow or jerky performance in a 3D application caused by an overworked processor, memory bandwidth, video card, or hard drive. 4) Any situation in which part of the *Second Life* experience is not performing as desired.

land baron: A resident who owns a significant quantity of land, especially with the intent to sell it at a profit.

land owner: A resident who owns land—anything from a parcel to multiple estates.

landmark: A beacon marking a specific location in-world, *and* the teleport shortcut to that location stored in the Landmarks folder in your avatar's Inventory.

liaison: A Linden Lab employee who serves as an in-world representative and contact for all residents, especially newcomers. They're the people you see with names like Liaison Ralph Linden.

IM: Instant message.

landmark: A beacon marking a specific location in the *SL* world, *and* the teleport shortcut to that location stored in the Landmarks folder in your avatar's Inventory.

LindeX Currency Exchange: The online currency exchange where you can change real-world money into Linden dollars, and vice versa.

LL: Linden Lab—the creators of *Second Life*.

LSL: Linden Scripting Language, used to animate objects in the *SL* world.

machinima: A computer movie made using a real-time, 3D game/virtual-world engine instead of a special application dedicated to making computer movies. The term has its origins in "machine animation" and "machine cinema."

Mature: A region rating permitting adult-only activities such as explicit sexuality.

mouselook: The first-person camera view. The mouse is used to move the camera around. Often used for weapons, vehicles, and grabbing objects.

newbie, noobie: A newcomer to *Second Life*; a resident who has been in-world for a relatively short period of time and/or is not familiar or comfortable with *Second Life*'s nuances. Also spelled "noob" or "nOOb."

no-copy: An object permission that forbids the object's current owner to make additional copies of it. These objects have "(no-copy)" in their name in the Inventory.

no-fly: Any land parcel that does not permit flying. You can fly through no-fly parcels, but as soon as you touch down and stop flying, you'll be unable to fly again until you exit the no-fly parcel. If you get really stuck, teleport somewhere else.

no-modify: An object permission that forbids the object's current owner to modify it. These objects have "(no-modify)" in their name in the Inventory.

no-transfer: An object permission that forbids the object's current owner to transfer it to another *SL* resident. These objects have "(no-transfer)" in their name in the Inventory.

notecard: An in-world text document, such as the instructions attached to an object.

object: Anything that exists in the virtual world and is built of one or more prims.

OI, Orientation Island: the first place most new residents see when they enter *Second Life*. Teaches the basics of getting around, customizing your avatar, and communicating.

parcel: A piece of virtual land that can be bought or sold.

permissions: Rules and regulations that define what an object's owner can do with it (for example, copy or modify).

PG: Region rating banning "mature" activities.

pie menu: The round, context-sensitive menu opened by right-clicking inside the virtual world.

prim: Short for "primitive"—a virtual solid of any shape, used as a building block in the *SL* world. Also used as an adjective, as in "prim hair" to denote hair made out of prims instead of texture. "High-prim" and "low-prim" describe virtual objects containing a high/low number of prims. Note that high prim numbers may cause lag.

push script: A script, usually for a virtual weapon, that results in the targeted avatar being moved to another location—for example, many thousands of feet up in the sky.

INTRO
CHAPTER 1
CHAPTER 2
CHAPTER 3
CHAPTER 4
CHAPTER 5
CHAPTER 6
CHAPTER 7
CHAPTER 8
CHAPTER 9
CHAPTER 10
CHAPTER 11
CHAPTER 12
CHAPTER 13
APPENDICES

to rate: To award points to a resident for behavior, appearance, etc., as listed on the resident's Profile panel.

region: A named area within *Second Life*, also commonly called a *simulator* or a *sim* (see "simulator"). *Second Life* is divided into square regions, each 256m on a side and assigned a name. The regions are aligned and assembled so that the borders between them are, for all intents and purposes, seamless. You can stand a one side of a region border with your friend on the other. Despite the fact that the two of you are in different regions, you can chat freely, throw a baseball across, even drive a car back and forth without interruption.

relog: To log out of *Second Life* then log back in again. Usage: "I've got to relog, be right back."

reputation: Your in-world prestige, as rated by other players. (See "rate.")

resident: A person who uses *Second Life*. Can refer to the user of the account as well as their in-world avatar.

rez: This term is commonly attributed to the movie *Tron*. To bring an object into 3D space within *Second Life*, usually by dragging it from Inventory into the world; 2) To create a new primitive in *Second Life* through the building tools.

sandbox: A public area where *SL* residents are allowed to create new objects. There are many sandboxes scattered around the world; most are "safe" areas that don't allow selling, gambling, or combat.

security system: An elaborate script, usually contained within an object, used to protect privately owned land from griefers and virtual weapons.

shield: An attachment that protects an avatar from virtual weapons. There is no perfect shield; as soon as it's invented, new weapons appear.

simulator, sim: A square, named region that makes up part of the *Second Life* world (not an avatar or character).

snapshot: An in-world photo. You can take snapshots using *SL*'s Snapshot button.

skin: What you see when you strip your avatar naked. May include body shape and features such as eyes and tattoos in addition to the avatar's actual skin. Often used to denote a custom-made avatar skin of superior appearance.

snap, snapshot: A screenshot or photograph taken in-world using *SL* software.

stipend: A weekly allowance paid in L$ to qualifying residents. Stipend rules change frequently; at the time of writing, they're limited to Premium-account holders.

storage: Space where virtual objects built out of prims may be stored. Each region can support a limited number of prims.

suspension: The temporary removal of someone from *Second Life*. A suspended resident will be unable to log into *Second Life*. The resident will receive an email stating the reason for suspension. A suspension is not to be confused with an administrative kick, which includes a short time-out from *Second Life* that's usually not accompanied by an email.

Teen *Second Life*; Teen Grid: A special *SL* area for 13- to 17-year-old members only; more info at `http://teen.secondlife.com`.

Telehub: Originally a teleporting "port" or location in the *SL* world. At the time of writing, Telehubs are used to direct teleporting traffic on private estates.

texture: An image or graphic applied to an object or avatar. You can create your own textures in any third-party graphics program and upload them to *Second Life* for L$10 per image.

themed community: An area, frequently an entire region or more, built to represent a specific entity—for instance, a medieval Japanese village or a Polynesian island. Many themed communities are also historical communities—the Victorian-inspired community of Caledon is a famous example.

tier; tier up: 1) One of *Second Life*'s levels of land ownership and land-use fees. Each tier has a monthly price and a maximum amount of land that can be held. 2) To make a land purchase that increases your monthly Land Use Cost.

Town Hall: Events at which the *SL* governing staff (the Lindens) meets with *SL* residents to introduce and discuss virtual-world issues.

tp: Short for "teleport," often used in teleport requests by residents (as in "Can you tp me to your location?").

vendor: A *Second Life* resident or a scripted object that sells objects, clothing, or other items.

sim, simulator: Originally the term for an *SL* region, created back in the ancient times when one LL server or simulator supported one region. Still used to denote a region, although servers now support two or more regions each.

welcome area, InfoHub: A location serving new residents, featuring numerous notecard dispensers, freebies, and *SL* mentors providing guidance and answering newbies' questions.

INTRO
CHAPTER 1
CHAPTER 2
CHAPTER 3
CHAPTER 4
CHAPTER 5
CHAPTER 6
CHAPTER 7
CHAPTER 8
CHAPTER 9
CHAPTER 10
CHAPTER 11
CHAPTER 12
CHAPTER 13
APPENDICES

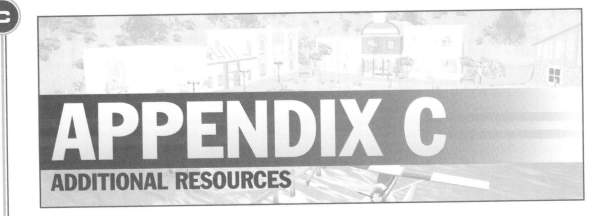

APPENDIX C
ADDITIONAL RESOURCES

This appendix presents selected URLs that will come in handy when you want to find out more about an aspect of *Second Life*. Most of the sites included here have been around for a long while and are likely to be there for long while more, and all contain links to other sites of *SL* interest—several hundred of them. For more resources, please check out the enclosed CD.

http://secondlife.com/
This, as you might have guessed, will take you to the home page of the official *SL* site. Generally speaking, this is the site you should visit first when seeking clarification about any *SL* issue: it contains late-breaking information plus a series of links to other very useful sites.

http://secondlife.com/knowledgebase/
This takes you to a treasure trove of information on just about every aspect of *Second Life*. Be sure to visit the site and glance through the topics even if you do not need info on a specific problem; new residents particularly may discover—just by looking at the topics covered!—new issues and possibilities they've been unaware of.

http://forums.secondlife.com/index.php
This is the main page of the Linden Lab–sponsored *SL* forums. You'll find a wealth of info there, and it's a great place to go to when you need help with a specific issue.

http://blog.secondlife.com/
The site of the official Linden blog contains the most up-to-date info about changes that affect *Second Life*. This is the link to use when you're looking for news about the latest *SL* updates, as well as fresh info on miscellaneous developments.

http://lslwiki.com/
The LSL Wiki is a great source for tutorials and plenty of general info on writing scripts in the Linden Scripting Language. Chapter 8 provides additional LSL-specific URLs.

http://secondlife.com/community/

This page links to hundreds of useful sites. A table of contents lets you choose websites by topic.

http://secondlife.com/community/fansites.php

This is a particularly important section of the community website. It lists a multitude of *SL*-related sites run by residents, including resident-run *SL* forums, blogs, etc. A sidebar contains links that will let you view even more *SL* websites—they're listed by topic, from architecture to videos.

http://secondlife.com/developers/resources.php

Want to create a unique outfit for your avatar but don't know how? Developer Resources is the place to go. Learn everything from how to animate your avatar to how to stream music onto your land.

INTRO
CHAPTER 1
CHAPTER 2
CHAPTER 3
CHAPTER 4
CHAPTER 5
CHAPTER 6
CHAPTER 7
CHAPTER 8
CHAPTER 9
CHAPTER 10
CHAPTER 11
CHAPTER 12
CHAPTER 13
APPENDICES

333

APPENDIX D
MENU COMMANDS AND FUNCTIONS

This appendix reviews the commands in the *SL* top-bar pull-down menus. All information is accurate at the time of writing, but things may change slightly as *SL* continues to evolve.

In many cases the commands in the pull-down menus duplicate commands available elsewhere; for example, a number of commands are also available through the pie menu that pops up when you right-click on your avatar. If you choose to hide the bottom bar and its button menu, you can still issue the button commands through the pull-down menus. The *Second Life* Knowledge Base contains more info on this and other *SL* interface issues.

The first four pull-down menus (File, Edit, View, World) contain a mix of commands that may be a little confusing to new *Second Life* residents. By contrast, the Tools menu contains only commands for managing, building, and editing objects, including object scripts—in this context, all the commands are self-explanatory. The Help menu includes shortcuts to internal and external *SL* info sources as well as a variety of other options, such as reporting bugs and abuse of *SL* regulations, and *Second Life's* Message of the Day.

FILE

Upload Image lets you import a graphics file into *SL*. Selecting it takes you to your operating system's Browse Files window, where you can find the image you want to upload. Select the file you want to upload to see a preview. At the time of writing, upload costs L$10 per file. The uploaded file is saved in your Inventory in the Textures folder.

Upload Sound lets you import a sound file into *SL*. Procedure and price are similar to the ones described above. However, you can import only .wav files with a 44.1k sample rate, and the file will be saved in the Sounds folder in your Inventory.

Upload Animation lets you upload animation files created in an external application such as Poser. Procedure and price are the same as above, except that the file gets saved in your Animations Inventory folder.

Bulk Upload lets you import all files contained in the selected folder. You are charged L$10 per file contained in the folder. Note that only files meeting *SL* criteria will be uploaded, and that each type of file will be saved in a corresponding folder—for example, images will be saved in the Textures folder.

Close Window closes the topmost window you have open in your *SL* client (an Inventory window, for instance).

Save Texture As saves the currently active texture file to your hard drive.

Take Snapshot opens the snapshot Preview panel.

Snapshot to Disk takes a snapshot and saves it on your hard drive after letting you choose the folder and name the file. Selecting this command again retains the original name, followed by 002, 003, etc.

Start/Stop Movie to Disk gets the camera rolling! What you see onscreen is saved as a Windows Media Player file on your hard drive. Manipulate views using *SL* camera controls—mouselook works best. Select this command again when you're ready to yell "Cut!"

Set Window Size lets you select screen resolution/monitor type to optimize *SL* performance on your system.

Quit exits *Second Life*.

EDIT

Undo becomes active only when you're in the building mode, letting you undo your last action. It won't let you undo other *SL* actions, so consider yourself warned.

Redo (aka "I've changed my mind again") is another command that applies to building mode only. It lets you redo the last action you undid.

Cut, **Copy**, and **Paste** become active when you're working with text within *SL*. You can also use them to import/export text. For instance, you'll use Paste to insert text you've cut or copied from an external application such as Microsoft Word, and Cut or Copy when you want to export text to an external application.

Delete works for both text and objects that you're permitted to delete.

Search doubles for the Search button in the bottom bar and opens the Search panel. Use tabs within the panel to refine your search after typing or pasting keywords into the text box.

INTRO
CHAPTER 1
CHAPTER 2
CHAPTER 3
CHAPTER 4
CHAPTER 5
CHAPTER 6
CHAPTER 7
CHAPTER 8
CHAPTER 9
CHAPTER 10
CHAPTER 11
CHAPTER 12
CHAPTER 13
APPENDICES

APPENDIX

D

INTRO

PART I

PART II

PART III

APPENDICES

APPENDIX D

Select All, **Deselect**, and **Duplicate** become active when you're in the building mode.

Attach Object and **Detach Object** open a submenu that lists attachment points: spots where objects can be attached to your avatar, such as on the right hand or the nose. The submenu choices become active only when you have an object selected *in the world*—it doesn't work for objects that are still in your Inventory; you have to take 'em out first!

Take Off Clothing—poof, and you're naked.

Gestures opens the Active Gestures panel, which lists gestures you have activated. If you haven't activated any (by checking the Active box in the Gesture panel), the list will be empty.

Profile opens your *SL* Profile panel.

Appearance switches to avatar-appearance-editing mode, just like the same command in the pie menu that pops up when you right-click on your avatar.

Friends opens a panel that lists the friends you've made in *SL* by offering them friendship and having them accept. You can add new friends by clicking Add Friend on the Friends panel.

Groups opens a panel listing all the groups to which you belong.

Preferences opens the Preferences panel that's also available through the Preferences button on the *SL* login screen.

VIEW

Mouselook switches to first-person view. Note that the quickest and easiest way of switching to mouselook is simply to use the mouse wheel to zoom in on your avatar until your view actually enters its head.

Build activates the building mode.

Reset View sets the camera to its default position in your current view mode.

Look at Last Chatter turns your avatar's head so that it is looking at the avatar that most recently spoke in an open (i.e., not private) conversation within hearing distance.

Toolbar can be toggled to hide/show the bottom-bar button menu.

Chat History opens a panel listing all dialogue and messages, spoken or otherwise, that took place within hearing distance or were received during your current *SL* session.

Instant Message opens the Instant Message panel.

Inventory opens the Inventory panel.

Mute List opens a list of people and/or objects you've muted because you just don't wanna hear anymore. Useful if you've changed your mind and don't want to give them the silent treatment anymore.

Camera Controls opens a panel that lets you move the camera or your point of view. Mastering camera controls is worth the trouble: you'll be able to see what goes on behind walls and closed doors.

Movement Controls opens a small panel with an assortment of clickable arrows, and its very own Fly button. Useful if you dislike mouselook and using the arrow keys, which most people find the easiest way to move exactly where you want to.

World Map opens the World Map panel, just like when you click on the Map button on the button menu.

Mini Map activates a small map in the upper-right corner of the screen—you can move the map around by clicking on the top bar and dragging it to your preferred spot. The map shows your nearby environment; clicking on it opens the World Map panel.

Statistics Bar opens a transparent panel that displays hard *SL* data—among others, current connection speed and quality (packet loss), and (importantly) the number of current active objects and running scripts.

Property Lines toggles on nifty colored lines showing land-parcel boundaries.

Land Owners paints land parcels by putting a color overlay on land. Your own land is green, land owned by someone else is a rusty red. Land for sale is yellow.

Hover Tips opens a little submenu where you can switch on hover tips for land parcels and objects that you point out with your cursor; this can be very useful. Note that hover tips do not appear in mouselook view.

Alt Shows Physical causes all physics-enabled objects to be colored red when you hold down the Alt key.

Highlight Transparent highlights all transparent surfaces within your view with a rusty red.

Beacons opens a small submenu that lets you set up beacons (thin red lines) for scripted objects, physical objects, plus sound and particle sources. Can be very useful when you're managing an environment in which too many things are happening and causing lag. You can also turn off particles here to improve performance, but watch out—that waterfall you've been admiring may suddenly disappear!

INTRO
CHAPTER 1
CHAPTER 2
CHAPTER 3
CHAPTER 4
CHAPTER 5
CHAPTER 6
CHAPTER 7
CHAPTER 8
CHAPTER 9
CHAPTER 10
CHAPTER 11
CHAPTER 12
CHAPTER 13
APPENDICES

APPENDIX

D

INTRO

PART I

PART II

PART III

APPENDICES

Show HUD Attachments controls whether HUDs will show on your screen; even when this option is unchecked, HUDs will respond to commands.

Zoom In, **Zoom Default**, and **Zoom Out** reposition the camera slightly; useful if you don't have a mouse wheel.

More opens a tiny submenu with two options (at the time of writing): Toggle Fullscreen (*SL* in full screen or windowed mode) and Set UI Size to Default. The second option is useful if you've moved the UI size slider a bit too far on the Preferences panel (Graphics tab).

WORLD

Chat opens the Chat window; usually it's easier just to hit the Enter key.

Start Gesture opens the Chat window and inserts a slash, so all you need to do is type in a gesture name (/bow, /clap, and so on). Remember that you need to precede the gesture name with a forward slash to mark it as a gesture command as opposed to a chat.

Always Run makes your avatar run instead of walking when you press the forward-arrow key.

Fly toggles between flying and falling down to earth with a bump.

Create Landmark Here sets a landmark for your current location on the world map and adds it to the contents of your Landmark Inventory folder.

Set Home to Here is where you enter into *Second Life* when you log in, if you so choose (not necessarily your home). Could be a money tree, could be a swingers' club—it's your choice, as long as it's land you own or has been deeded to a group you belong to. Home is the landmark marked with a little blue house on the world map.

Teleport Home teleports you to the place you call home (see "Set Home to Here").

Set Away instructs your avatar to instantly adopt the pose it assumes when you haven't been active for a while: head forward, shoulders slumped as if it were sleeping on its feet.

Set Busy is the *SL* equivalent of a Do Not Disturb sign. All messages are hidden and all offers are automatically declined. A Set Not Busy button appears onscreen to remind you that you're incommunicado.

Account History opens a panel that does not deal with your *SL* account, but rather with your *SL* finances. Tabs open info screens that help you keep track of what money went where, and why.

Manage My Account takes you to your *SL* account web page for account-management purposes.

Buy opens a LindeX currency exchange panel that lets you buy *SL* currency for real dollars.

My Land opens a panel with your personal real-estate info. The panel lists your current land holdings and their locations, as well as how much more land you can acquire within your land-fee tier; if you get more, you'll pay higher Land Use Costs.

About Land opens the About Land panel with info about the land parcel your avatar's currently in. Note that you can bring up the About Land panel for any parcel within view by right-clicking on the parcel's land—this opens a pie menu that contains an About Land option.

Buy Land is active only when you're on a land parcel that's being offered for sale. Selecting it marks the parcel boundary in yellow and opens the Buy Land panel.

Region/Estate opens a Region/Estate management and info panel that lets the estate manager (owner or designated person) exercise ownership rights and options. The tabs open submenus that deal with specific aspects of land ownership and management, including the land covenant.

Force Sun lets you issue orders to the sun; how's that? Selecting this command opens a submenu that lets you experience continuous sunrise, noon, sunset, or midnight (that last option is particularly useful for vampires). You can also reset the sun to the region default.

TOOLS

Select Tool contains the following options: Focus, Move, Edit, Create, Land. When you select one of them you'll open the Build window and enter the appropriate mode.

Select Only My Objects allows you to toggle your ability to select other users' or groups' objects when building. This ensures easy cleanup of your objects, as well as easy object linking when surrounded by others' objects.

Select Only Movable Objects allows you to toggle whether you select locked objects when building.

Select by Surrounding lets you select multiple objects by dragging a selection box around them. Using this in conjunction with Select Only My Objects or Select Only Movable Objects allows for quick and easy object selection for builders.

INTRO
CHAPTER 1
CHAPTER 2
CHAPTER 3
CHAPTER 4
CHAPTER 5
CHAPTER 6
CHAPTER 7
CHAPTER 8
CHAPTER 9
CHAPTER 10
CHAPTER 11
CHAPTER 12
CHAPTER 13
APPENDICES

339

Show Hidden Selection allows you to see objects that are ordinarily invisible when building.

Show Light Radius for Selection toggles your ability to see the extent of the light emitted by that object (when you're editing a light-emissive object).

Show Selection Beam toggles whether your avatar extends its hand and shoots a beam of particles toward the object you're editing (thereby indicating to everyone else that you're editing that object).

Snap to Grid toggles "snap to grid" when building. When it's on, you can quickly position an object to exact grid coordinates. When it's off, you can position an object anywhere you like.

Snap Object XY to Grid moves an object to the nearest grid intersection, as if you manipulated it with Sna to Grid manually. It doesn't matter if Snap to Grid is active or not; it'll do it either way.

Use Selection for Grid allows you to use the selected object as the origin for the grid rather than using the region's default.

Grid Options opens the Grid Options window, allowing you to set the building grid frequency, extents, and opacity.

Link allows you to combine two or more open objects into a single object.

Unlink breaks a selected linked object apart into its component prims.

Stop All Animations allows you to stop all the animations currently running on your avatar. This can be useful if you get stuck running or dancing.

Focus on Selection repositions the camera to focus on the object currently being edited.

Zoom to Selection repositions the camera to zoom in on the object currently being edited.

Take moves the selected object(s) into your inventory, removing them from the world. (You must have the proper permissions, however.)

Take Copy copies the selected object(s) into your inventory, leaving the original copy in the world. (You must have the proper permissions, however.)

Save Object Back to My Inventory is handy when rezzing a copy of an object from your Inventory. This option allows you to save any changes you've made to the version of an object you have in the world to the version that exists within your Inventory. This is useful because it avoids cluttering up your Inventory with old versions of an object.

Save Object Back to Object Contents is useful when working with an object that normally resides within another. This option allows you to update the copy that exists within the other object without having to copy it manually.

Show Script Warning/Error Window opens the Script Errors/Warning window, where you can see errors and debug messages from all scripts running in the region.

Recompile Scripts in Selection lets you recompile all the scripts in all the primitives you currently have selected. This puts them back to their initial state.

Reset Scripts in Selection resets all the scripts in all the primitives you currently have selected. This puts them back to their initial state.

Set Scripts to Running in Selection sets all the scripts in all the primitives you currently have selected to "Running," turning them on.

Set Scripts to Not Running in Selection sets all the scripts in all the primitives you currently have selected to "Not Running," turning them off.

HELP

Second Life Help opens a panel that contains general information. Click on the Getting More Help link on the panel to see a very helpful list of *SL* resources; Common Terms opens a glossary of *SL* terms and language, including evolved *SL*-speak such as rezzing, as well as standard online-speak abbreviations such as afk ("away from keyboard").

Knowledge Base takes you outside *SL* and to the specified website.

Live Help is handy when you have a question. Select Live Help, type in your query, and if you're both lucky and patient, someone might answer. Do not depend too heavily on Live Help; search the Knowledge Base while you're waiting for someone to answer, and chances are you'll find your answer there before anyone contacts you.

Official Linden Blog takes you outside *SL* and to the indicated website. Checking out the Official Linden Blog on a regular basis is mandatory if you're serious about your virtual existence: it contains the latest news on issues that affect *Second Life*, including upcoming application and membership plan changes.

Scripting Guide and **Scripting Wiki** take you to the associated websites—useful if you've run into a problem while writing a script in LSL (Linden Scripting Language).

Message of the Day displays the message that's shown as you log in. Messages of the Day often contain very helpful tips, so make sure you read them!

INTRO
CHAPTER 1
CHAPTER 2
CHAPTER 3
CHAPTER 4
CHAPTER 5
CHAPTER 6
CHAPTER 7
CHAPTER 8
CHAPTER 9
CHAPTER 10
CHAPTER 11
CHAPTER 12
CHAPTER 13
APPENDICES

Report Abuse opens a panel that's the *SL* equivalent of a complaint form. If someone's making you suffer, fill in the details and file your grievance.

Bumps, Pushes, and Hits lists the abuse you've suffered during your current online session so that you can include it in your report.

Report Bug opens a panel that lets you enter the details of an encountered application bug and send them in.

Release Notes takes you to the website that contains the latest *SL* update release notes. Changes are introduced fairly frequently, and it's a good idea to keep up-to-date. If something in your virtual life is not quite the way it used to be, check the release notes before filing a bug report.

About Second Life shows you more than just *SL* info such as version number and a credits list; you'll also see you own system info—processor, operating system, graphics card, etc.

The right thing to do, of course, is not to leave the world, but simply find something that you *do* like. There's no shortage of choices—shopping, visiting art galleries, skydiving, bowling, and attending live shows and concerts are just some of the options available. Note also that not all the people you meet in *SL* are there just to have fun. Increasingly, the virtual world of *Second Life* is the venue for real-world study and research programs—a place where scientists, teachers, and students can meet even though they're thousands of miles apart in the real world.

Figure 1.4: *You'll see plenty of interesting new faces in Second Life.*

NOTE

ADDITIONAL INFO:
SECOND LIFE EVENTS

Second Life is rich in events of all kinds—from movie festivals and shows by major real-life artists to local events organized by individual residents. Locations of current and upcoming events are marked by a pink or purple star on the world map, and advertised both in the SL Classifieds and at `http://secondlife.com/events/`. For a full list of SL events, click the Search button and select the Events tab on the Search panel.

Second Life does contain rules and regulations that limit resident activities: different areas allow different types of activity. Areas listed as Mature allow activities euphemistically known as adult behavior, while PG areas impose stricter rules. Many areas are dedicated to pursuing a specific kind of activity within a specific environment.